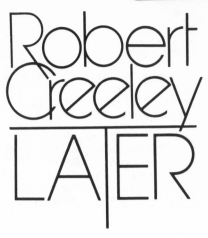

Robert Creeley
LATER

Count then your blessings, hold in mind
All that has loved you or been kind . . .
Gather the bits of road that were
Not gravel to the traveller
But eternal lanes of joy
On which no man who walks can die.

—from Patrick Kavanagh, "Prelude"

A NEW DIRECTIONS BOOK

Later (1-10) was originally published by Toothpaste Press, West Branch, Iowa, in 1978. Several poems in the present volume were first brought out as broadsides and in booklets, titled as follows: **John Chamberlin**, Contemporary Arts Museum, Houston, 1975; **Thanks**, Deerfield Press/The Gallery Press, Deerfield, Mass., and Dublin, Ireland, 1977; **Just Buffalo**, Buffalo, N.Y., 1978; **Desultory Days**, The Sceptre Press, Knotting, England, 1978. Further acknowledgment is made to the various magazines and newspapers in which other of the poems included here had their first appearance: **Agenda** (London), **American Poetry Review, The Atlantic Review** (England), **Attaboy, Atropos** (Montreal), **Bezoar, Bombay Gin, Boundary 2, The CoEvolution Quarterly/Journal for the Protection of All Beings, Foot, Harvard Magazine, Impact, International Herald Tribune, Little Caesar, Milk Quarterly, Paris Review, Perceptions, Purchase Poetry Review, The Southwestern Review.**

The lines from Patrick Kavanagh's "Prelude" (Copyright © 1964 by Patrick Kavanagh) quoted on the title page are reprinted by permission of The Devin-Adair Co., Inc., publisher of the **Collected Poems of Patrick Kavanagh.**

Manufactured in the United States of America
First published as New Directions Paperbook 488 in 1979
Published simultaneously in Canada by George J. McLeod Ltd., Toronto

Library of Congress Cataloging in Publication Data

Creeley, Robert, 1926-
    Later.
    (A New Directions Book)
    I. Title
PS3505.R43L3   1979   811'.5'4   79-15600
ISBN 0-8112-0736-6

New Directions Books are published for James Laughlin
by New Directions Publishing Corporation,
80 Eighth Avenue, New York 10011

SECOND PRINTING

I

MYSELF

What, younger, felt
was possible, now knows
is not—but still
not changed enough—

Walked by the sea,
unchanged in memory—
evening, as clouds
on the far-off rim

of water float,
pictures of time,
smoke, faintness—
still the dream.

I want, if older,
still to know
why, human, men
and women are

so torn, so lost,
why hopes cannot
find better world
than this.

Shelley is dead and gone,
who said,
"Taught them not this—
to know themselves;

their might Could not repress
the mutiny within,
And for the morn
of truth they feigned,

deep night
Caught them ere evening . . ."

THIS WORLD

If night's the harder,
closer time, days
come. The morning
opens with light

at the window.
Then, as now, sun
climbs in blue sky.
At noon

on the beach
I could watch
these glittering
waves forever,

follow their sound
deep into mind
and echoes—
let light

as air
be relief.
The wind
pulls at face

and hands,
grows cold. What
can one think—
the beach

is myriad stone.
Clouds pass,
grey undersides,
white clusters

of air, all
air. Water
moves at the edges,
blue, green,

white twists
of foam.
What then
will be lost,

recovered.
What
matters as one
in this world?

THE HOUSE

Mas-Soñer
Restaurat—Any—
1920 . . . Old
slope of roof,

gutted windows,
doors, the walls,
with crumbling stucco
shows the mortar

and stones
underneath. Sit
on stone wall adjacent
topped with brick,

ground roundabout's weeds,
red dirt, bare rock.
Then look east
down through valley—

fruit trees in their rows,
the careful fields,
the tops of the other
farmhouses below—

then the city, in haze,
the sea. Look
back in time
if you can—

think of the
myriad people
contained in this instant
in mind. But the well

top's gone, and debris
litters entrance.
Yet no sadness,
no fears

life's gone out.
Could put it all right,
given time,
and need, and money,

make this place sing,
the rooms open
and warm, and spring
come in at the windows

with the breeze—
the white blossom
of apple
still make this song.

LA CONCA

Sand here's like meal—
oats, barley, or wheat—
feels round and specific.

Sun's hot,
just past noon, and sound
of small boat clearing headland

chugs against wash.
Light slants
now on rocks, makes shadows.

Beach is a half-moon's
curve, with bluff,
at far end, of rock—

and firs look like garden
so sharply their tops
make line against sky.

All quiet here,
all small
and comfortable. Boat goes by,

beyond, where sky
and sea meet
far away.

SEA

Ever
to sleep,
returning water.

•

Rock's upright,
thinking.

•

Boy and dog
following
the edge.

•

Come back, first
wave I saw.

•

Older man at
water's edge, brown
pants rolled up,
white legs, and hair.

•

Thin faint
clouds begin
to drift over
sun, im-
perceptibly.

•

Stick stuck
in sand, shoes,
sweater, cigarettes.

•

No home more
to go to.

•

But that line,
sky and sea's,
something else.

•

Adios, water—
for another day.

FLAUBERT'S EARLY PROSE

"Eventually he dies
out of a lack of will to live,
out of mere weariness and sadness . . ."

And then he is hit by a truck
on his way home from work,

and/or a boulder
pushed down onto him
by lifelong friends of the family
writes FINIS to his suffering—

Or he goes to college,
gets married,
and *then* he dies!

Or finally he doesn't die at all,
just goes on living,
day after day in the same old way . . .

He is a very interesting man,
this intensively sensitive person,
but he has to die somehow—

so he goes by himself to the beach,
and sits down and thinks,
looking at the water to be found there,

"Why was I born? Why
am I living?"—like
an old song, *cheri*—
and then he dies.

BARCELONA: FEBRUARY 13, 1977

Grave, to the will
of the people,
in the plaza
in front of the cathedral,
at noon dance
the *sardana*—

"two policemen dead,
four arrested"—

ritual, formal,
grave, old and young,
coats left in heap
in the middle
of the circle, wind chill—
dance, to find will.

PLACE

This is an empty landscape,
in spite of its light,
air, water—
the people walking the streets.

I feel faint here,
too far off, too
enclosed in myself,
can't make love a way out.

I need the oldtime density,
the dirt, the cold,
the noise through the floor—
my love in company.

SPEECH

Simple things
one wants to say
like, what's the day
like, out there—
who am I
and where.

BEACH

Across bay's loop
of white caps,
small seeming black
figures at edge—

one, the smallest,
to the water goes.
Others, behind,
sit down.

AFTER

I'll not write again
things a young man
thinks, not the words
of that feeling.

There is no world
except felt, no
one there but
must be here also.

If that time was
echoing, a vindication
apparent, if flesh
and bone coincided—

let the body be.
See faces float
over the horizon let
the day end.

FOR PEN

Reading, in the chair
in front of the fire
keeps the room both warm
and sparely human—

thinking, to where I've come,
where come from,
from what, from whom—
wanting a meaning.

None to hand but the days
pass here,
in dear company
takes mind of shy comfort.

I want the world
I did always,
small pieces
and clear acknowledgments.

I want to be useful
to someone, I think,
always—if not many,
then one.

But to have it
be echo, feeling
that was years ago—
now my hands are

wrinkled and my hair
goes grey—seems
ugly burden
and mistake of it.

So sing this
weather, passing,
grey and blue
together, rain and sun.

LOVE

There are words voluptuous
as the flesh
in its moisture,
its warmth.

Tangible, they tell
the reassurances,
the comforts,
of being human.

Not to speak them
makes abstract
all desire
and its death at last.

EROTICA

On the path
down here, to the sea,
there are bits

of pages
from a magazine, scattered,
the *big tits*

of my adolescence
caught on bushes,
stepped on, faces

of the women, naked,
still smiling out at me
from the grass.

In the factory,
beside which
this path goes,

there is
no one. The windows
are broken out.

A dump
sits in front of it.
Two piles of dirt

beyond that.
Do these
look like tits

too, some primordial
woman sunk
underground

breaking out,
up,
to get me—

shall I throw
myself down
upon it,

this ground
rolls and twists,
these pictures

I want still
to see. Coming back
a day later,

kids were stopped
at that spot
to look

as I would
and had—there the fact
of the mystery

at last—
"what they look like
underneath"—

paper shreds,
blurred pages,
dirty pictures.

NATURE

for R.B.K.

Out door here—
tall as wall
of usual room,
slight arch at top—

sunlight
in courtyard
beyond
settles on stump

of tree's trunk—
limbs all cut
to force growth,
come summer—

in blue and white
checkerboard tiled
square planter
at bottom

sits in cement,
thoughtful,
men's minded
complement.

THINKING OF WALTER BENJAMIN

What to say
these days
of crashing disjunct,
whine, of separation—

Not abstract—
"God's will," not
lost in clouds this
experienced wisdom.

Hand and mind
and heart one
ground to walk on,
field to plow.

I know
a story
I can tell
and will.

WAITING FOR A BUS
"EN FRENTE DE LA IGLESIA"

Here's the church,
here's the tower, the wall,
chopped off. *Open*

the door—no
people. This is
age, long time gone,

like town gate sits
at intersection
across—just façade

leading nowhere.
Zipzap, the cars
roar past. Three

faded flags flap
on top of Hotel
Florida. Old dog,

old friend, walks toward us,
legs rachitic, stiff,
reddish hair all fuzzed.

Long grey bus
still parked to go
to Gerona

which, 8th century,
Charlemagne came personally
to take back from Moors.

You can *read*
all about it!
but wind's cold

in this early spring sun,
and this bench's
lost its bars

on the back
but for one—
and bus

now starts up,
and we're on,
and we're gone.

NEWS OF THE WORLD

Topical questions,
as the world swirls,
and never

enough in hand,
head, to know
if Amin

will truly become
"Jimmy Carter's best friend"
as he professes. The facts

are literal daily horror:
1/5 of world's population has no access
to processed drinking water;

"women in rural Burma
walk 15 miles a day to get some
and bring it home,
a six hour trip." Or

Romania's earthquake dead—
"What day is today
and how are my parents?"

were the first words of Sorin Crainic
when he emerged from the rubble
after eleven days. "I kept

hoping all the time.
My hope has come true.
I shall be able to walk again

and breath fresh air, much
fresh air.
I shall go back to work."

Meanwhile, same page, "Goldwater
Denounces Report Linking Him
To Gang Figures"—"A 36-member

team of journalists from 23 newspapers
and broadcast outlets . . . continuing
work begun by reporter Don Bolles . . .

who was murdered last June. One man
has pleaded guilty to second-degree
murder in the killing; two

are awaiting trial." G. believes
"that the reporters had gone to Arizona
hoping to solve the Bolles murder"

but when "they could not" did
"a job" on said state. Too late,
too little. But not for you, Mr. G.,

as hate grows, lies, the same
investment of the nice and tidy
ways to get "rich,"

in this "world,"
wer eld, the length
of a human life.

MORNING

Shadows, on the far wall,
of courtyard, from the sun
back of house, faint

traceries, of the leaves,
the arch of the balcony—
greens, faded white,

high space of flat
blind-sided building
sits opposite this

window, in high door,
across the floor here
from this table

where I'm sitting, writing,
feet on cold floor's
tiles, watching this light.

THE TABLE

Two weeks from now
we'll be gone. Think,
problems will be
over, the time here

done. What's the time
left to be.
Sky's grey again,
electric stove whirs

by the wall with its
snowflake, flowerlike
yellow, blue and green
tile design. On the table

the iris have opened,
two wither and close.
Small jug holds them,
green stalks, husks and buds.

Paper, yesterday's, book
to read face down, ashtray,
cigarettes, letter from
your mother, roll now

of thunder outside. You
put down the papers,
go back to reading
your book, head bent.

Sarah's cap on your hair
holds it close—red at top,
in a circle, first ring French
blue, then one lighter,

then the darker repeated.
Think of the sounds,
outside, now quiet,
the kids gone back to school.

It's a day we may
live forever, this
simple one. Nothing
more, nothing less.

CHILDISH

Great stories matter—
but the one who tells them
hands them on
in turn to another

who also will.
What's in the world
is water, earth,
and fire, some people,

animals, trees, birds,
etc. I can see
as far as you,
and what I see I tell

as you told me
or have or will.
You'll see too
as well.

ECHOES

Eight panes
in this window
for God's light,
for the outside,

comes through door
this morning.
Sun makes laced
shadows on wall

through imperfect glass.
Mind follows,
finds the lines,
the wavering places.

Rest wants
to lie down
in the sun,
make resolution.

Body sits single,
waiting—
but for what
it knows not.

Old words
echoing what
the physical
can't—

"Leave love,
leave day,
come
with me."

REFLECTIONS

What pomposity
could say only—
Look
at what's happened to me.

All those others
surrounding
know
the same bounds.

Happiness
finds itself
in one or many
the same—

and dead,
no more than one
or less
makes a difference.

I was thinking
this morning
again—
So be it.

NEW MOON

Are there still some
"quiet craters of the moon"—
seeing that edge of it
you were pointing to,

stopped, in the street,
looking past the wires
on those poles, all
the stores, open, people,

cars, going past, to see
in that space, faint sliver
of its visible edge. What
advice then remembered,

what had she said?
Turn your money over
and bow three times
to make it increase.

LATER

If I could get
my hands on
a little bit
of it—neither fish,

flesh, nor fowl. Not
you, Harry. No one's
mother—or father,
or children. Not

me again. Not
earth, sky, water—
no mind, no time.
No islands in the sun.

Money I don't want.
No place more
than another—
I'm not here

by myself. But,
if you want to give
me something for Xmas,
I'll be around.

NIGHT TIME

When the light leaves
and sky's black,
no nothing
to look at,

day's done.
That's it.

PEACE

You're looking at a chopper,
brother—no words to say.
Just step on
the gas, man, up and away.

That's dead, I know,
I don't even talk like that
any more. My teeth
are hurting.

But if you'll wait
out back, and
hit yourself over the head
with a hard object,

you'll dig, like, you
like me were young once,
jesus, here come
the creeps. I wrote

a book once, and was
in love with
substantial objects.
No more, I can

get out of here
or come here
or go there
or here, in five minutes.

Later. This
is just to say I was
something or other, and you dig it,
that's it, brother.

BLUES

for Tom Pickard

Old time blues
and things to say—
not going home
till they come to get me.

See the sky
black as night,
drink what's
there to drink.

God's dead,
men take over,
world's round,
all over.

Think of it,
all those years,
no one's the wiser
even older.

Flesh, flesh,
screams in body,
you know,
got to sleep.

Got to eat, baby,
got to.
No way
you won't.

When I lay down
big bed
going to pillow
my sleeping head.

When I fall,
I fall,
straight down
deep I'm going.

No one
touch me
with
their doubting mind.

You don't
love me
like you
say you do, you

don't do me
like you
said
you would.

What I say
to people
don't mean
I don't love,

what I
do don't
do, don't don't
do enough.

Think I drink
this little glass,
sit on my ass,
think about

life, all
those things,
substance.
I could touch you.

Times in jail
I was scared
not of being hurt
but that people lock you up,

what's got to be
cruel is you know,
and I don't, you say
you got the truth.

I wouldn't listen
if I was drunk, couldn't hear
if I was stoned,
you tell me right or don't.

Come on home, brother,
you make a fool,
get in trouble, end up
in jail.

I'm in the jailhouse now.
When they lock the door,
how long is what
you think of.

Believe in what's there,
nowhere else it will be.
They kill you,
they kill me.

Both dead,
we'll rise again.
They believe in Christ,
they'll believe in men.

SPRING IN SAN FELIU

Think of the good times—
again. Can't let it all
fail, fall apart, at
that always vague edge is

the public so-called condition,
which nobody knows enough
ever, even those
are supposed to be it.

I could identify that man,
say, bummed us out, or
the woman took the whole
street to walk in. They are

familiar faces, anywhere. They
don't need a place. But,
quieter, the kid took the running
leap past us, to show off,

the one then asked to look in
to the courtyard, saw the house,
said, *que casa grande!*, sans malice
or envy, the ones let us off

the hook of the randomly purposive
traveler, the dogs that
came with us, over hill,
over dale, the country men and women

could look up from those
rows of stuff they had planted,
showed now green, in the sun,
—how modest those farms and those lives.

Well, walk on . . . We'll be gone
soon enough. I'll have got
all I wanted—your time and your love
and yourself—like, *poco a poco.*

That sea never cared about us.
Nor those rocks nor those hills,
nor the far-off mountains still
white with snow. The sun

came with springtime—*la
primavera,* they'll say, when
we've gone. But we came.
We've been here.

4/1/77

SPARROWS

Small birds fly up
shaft of stairwell,

sit, chirping,
where sun strikes in at top.

Last time we'll see them,
hear their feisty greeting

to the day's first light,
the coming of each night.

II

END

End of page,
end of this

company—wee
notebook kept

my mind in hand,
let the world stay

open to me
day after day,

words to say,
things to be.

FOR JOHN CHAMBERLAIN

They paid my way here
and I'll get myself home.
Old saying:
Let the good times roll.

. . .

This is *Austin*
spelled with an H? This is
Houston, Texas—
Houston Street is back there—

ways in and out
of New York. The billboards
are better than the natural view,
you dig. I came here

just to see you, personal
as God and just as real.
I may never go home
again. Meantime

the lead room with the x
number of people
under the street
is probably empty tonight.

In New York, in
some other place.
Many forms.
Many farms, ranches

in Texas—many places,
many miles, big
endless spaces they say.
This is Marlboro Country

47

with box those dimensions,
module. Old movie of you
using baler with the crunchers
coming down so delicately.

The kids in the loft, long space.
The Oldenbergs going to work,
eight o'clock. Viva
talking and talking. Now I'm

stoned again, I was
stoned again, all that
past, years
also insistent dimension.

If I could take the world,
and put it on its side, man,
and squeeze just in the right
places. Wow. I don't think

much of interest would happen.
Like the lion coming into the room
with two heads, we'd all end up
killing it to see it.

So this is Art and here we are.
Who would have thought it?
I'll go sooner than you.
I can always tell

no matter how long I sit
after they've all gone, but the bottle
isn't empty.
No one's going to throw me out.

Let's sit in a bar and cry again.
Fuck it! Let's go out on your boat
and I'll fall asleep just like
they all do you tell me.

Terrific. Water's
an obvious material.
You could even make
a suit out of it. You could

do anything you wanted to,
possibly, if you wanted to.
Like coming through customs
with the grey leather hat.

It's all so serious and wonderful.
It's all so big and small.
Upended, it begins again, all the way
from the end to the very beginning,

again. I want it two ways,
she said, in a book
someone wrote. I want it all.
I want to take it all home.

But there's too much already
of everything, and something
I have to let go
and that's me, here and now.

But before leaving, may I say
that you are a great artist
whatever that turns out to be,
and art is art because of you.

I LOVE YOU

I see you, Aunt Bernice—
and your smile anticipating reality.
I don't care any longer that you're older.
There are times all the time the same.

I'm a young old man here on earth,
sticks, dust, rain, trees, people.
Your cat killing rats in Florida was
    incredible—
Pete—weird, sweet presence. Strong.

You were good to me. You had *wit*—
value beyond all other human possibility.
You could smile at the kids, the old cars.
Your house in N.H. was lovely.

FOUR YEARS LATER

When my mother
died, her things were
distributed

so quickly. Nothing
harsh about it,
just gone,

it seemed, but
for small
mementos, pictures

of family, dresses,
a sweater,
clock.

Looking back
now, wish
I'd talked

more to her.
I tried
in the hospital

but our habit
was too deep—
we didn't

speak easily.
Sitting
now, here,

early morning,
by myself,
can hear her—

as, "Bob,
do what you have to—
I trust you—"

words like
"presumption," possibly
"discretion"—some

insistent demand to
cover living
with clothes—not

"dressed up" but
common, faithful—
what no other can know.

HEAVEN

If life were easy
and it all worked out,
what would this sadness
be about.

If it was happy
day after day,
what would happen
anyway.

NEIGHBORS

Small horses on windowsill
adjacent, 'cross street,
kid's apparent

window, three point
one way, one
another, to face

babydoll, sits there,
with curtains drawn.
Everyone's gone.

JULY: FARGO STREET

Bangs in street.
Fourth's here again,
200th yet,

useless as ever,
'cept for energies
of kids, and the

respite from work
for all these
surrounding neighbors.

THINKING OF YEATS

Break down
"innocence"—
tell truth,

be *small*
in world's
wilderness.

P—

Swim
on her
as in
an ocean.

•

Think out
of it—

be here.

•

Hair's
all around,

floats
in flesh.

• ..

Eyes'
measure,

mouth's small
discretion.

Smiles.

•

Long warmth,
speaks
too.

•

Couldn't
do it
better.

·

Can walk
along.

BLUE SKIES MOTEL

Look at
that mother-fucking smoke stack

pointing
straight up.

See those clouds,
old time fleecy pillows,

like they say, whites and greys,
float by.

There's cars
on the street,

there's a swimming pool
out front—

and the trees
go yellow

now
it's the fall.

RIDDLE

What'd you throw it on the floor for?
Who the hell you think you are

come in here
push me around.

FOR PEN

Thinking out
of the heart—

it's up,
it's down . . .

It's that time
of day light

echoes the sun
setting west

over mountains.
I want to come home.

CIANO'S

Walking
off street

into Ciano's—
last sun

yellow
through door.

The bar
an oval, people—

behind is
pool table.

Sitting
and thinking.

Dreaming
again

of blue eyes,
actually green—

whose head's
red, mouth's

round, soft
sounds—

whose waist is
an arrow

points down
to earth.

TRAIN GOING BY

for Rosalie Sorrels

When I was a kid
I wanted to get educated
and to college go
to learn how to know.

Now old I've found
train going by
will take me along
but I still don't know why.

Not just for money
not for love
not for anything thought
for nothing I've done—

it's got to be luck
keeps the world going round
myself moving on
on that train going by.

FOR PEN

Last day of year,
sky's a light

open grey, blue
spaces appear

in lateral tiers.
Snow's fallen,

will again. Morning
sounds hum, inside,

outside, roosters squawk,
dog barks, birds squeak.

—"Be happy with me."

LONER

Sounds, crank
of kid's cart's axle

on street, one
floor down.

Heat's thick,
sun's bright

in window still
early morning,

May, fifty first
birthday. What

time will the
car be done, time—

ready? Sits opposite,
love, in red wrapper,

sheen of silk,
sideways, hair, hands,

breasts, young
flight of fancy,

long fingers, here
in a way

wants the dream back,
keeps walking.

B.B.

What's gone,
bugger all—

nothing lost
in mind till

it's all
forgotten.

MORNING

Light's bright glimmer,
through green bottle

on shelf
above. Light's white

fair air,
shimmer,

blue summer's
come.

THANKS

Here's to Eddie—
not unsteady
when drunk,
just thoughtful.

Here's to his mind
can remember
in the blur
his own forgotten line.

Or, too, lest
forgot, him in the traffic
at Cambridge, outside,
lurching, confident.

He told me later,
"I'm Catholic,
I'm queer,
I'm a poet."

God bless him,
God love him,
I say,
praise him

who saves you time,
saves you money,
takes on the burden
of your own confessions.

And my thanks again
for the cigarettes
he gave me
someone else had left.

I won't escape
his conversation
but will listen
as I've learned to,

and drink
and think again
with this dear man
of the true, the good, the dead.

THERESA'S FRIENDS

From the outset charmed
by the soft, quick speech
of those men and women,
Theresa's friends—and the church

she went to, the "other,"
not the white plain Baptist
I tried to learn God in.
Or, later, in Boston the legend

of "being Irish," the lore, the magic,
the violence, the comfortable
or uncomfortable drunkenness.
But most, that endlessly present talking,

as Mr. Connealy's, the ironmonger,
sat so patient in Cronin's Bar,
and told me sad, emotional stories
with the quiet air of an elder

does talk to a younger man.
Then, when at last I was twenty-one,
my mother finally told me
indeed the name *Creeley* was Irish—

and the heavens opened, birds sang,
and the trees and the ladies spoke
with wondrous voices. The power of the glory
of poetry—was at last mine.

LATER

LATER (1)

Shan't be winding
back in blue
gone time ridiculous,
nor lonely

anymore. Gone,
gone—wee thin
delights, hands
held me, mouths

winked with white
clean teeth. Those
clothes have fluttered
their last regard

to this passing
person walks by
that flat back-
yard once and for all.

LATER (2)

You won't want to be early
for passage of grey mist
now rising from the faint

river alongside the childhood
fields. School bell rings,
to bring you all in again.

That's mother sitting there,
a father dead in heaven,
a dog barks, steam of

drying mittens on the stove,
blue hands, two doughnuts
on a plate.

LATER (3)

The small
spaces of existence,
sudden

smell of burning
leaves makes
place in time

these days
(these days)
passing,

common
to one
and all.

LATER (4)

Opening
the boxes packed
in the shed,

at the edge
of the porch
was to be

place to sit
in the sun,
glassed over,

in the winter
for looking out
to the west,

see the shadows
in the early
morning lengthen,

sharp cold
dryness of air,
sounds of cars,

dogs, neighbors,
persons
of house, toilet

flush, pan
rattle, door
open, never done.

LATER (5)

Eloquent,
my heart,

thump bump—
My Funny Valentine

LATER (6)

If you saw
dog pass, in car—

looking out, possibly
indifferently, at you—

would you—*could* you—
shout, "Hey, Spot!

It's me!" After all
these years,

no dog's coming home
again. Its skin's

moldered
through rain, dirt,

to dust, hair alone
survives, matted tangle.

Your own, changed,
your hair, greyed,

your voice not the one
used to call him home,

"Hey Spot!" *The world's
greatest dog*'s got

lost in the world,
got lost long ago.

LATER (7)

Oh sadness,
boring

preoccupation—
rain's wet,

clouds
pass.

LATER (8)

Nothing "late" about the
"no place to go" old folks—

or "hell," or
"Florida this winter."

No "past" to be
inspired by "futures,"

scales of the imperium,
wonders of what's next.

When I was a kid, I
thought like a kid—

I *was* a kid,
you dig it. But

a hundred and fifty years later,
that's a whole long time to

wait for the train.
No doubt West Acton

was improved by the discontinuance
of service, the depot taken down,

the hangers-around there moved
at least back a street to Mac's Garage.

And you'll have to drive your own car
to get to Boston—or take the bus.

These days, call it "last Tuesday,"
1887, my mother was born,

and now, sad to say,
she's dead. And especially "you"

can't argue
with the facts.

LATER (9)

Sitting up here in
newly constituted

attic room 'mid
pipes, scarred walls,

the battered window
adjacent looks out

to street below. It's fall,
sign woven in iron

rails of neighbor's porch:
"Elect Pat Sole."

O sole mio, mother,
thinking of old attic,

West Acton farmhouse,
same treasures here, the boxes,

old carpets, the smell.
On wall facing, in chalk:

KISS ME. I love you.
Small world of these pinnacles,

places ride up in these
houses like clouds,

and I've come as far,
as high, as I'll go.

Sweet weather, turn
now of year . . .

The old horse chestnut,
with trunk a stalk like a flower's,

gathers strength to face winter.
The spiked pods of its seeds

start to split, soon will drop.
The patience, of small lawns, small hedges,

papers blown by the wind,
the light fading, gives way

to the season. School's
started again. Footsteps fall

on sidewalk down three
stories. It's man-made

endurance I'm after,
it's love for the wear

and the tear here,
goes under, gets broken, but stays.

Where finally else
in the world come to rest—

by a brook, by a
view with a farm

like a dream—in
a forest? In a house

has walls all around it?
There's more always here

than just me, in this room,
this attic, apartment,

this house, this world,
can't escape.

LATER (10)

In testament
to a willingness

to *live*, I,
Robert Creeley,

being of sound body
and mind, admit

to other preoccupations—
with the future, with

the past. But now—
but now the wonder of life is

that *it is* at all,
this sticky sentimental

warm enclosure,
feels place in the physical

with others,
lets mind wander

to wondering thought,
then lets go of itself,

finds a home
on earth.

> —*400 Fargo*
> *Buffalo, N.Y.*
> *September 3rd to 13th, 1977—*

FOR RENE RICARD

Remote control factors
of existence, like
"I wanted it this way!"

And hence to Lenox
one summer's day
with old friend, Warren Tallman,

past charming hills
and valleys give class
to that part of western Mass.

I can get funny—
and I can get lost,
go wandering on,

with friends like signboards
flashing past
in those dark nights of the soul.

All one world, Rene,
no matter one's half
of all it is or was.

So walking with you and Pepi,
talking, gossiping,
thank god—the useful news—

what's presently the word
of X, Y, and Z
in NYC, the breezes

on the hill, by the orchard
where Neil sits under tree,
blow the words away,

while he watches me talk,
mouth poems for them,
though he can't hear a word.

This is art,
the public act
that all those dirt roads lead to,

all those fucking bogs
and blown out tires
and broken fan belts—

willed decision—
call it,
though one's too dumb to know.

For me—and possibly
for only me—a bird
sits in a lousy tree,

and sings and sings
all goddamn day,
and what I do

is write it down,
in words
they call them:

him, and *it,* and *her,*
some story this
will sometimes tell

or not. The bird
can't care, the
tree can hardly hold it up—

and me is least of all
its worry. What then
is this life all about.

Simple. It's garbage
dumped in street,
a friend's quick care,

someone who hates you
and won't go way,
a breeze

blowing past Neil's
malfunctioning dear ears,
a blown-out dusty room,

an empty echoing kitchen,
a physical heart
which goes or stops.

For you—
because you carry wit with you,
and you are there somehow

at the hard real times,
and you know them too—
a necessary love.

THE PLACE

. . . Swoop of hawk—
or mind's adjustment

to sight—*memory?*
Air unrelieved, *unlived?*

Begun again, begin
again the play

of cloud, the lift
of sudden cliff,

the place in place—
the way it was again.

Go back a day,
take everything, take time

and play it back
again, the staggering

path, ridiculous, uncertain
bird, blurred, fuzzy

fog—or rocks which
seem to hang in

imperceptible substance
there, or here,

in thought? This thinking
is a place itself

unthought, which comes
to be the world.

LEARNING

"Suggestion/recognition . . ."
The horse
at the edge of the pool,

or the horse's ass,
the fool,
either end, sits

waiting for world
to resolve it—
Or in swirl

of these apparent facts,
contexts, states,
of possible being,

among all others,
of numbered time,
one or two

gleam clearly
there, now *here*—
in mind.

CORN CLOSE

for Basil Bunting

Words again, rehearsal—
"Are we going to
get up *into*

heaven—after all?"
What's
the sound of *that,*

who, where—
and how.
One wonder,

one wonders, sees
the world—
specifically, this one.

Sheep, many
with lambs,
of a spring morning,

on sharp slope of hill's side,
run up it
in chill rain.

Below's brook,
as I'd say,
a *burn?* a *beck?*

Goddamnit, *learn* it.
Fell fills eye,
as we lie abed.

Basil's up and out
walking
with the weather's

vagaries. His home is
this world's
wetness

or any's, feet
planted on ground,
and but

for trash can takes
weekly hauling
up and down,

no seeming fact
of age presently
bothers him.

Vague palaver.
Can I get the fire
to burn with wet wood?

Am I useful
today? Will I fuck up
the fireplace?

Drop
log
on my foot.

At breakfast we sit,
provided, tea's steam,
hot scones, butter,

marmalade—Basil's
incurious, reassuring
smile—*and* stories

of Queen E's
garden party, the thousands
jammed into garden—

style
of a damned poor
sort . . . Consider

(at night) Corelli
gives lifetime
to getting it right:

the *Twelve Concerti Grossi,*
not Ives
(whom I love),

not makeshift,
tonal blather—
but sound meets sound

with clear edge,
finds place,
precise, in the mind.

Have you seen a hawk—
look out! It
will get you,

blurred,
patient person,
drinking, eating,

sans body, sans
history, in-
telligence, etc.

Oh, I think
the words come from
the world and go

"I know
not
where . . ."

Their breasts banging—
flap—on their breastbones
makes the dear *sound*—

like tire tread
pulled from the shoe—
flap flap, bangs the body,

chortles, gurgles,
wheezes, breathes,
"Camptown race is (?)

five miles long!"
Back on the track,
you asshole.

No excuses,
no
"other things to do"—

And Wyatt's
flight through the night
is an honest

apprehension:
They *flee*
from *me*

that sometime did me seek . . .
When we'd first come,
our thought

was to help him,
old friend, and brought
such scanty makeshift

provision, in retrospect
I blush—as who
would give to Northumbrian

Teacher's
as against Glenfiddich—
which he had.

Was I scared
old friend
would be broken

by world
all his life
had lived in,

or that art,
his luck,
had gone sour?

My fear
is my own.
He got

the car started
after I tried
and tried, felt

battery fading,
mist-sodden spark plugs—
despair!

He had a wee can
in his hand,
and he sprayed

minute part
of its contents—
phfft!—on car's motor,

and car starts,
by god. What wonder
more than

to be where you are,
and to know it?
All's here.

THE CHILDREN

after Patrick Kavanagh

Down on the sidewalk recurrent
children's forms, reds, greens,
walking along with the watching
elders not their own.

It's winter, grows colder and colder.
How to play today without sun?
Will summer, gone, come again?
Will I only grow older and older?

Not wise enough yet to know
you're only here at all
as the wind blows, now
as the fire burns low.

III

DESULTORY DAYS

for Peter Warshall

Desultory days,
time's wandering
impermanences—

like, *what's for lunch,*
Mabel? Hunks
of unwilling

meat got chopped
from recalcitrant
beasts? "No tears

for this vision"—
nor huge strawberries
zapped from forlorn Texas,

too soon, too soon . . .
We will meet again
one day, we will

gather at the river
(Paterson perchance)
so turgidly oozes by,

etc. Nothing new in the world
but us, the human
parasite eats up

that self-defined reality
we talked about in
ages past. Now prophecy declares,

got to get on with it,
back to the farm, else die
in streets inhuman

'spite we made them every one.
Ah friends, before I die,
I want to sit awhile

upon this old world's knee,
yon charming hill, you see,
and dig the ambient breezes,

make of life
such gentle passing pleasure!
Were it then wrong

to avoid, as might be said,
the heaped-up canyons of the dead—
L.A.'s drear smut, and N.Y.C.'s

crunched millions? I don't know.
It seems to me
what can salvation be

for less than 1%
of so-called population
is somehow latent fascism

of the soul. What leaves behind
those other people,
like they say,

reneges on Walter Whitman's
19th century Mr. Goodheart's
Lazy Days and Ways In Which

we might still *save the world.*
I loved it but
I never could believe it—

rather, the existential
terror of New England
countrywoman, Ms.

Dickinson: "The Brain, within its Groove
Runs evenly—and true—
But let a Splinter swerve—

" 'Twere easier for You—//
To put a Current back—
When Floods have slit the Hills—

"And scooped a Turnpike for Themselves—
And Trodden out the Mills—"
moves me. My mind

to me a nightmare is—
that thought of days,
years, went its apparent way

without itself, with
no other company than thought.
So—*born to die*—why

take everything with us?
Why the meagerness
of life deliberately,

why the patience
when of no use,
and the anger, when it is?

I am no longer
one man—
but an old one

who is human again
after a long time,
feels the meat contract,

or stretch, upon bones,
hates to be alone
but can't stand interruption.

Funny
how it all works out,
and Asia is

after all *how much money*
it costs—
either to buy or to sell it.

Didn't they have a
world too? But then
they don't look like us,

do they? But they'll get us,
someone will—they'll find us,
they won't leave us here

just to die
by ourselves
all alone?

ARROYO

Out the window,
across the ground there,
persons walk
in the hard sun—

Like years ago we'd watch
the children go to school
in the vacant building now
across the arroyo.

Same persons,
Mr. Gutierrez and,
presumably, his son,
Victor, back from the army—

Would wave to me
if I did to them,
call *que tal, hello,*
across the arroyo.

How sentimental,
heartfelt, this life becomes
when you try to think of it,
say it in simple words—

How far in time and space
the distance,
the simple division of a ditch,
between people.

FOR JOHN DUFF

"I placed a jar in Tennessee . . ."
—Wallace Stevens,
"Anecdote of the Jar"

Blast of harsh
flat sunlight

on recalcitrant ground
after rain. Ok.

Life in N.M. is
not a tourist's paradise,

not the solar
energy capital

of the world, not
your place in the sun. If

I had my way,
I'd be no doubt

long gone. But
here I am and we talk

of plastic America,
of other friends

other places. What
will we do

today. When
will heart's peace

descend in rippling, convenient
waves. Why

is the sky still
so high.

What's
underfoot.

I don't
feel comfortable with Indians—

and the Mexican
neighbors with

seventeen kids—
what time exists

now still to
include them.

Ok. A day
goes by. Night

follows. On the slight
lip of earth

down from the gate
at the edge of

the arroyo
sits

a *menhir*—
remember

that oar
you could screw into

ground, say,
here I'll build a city?

No way.
This column

is common
old stretcher

cement blocks.
Put one on one

in pairs, first this way,
then that, you get

a house,
explicit, of the mind,

both thought
and the senses provoke it—

you see it—
you feel and think

this world.
It's a quiet

grey column,
handsome—"the one

missing color"—
and it's here now

forever,
no matter

it falls in a day.
Ok, John.

When you're gone,
I'll remember

also forever
the tough dear

sentiment, the clarity,
of your talking, the care.

And this *it*
you gave us:

here
is all the wonder,

there
is all there is.

TALK

One thing, strikes in,
recall, anyone talking
got to be to human

or something, like a rock,
a "song," a thing to
talk to, to talk to.

POOR

Nothing's
today and
tomorrow only.

.

Slow-
er.

.

Place-
ss.

.

POOR
Pur-
pose por-
puss.

.

Sore hand.

.

Got
to get going.

.

And I was
not asleep

and I was
not alone.

TOUCHSTONE

for L.Z.

"Something
by which
all else
can be measured."

Something
by which
to measure
all else.

MORNING (8:10 AM)

In sun's
slow rising
this morning

antenna tower
catches
the first light,

shines
for an instant
silver

white,
separate
from the houses,

the trees,
old woman walking
on street out front.

EYE O' THE STORM

Weather's a funny
factor, like once

day breaks, storm's
lifted, or come,

faces, eyes,
like clouds drift

over this world,
are all there is

of whatever there is.

ON A THEME BY LAWRENCE, HEARING PURCELL

Knowing what
knowing is,

think less
of your life as labor.

Pain's increase,
thought's random torture,

grow with intent.
Simply live.

THIS DAY

This day after
Thanksgiving the edge
of winter
comes closer.

This grey, dulled
morning the sky
closes down on
the horizon to make

one wonder
if a life lives more
than just looking,
knowing nothing more.

Yet such a gentle
light, faded,
domestic,
impermanent—

one will not
go farther than home
to see this world
so quietly, greyly, shrunken.

THE LAST MILE

for Jack Clarke

What's to be said
of friend dead—
eight years later?

Should he have waited
for whatever
here comes together

to make a use
for these friends and fools
must need excuse

for testament, for
interpretation,
for their own investment?

You know the world
is one *big blow*—
that's all.

I'm here as well, now
unable to say
what it is or was,

he said, more than to stay
in the body
all the way

to the grave, as it happens,
which is what scares us
then and now.

So much for the human.
No one more than any
ever did anything.

But we'll still talk about it,
as if to get out of it,
be God's little symbols . . .

At least to *stand forth*—
walk up the path,
kick the goddamn rock.

Then take deep breath
and cry—
Thank god I'm alive!

IF I HAD MY WAY

If I had my way, dear,
all these fears, these insistent
blurs of discontent would fade,

and there be
old time meadows
with brown and white cows,

and those boulders,
still in mind, marked
the solid world. I'd

show you these ridiculous,
simple happinesses, the wonders
I've kept hold on

to steady the world—
the brook, the woods,
the paths, the clouds, the house

I lived in,
with the big barn
with my father's sign on it:

FOUR WINDS FARM.
What life ever is
stays in them.

You're young, like
they say. Your life
still comes to find

me—my honor
its choice. Here is the place
we live in

day by day, to learn
love, having it,
to begin again

again. Looking up,
this sweet room
with its colors, its forms,

has become you—
as my own life
finds its way

to you also,
wants to haul
all forward

but learns to let go,
lets the presence
of you be.

If I had my way, dear,
forever there'd be
a garden of roses—

on the old player piano
was in the sitting room
you've never seen nor will now see,

nor my mother or father,
or all that came after,
was a life lived,

all the labor, the pain?
the deaths, the wars,
the births

of my children? On
and on then—
for you and for me.

ONE

There are no words I know
tell where to go and how,
or how to get back again
from wherever one's been.

They don't keep directions
as tacit information.
Years of doing this and that
stay in them, yet apart.

As if words were things,
like anything. Like this one—
s i n g l e—
sees itself so.

THE FACT

Think of a grand metaphor
for life's décor,
a party atmosphere
for all you love or fear—

let a daydream
make factual being,
nightmare be where
you live then.

When I'm sufficiently depressed,
I change the record,
crawl out into air,
still thankful it's there.

Elsewise the nuttiness of existence
truly confuses—
nowhere to eat
if thousands starving give you meat,

nowhere to sit
if thousands die for it,
nowhere to sleep
if thousands cannot.

Thousands, millions, billions
of people die, die,
happy or sad, starved, murdered,
or indifferent.

What's the burden then
to assume,
as 'twere load on back—
a simple fact?

Will it be right
later tonight,
when body's dumped its load
and grown silent,

when hairs grow on
in the blackness
on dead or living face,
when bones creak,

turning in bed, still alive?
What is the pattern,
the plan, makes it right
to be alive,

more than *you are,*
if dying's the onus
common to all of us?
No one gets more or less.

Can you hurry through it,
can you push and pull
all with you,
can you leave anything alone?

Do you dare to
live in the world,
this world,
equal with all—

or, thinking, remembering,
$1 + 1 = 2,$
that sign means one and one,
and two, are the same—

equality!
"God shed his grace on thee . . ."
How abstract
is that fucking fact.

PRAYER TO HERMES

for Rafael Lopez-Pedraza

Hermes, god
of crossed sticks,
crossed existence,
protect these feet

I offer. Imagination
is the wonder
of the real, and I am
sore afflicted with

the devil's doubles,
the twos, of this
half-life,
this twilight.

Neither one nor two
but a mixture
walks here
in me—

feels forward,
finds behind
the track, yet
cannot stand

still or be here
elemental, be more
or less a man,
a woman.

What I understand
of this life,
what was right
in it, what was wrong,

I have forgotten
in these days
of physical change.
I see the ways

of knowing, of
securing, life grow
ridiculous. A weakness,
a tormenting, relieving weakness

comes to me. My hand
I see at arm's end—
five fingers, fist—
is not mine?

Then must I forever
walk on, *walk on*—
as I have and
as I can?

Neither truth, nor love,
nor body itself—
nor anyone of any—
become me?

Yet questions
are tricks,
for me—
and always will be.

This moment the grey,
suffusing fog
floats in the quiet courtyard
beyond the window—

this morning grows now
to noon, and somewhere above
the sun warms the air
and wetness drips as ever

under the grey, diffusing
clouds. This weather,
this winter, comes closer.
This—*physical* sentence.

I give all
to you, hold
nothing back,
have no strength to.

My luck
is your gift,
my melodious
breath, my stumbling,

my twisted commitment,
my vagrant
drunkenness, my confused
flesh and blood.

All who know me
say, *why* this man's
persistent pain, the scarifying
openness he makes do with?

Agh! brother spirit,
what do they know
of whatever *is* the instant
cannot wait a minute—

will find heaven in hell,
will be there again even now,
and *will* tell of itself
all, *all* the world.

Some New Directions Paperbooks

The Real Life of Sebastian Knight. NDP432.
P. Neruda, The Captain's Verses.† NDP345.
    Residence on Earth.† NDP340.
New Directions in Prose & Poetry (Anthology).
    Available from #17 forward. #38, Spring 1979.
Robert Nichols, Arrival. NDP437.
    Garh City. NDP450.
    Harditts in Sawna. NDP470.
Charles Olson, Selected Writings. NDP231.
Toby Olson. The Life of Jesus. NDP417.
George Oppen, Collected Poems. NDP418.
Wilfred Owen, Collected Poems. NDP210.
Nicanor Parra, Emergency Poems.† NDP333.
    Poems and Antipoems.† NDP242.
Boris Pasternak, Safe Conduct. NDP77.
Kenneth Patchen, Aflame and Afun. NDP292.
    Because It Is. NDP83.
    But Even So. NDP265.
    Collected Poems. NDP284.
    Doubleheader. NDP211.
    Hallelujah Anyway. NDP219.
    In Quest of Candlelighters. NDP334.
    The Journal of Albion Moonlight. NDP99.
    Memoirs of a Shy Pornographer. NDP205.
    Selected Poems. NDP160.
    Wonderings. NDP320.
Octavio Paz, Configurations.† NDP303.
    Eagle or Sun?† NDP422.
    Early Poems.† NDP354.
Plays for a New Theater. (Anth.) NDP216.
J. A. Porter, Eelgrass. NDP438.
Ezra Pound, ABC of Reading. NDP89.
    Classic Noh Theatre of Japan. NDP79.
    Confucius. NDP285.
    Confucius to Cummings. (Anth.) NDP126.
    Gaudier Brzeska. NDP372.
    Guide to Kulchur. NDP257.
    Literary Essays. NDP250.
    Love Poems of Ancient Egypt. NDP178.
    Pavannes and Divagations. NDP397.
    Pound/Joyce. NDP296.
    Selected Cantos. NDP304.
    Selected Letters 1907-1941. NDP317.
    Selected Poems. NDP66.
    Selected Prose 1909-1965. NDP396.
    The Spirit of Romance. NDP266.
    Translations.† (Enlarged Edition) NDP145.
James Purdy, Children Is All. NDP327.
Raymond Queneau, The Bark Tree. NDP314.
    The Flight of Icarus. NDP358.
    The Sunday of Life. NDP433.
Mary de Rachewiltz, Ezra Pound. NDP405.
M. Randall, Part of the Solution. NDP350.
John Crove Ransom, Beating the Bushes.
    NDP324.
Raja Rao, Kanthapura. NDP224.
Herbert Read, The Green Child. NDP208.
P. Reverdy, Selected Poems.† NDP346.
Kenneth Rexroth, Beyond the Mountains.
    NDP384.
    Collected Longer Poems. NDP309.
    Collected Shorter Poems. NDP243.
    New Poems. NDP383.
    100 More Poems from the Chinese. NDP308.
    100 More Poems from the Japanese. NDP420.
    100 Poems from the Chinese. NDP192.
    100 Poems from the Japanese.† NDP147.
Rainer Maria Rilke, Poems from
    The Book of Hours. NDP408.
    Possibility of Being. NDP436.
    Where Silence Reigns. (Prose). NDP464.
Arthur Rimbaud, Illuminations.† NDP56.
    Season in Hell & Drunken Boat.† NDP97.
Edouard Roditi, Delights of Turkey. NDP445.
Selden Rodman, Tongues of Fallen Angels.
    NDP373.
Jerome Rothenberg, Poems for the Game
    of Silence. NRP406.
    Poland/1931. NDP379.
    Seneca Journal. NDP448.
Saikaku Ihara, The Life of an Amorous
    Woman. NDP270.

Saigyo. Mirror for the Moon.† NDP465.
St. John of the Cross, Poems.† NDP341.
Jean-Paul Sartre, Baudelaire. NDP233.
    Nausea. NDP82.
    The Wall (Intimacy). NDP272.
Delmore Schwartz, Selected Poems. NDP241.
    In Dreams Begin Responsibilities. NDP454.
Kazuko Shiraishi, Seasons of Sacred Lust.
    NDP453.
Stevie Smith, Selected Poems, NDP159.
Gary Snyder, The Back Country. NDP249.
    Earth House Hold. NDP267.
    Myths and Texts. NDP457.
    Regarding Wave. NDP306.
    Turtle Island. NDP381.
Gilbert Sorrentino, Splendide-Hôtel. NDP364.
Enid Starkie. Rimbaud. NDP254.
Stendhal, The Telegraph. NDP108.
Jules Supervielle, Selected Writings.† NDP209.
W. Sutton, American Free Verse. NDP351.
Nathaniel Tarn, Lyrics . . . Bride of God. NDP391.
Dylan Thomas, Adventures in the Skin Trade.
    NDP183.
    A Child's Christmas in Wales. NDP181.
    Collected Poems 1934-1952. NDP316.
    The Doctor and the Devils. NDP297.
    Portrait of the Artist as a Young Dog.
    NDP51.
    Quite Early One Morning. NDP90.
    Under Milk Wood. NDP73.
Martin Turnell, Art of French Fiction. NDP251.
    Baudelaire. NDP336.
    Rise of the French Novel. NDP474.
Paul Valéry, Selected Writings.† NDP184.
P. Van Ostaijen, Feasts of Fear & Agony.
    NDP411.
Elio Vittorini, A Vittorini Omnibus. NDP366.
    Women of Messina. NDP365.
Vernon Watkins, Selected Poems. NDP221.
Nathanael West, Miss Lonelyhearts &
    Day of the Locust. NDP125.
J. Williams, An Ear in Bartram's Tree. NDP335.
Tennessee Williams, Camino Real, NDP301.
    Cat on a Hot Tin Roof. NDP398.
    Dragon Country. NDP287.
    Eight Mortal Ladies Possessed, NDP374.
    The Glass Menagerie. NDP218.
    Hard Candy. NDP225.
    In the Winter of Cities. NDP154.
    One Arm & Other Stories. NDP237.
    The Roman Spring of Mrs. Stone. NDP271.
    Small Craft Warnings. NDP348.
    Sweet Bird of Youth. NDP409.
    Twenty-Seven Wagons Full of Cotton. NDP217.
    Vieux Carré. NDP482.
    Where I Live, NDP468.
William Carlos Williams.
    The Autobiography. NDP223.
    The Build-up. NDP259.
    Embodiment of Knowledge. NDP434.
    The Farmers' Daughters. NDP106.
    I Wanted to Write a Poem. NDP469.
    Imaginations. NDP329.
    In the American Grain. NDP53.
    In the Money. NDP240.
    Paterson. Complete. NDP152.
    Pictures from Brueghel. NDP118.
    The Selected Essays. NDP273.
    Selected Poems. NDP131.
    A Voyage to Pagany. NDP307.
    White Mule. NDP226.
    W. C. Williams Reader. NDP282.
Yvor Winters, E. A. Robinson. NDP326.
Wisdom Books: Ancient Egyptians, NDP467;
    Wisdom of the Desert, NDP295; Early
    Buddhists, NDP444; English Mystics, NDP466;
    Forest (Hindu), NDP414; Jewish Mystics,
    NDP423; Spanish Mystics, NDP442; Sufi,
    NDP424; Zen Masters, NDP415.

Complete descriptive catalog available free on request from
New Directions, 80 Eighth Avenue, New York 10011   † Bilingual

Reach for the Summit

Reach for

The **Definite Dozen System** for
Succeeding at Whatever You Do

the Summit

Pat Summitt

with Sally Jenkins

Three Rivers Press ● New York

Three Rivers Press and the Tugboat design are registered trademarks of Random House, Inc.

Originally published in hardcover in the United States by Broadway Books, New York, in
1998, and subsequently published in paperback by Broadway Paperbacks in 1999.

Three Rivers Press titles may be purchased for business or promotional use or for special
sales. For information, please contact: Premium Sales at (212) 572-2232 or email
specialmarkets@randomhouse.com.

Designed by Brian Mulligan

The Library of Congress has catalogued the hardcover edition as:

Summitt, Pat Head, 1952–
     Reach for the summit : the definite dozen system for succeeding at
whatever you do / Pat Summitt with Sally Jenkins. — 1st ed.
          p.   cm.
     ISBN 0-7679-0228-9 (hardcover)
     1. Success—Psychological aspects.   I. Jenkins, Sally.
II. Title.
BF637.S8S82   1998
158—dc21   97-52609
                                                              CIP

ISBN 978-0-7679-0229-8

20   19   18

For my family—for my mother and my father, the two people who have influenced me most, and for my husband, who is my best friend and generously supports me in a two-career household, and for my son, who has already taught me more than I've taught any player. Thanks to him, I am a better coach.

—PAT HEAD SUMMITT

For my actual goddaughters, Avery, Meredith, and Paige, and for my informal ones, Rachel and Bailey. Gorgeous children of a trillion toys, may you have a Pat in your lives.

—SALLY JENKINS

Acknowledgments

We are indebted to Bob Barnett of Williams & Connolly for proposing this book, to John Sterling of Broadway Books for his belief in it, and to Esther Newberg of ICM for helping to bring us together on it. Without them, these pages would not have been written or published.

We are especially grateful to five people who lived with the project every day: R.B. and Tyler Summitt and Tennessee assistant coaches Mickie DeMoss, Holly Warlick, and Al Brown. They endured the imposition gracefully and told their side of the story with honesty, affection, and hilarity.

Katie Wynn and Debby Jennings of the Tennessee women's athletic department and Jenny Minton and Luke Dempsey of Broadway Books each provided invaluable editorial advice and laughter from the trenches.

Pat was very fortunate to play for some knowledgeable and dedicated coaches who greatly influenced her life as she competed at the junior high, high school, college, and international level, and she would like to thank them.

But special thanks are reserved for the Lady Vol basketball family, immediate and extended, past and present, including each of those student athletes and assistants who have worked so hard over the last twenty-four years, as well as university president Dr. Joe Johnson, past president Dr. Ed Boling, women's athletic director Joan Cronan, and the Lady Vol team managers. Without such dedicated players, staff, and administrators, there would be no success story to tell.

—P.S. and S.J.

Contents

The Threepeat Season

Sometimes the best laid plan doesn't work, and sometimes, you don't have a plan at all, and things work out beautifully. Most of the time, you only have half a plan, and it about half works. But every once in awhile, a good plan works to utter perfection. When that happens, you don't write it off to luck or good fortune. You examine it, and ask yourself why things turned out so well.

I wrote *Reach for the Summit* in the summer and fall of 1997 with no idea of what the University of Tennessee women's basketball team was about to accomplish. It was a peculiar process. When I began the book, Tennessee had just experienced one of its most difficult, if rewarding seasons, struggling to a 27–10 mark, and setting a record for the most losses ever by a team that still managed to claim a national championship. Then, on the heels of that team and shortly after the publication of *Reach*

for the Summit, came the 1997–98 Lady Vols. A team starring four fresh-
men and an All-American named Chamique Holdsclaw went 39–0, estab-
lishing a record for the most victories by a collegiate team ever, men or
women, and along the way won a third consecutive national champion-
ship, Tennessee's sixth overall. Some called it the greatest women's col-
legiate basketball team ever.

In short, in the space of two seasons, Tennessee managed to set records
for both losses and victories.

Strangely enough, after writing a how-to-succeed book, and concluding
that I knew all there was to know about success, the 1997–1998 Lady Vols
were the single most successful experience of my career.

Why?

The extraordinary but very different achievements of those back-to-back
championship teams forced me to think again about *Reach for the Sum-
mit*, and the set of principles it outlines. The one thing those teams had in
common, I realized, was the Definite Dozen. While the players have
changed at Tennessee, The Definite Dozen has remained a fixture. It has
evolved over several years, with many of the rules in place for more than a
decade, while some of them have been refined or reworded.

Reach for the Summit opens with the 1997–98 squad reporting to cam-
pus, and our first team meeting. What none of us could know then was
that the Lady Vols would go on to exemplify every principle contained in
the Definite Dozen. Our plan was fully realized.

But in the beginning, we didn't even know if they would get along. We
had a puzzling mix of new players and veterans. We had four pure fresh-
men, and not a single senior. How could we hope to repeat our previous
success? Would they respect each other? The more talented people you
put in the same room, the bigger the potential problem.

But ultimately, their desire to win was strong enough to overcome
personal concerns in the name of team, and that in turn created the
intangible thing called chemistry.

Of course, there are a million different motivational formulas and
prescriptives for winning, from the Definite Dozen to John Wooden's
Pyramid of Success. But I have noticed that they tend to have common
denominators. Any realistic formula must include five things: people, sys-

tem, communication, work ethic, and discipline. The Definite Dozen is simply a proven plan for incorporating each of these.

I've always believed you win with people. You cannot succeed at any level without talented people around you. The Lady Vols came in highly motivated. They weren't only talented, they took responsibility for themselves before they ever reported to campus. Once they arrived, they committed to the system. But they never lost that creative individual spark. They were respectful of the program, but never intimidated by it.

Next, you have to have a system. The Lady Vols were one of the most principled teams I've ever encountered. Despite the presence of huge competitive egos and almost too much talent for one bench, they never quarreled over playing time. They each accepted their role in the overall scheme.

You can have the brightest, most creative people in the world, but if they can't communicate you won't fully comprehend what they're capable of. They have to understand the system and each other. The '97–98 Lady Vols, it gradually dawned on me, were an especially uninhibited group. If they thought it, they said it. If they felt it, they expressed it.

Without hard work, you won't get anywhere. What's more, you have to be willing to work even after you have achieved success. One of the most impressive attributes of that unbeaten team was that they continued to work hard even when they were winning. In the end, they won games by an average of more than 20 points.

At that first team meeting, I challenged the Lady Vols to be the first team in my career not to have a discipline problem. We never had a single serious instance of one.

People often ask me if the Lady Vols felt extra pressure as we approached the end of what could be a perfect season. No, we really didn't. We felt an excitement. We felt an opportunity. Our goal every year is to win a title. You have to aim that high if you expect to reach a goal. If you expect to be No. 1, you might wind up No. 4. But if you just want to be somewhere in the top 10, you'll probably wind up a lot lower.

Above all, the experience of going undefeated with the 1997–98 Lady Vols reaffirmed the importance of doing the little things. The Definite Dozen is ultimately about paying attention to basics, those things that enable you to achieve a larger, more profound goal. When you want to win a championship, you don't focus on winning. You focus on the small tasks you have to do in order to win.

And once you have won a championship, what then? You try to win another one, of course. A funny thing happened in the aftermath of our 1997–98 NCAA championship. Someone asked Chamique Holdsclaw if she thought the Lady Vols were the greatest team ever.

"You know what?" she said. "I think next year's team will be the best ever."

Never Wait 'Til Next Year

When I get after something, the veins in my neck stand out. The color begins to rise up from my collarbone, and you can see the pulse going in my throat, and my eyes look like the high beams of an oncoming car. I am what you would call a classic Type A personality. An extremely demanding person. Certainly the people close to me would tell you that, including my seven-year-old son, Tyler. In whom, may I just say, I have met my match. The other night, Tyler pulled out his own front tooth, and it wasn't even that loose. The fact that it was his *only* remaining front tooth, and that it bled like a slaughtered hog, and that he reminded me more than a little bit of myself, may have accounted for the exorbitant fee of seven dollars he received from the tooth fairy.

"Mama," Tyler says, when I get that look in my eye. "Please put your sunglasses back on."

That's who you're dealing with here. Someone who will sell her house to own your farm. Someone who will push you beyond all reasonable limits. Someone who will ask you to not just fulfill your potential, but to exceed it. Someone who will expect more from you than you may believe you are capable of. So if you aren't ready to go to work, shut this book.

They tell a story about me back in Henrietta, Tennessee. One day when I was about fourteen years old, I passed a neighbor boy who was struggling to load a forty-five-pound bale of hay on to a truck. He was hot and sweaty, and trying to push the bale up onto the flatbed. I was just a tall, stick-legged girl everybody called Bone.

I watched him for a minute, and then I said, "You want me to show you how to do that?"

I grabbed the bale from him and threw it four stacks high.

You're wondering what a bale of hay has to do with success. Well, there's a trick to loading hay. You have to use your knee. What you do is, you put your right knee behind it and half kick it up in the air. That way you get some loft on it. It works with luggage, too.

My point is, there are certain ways to make a hard job easier. Which is what this book is all about. It's about some tried-and-true methods of success, applicable to any job, that I have found over the course of my career.

I can fix a tractor, mow hay, plow a field, chop tobacco, fire a barn, and call cows. I can also teach, cook, and raise a child. But what I'm known for is winning. I wrote this book because I believe the winning formula we have created at Tennessee deserves to be documented.

I also wrote it because I'm not happy unless I'm driving myself to my limit, and driving everybody around me crazy while I'm doing it. Fortunately, I have a loyal, long-suffering staff in my assistants Mickie DeMoss, Holly Warlick, and Al Brown, and my secretary of seventeen years, Katie Wynn. I usually try to do five things at once—in fact, we remodeled our house at the same time I was working on this book.

I'm famous for putting my makeup on at stoplights. I constantly drive barefoot, changing my shoes in the car. I seem to arrive at my latest appointment still screwing in one earring.

My attitude is, why do things one at a time, when you can do two at once? The more work I have to do, the happier I am.

In my opinion, too many people in this world are born on third base and think they've hit a triple. They think winning is a natural state of being. Take our team, the 1998 University of Tennessee Lady Volunteers. Every year, we get one or two players who think that just being at Tennessee is enough, that all they have to do is stand on the basketball court, and breathe in and out, and we will win titles. And why shouldn't they think that? We've won five titles in ten years, and two back-to-back in 1996–97. Fourteen times the Lady Vols have finished among the Final Four in the nation. You could pull a heist in our locker room, it's so jammed with silver and gold hardware.

I promise you, I cure our players of this type of thinking. It starts the moment they arrive.

On a mild Sunday this past August, the 1998 Tennessee women's basketball team reported to campus. They gathered in a locker room that still bore the signs and slogans and newspaper clippings of the '97 national championship season. The Lady Volunteers hadn't really been together since we had done the so-called impossible the previous March, when a team no one believed in, a group of classic overachievers, defeated Old Dominion, 68–59, to win a second straight NCAA title.

Now we were joined by four new players, a group that was being called the single best recruiting class in the history of women's collegiate basketball: Tamika Catchings, the Naismith Award winner for best high school player in the country; Semeka Randall, *USA Today*'s Player of the Year; Kristen "Ace" Clement, a fluid point guard out of Broomall, Pennsylvania, who we jokingly call "Aceika"; Teresa Geter, the best player in the state of South Carolina. The rest of the team was an assortment of underclassmen, led by junior All American Chamique Holdsclaw, the clear candidate for collegiate player of the year.

I had a lot to say to these young ladies. A whole lot. I knew that before the '98 season was over, I would probably say it with those veins standing out in my neck.

Everybody was talking "three-peat"—an unprecedented third straight national championship. But how could I explain what we would have to go through if we wanted to win another? How could I explain to them just how tired and hoarse I would grow from the daily exertion of trying to convince a team that isn't very good—no one ever is, not at the beginning—to become great? How could I convince them, in a simple welcome speech, of what it has taken me forty-five years to learn:

Winners are not born, they are *self-made*.

●   ●   ●

If ever there was proof of this, it was Tennessee's '97 team. No team had ever won a title with ten losses. But somehow they managed to win it all. As I looked around the locker room that following fall, the whole story was right there in front of me. The walls yelled it out, and I heard my own voice coming back at me. I saw the spot on the wall where I had thrown a cup of water in frustration with my center, Abby Conklin. They had been called "losers" and "pretenders" in the press. I had added my own taunts.

Abby Conklin, everybody wants to guard you. They can't wait.

Ya'll better get back out there quick, because if I was a paying spectator, I'd leave.

To be perfectly honest, I hadn't liked the personality of the '97 team to begin with. They were too quiet, they were listless, they had no attitude. I felt like a dentist pulling teeth. The misery started the day before our first practice, when I learned that our point guard, Kellie Jolly, had torn her anterior cruciate ligament. I knew then that we were in serious trouble. I could look at our schedule and count the games we would lose.

Of course, I didn't dare let the team know it. But I told my husband, R.B., "This is gonna be a long year."

I was right. We didn't just lose. We lost badly. On December 15, we were humiliated by Stanford, 82–65. *On our home court.* It was our worst loss in Knoxville in a decade. It gave us a 7–3 record, our slowest start since 1984.

Chamique Holdsclaw was not used to losing. Chamique had never lost at anything. She had finished every year of her career so far as a champion. She had won state championships all four years at her New York

City high school, Christ the King. Then she had won a national title as a freshman at Tennessee.

And she was completely demoralized after that Stanford game.

As we were walking back to the press room, Chamique dragged alongside of me. "I can't wait 'til next year," she muttered.

And we were only ten games into the season.

I didn't want to reveal how concerned I was, so I said, "Chamique, we're going to be all right."

But a few games later we got killed again, this time by top-ranked Connecticut, 72–57. In that game, we racked up season lows for points and shooting percentage. Now we had five losses, and we were on our way to play Old Dominion, ranked second in the country. On the night of January 5, we changed planes in Washington, D.C. I sat there in the airport, exhausted, in the same clothes I had coached in against UConn. Tyler was asleep on my lap, and I was too tired to move. I was in a daze. All of a sudden I saw the North Carolina basketball team, and their coach, Sylvia Hatchell, passing through the airport. I must have looked awful, because she put a hand on my shoulder as she went by.

"How you doing, Pat?" she asked sympathetically.

"Oh, I'm doing all right," I said.

Sylvia said, "Well, just hang in there 'til next year."

Right, I thought, wait 'til next year. It was like everyone had given up on us. Home Box Office had come to campus to film a documentary, but now the producers were being told to pull off the story and find another team, because we were losers. Even my own assistants were worried that we might not make the post-season tournament. I looked at our schedule, at where we still had to go, and thought, *How are we ever going to get through this?*

The next day I had a five-hour meeting with the team. Actually, this meeting, like others we have from time to time, was more like a knock-down-drag-out. I critiqued each and every one of them—and they critiqued me back. Chamique said straight out to her teammates, "I've got to have help." She had been doing it alone.

That night against Old Dominion, I was really proud of them. They fought, they made things happen, they were on top of every loose ball. But we lost again, 83–72.

Now we were 10–6.

Our players were devastated. In the post-game locker room, everyone was sobbing. Some of them to the point that they couldn't speak or breathe. They were so distraught that I was actually concerned. I put my arms around Chamique Holdsclaw, and her shoulders would not stop shaking.

I had never seen a team react so strongly. I was both moved and bothered by the depth of their emotion. So I made them a promise.

"Get your heads up," I said.

They looked at me, their eyes swollen.

"If you give effort like this all the time," I said, "if you fight like this, I'm telling you, I *promise* you, we'll be there in March."

I said it, and I believed it.

What had happened was, they had taken ownership of their team, and for the first time they all felt responsible.

When you take ownership of a project and make a commitment to it and then you fail, it hurts so deeply. If you never make that commitment—if you just stand around waiting for things to happen—failure won't affect you so much. You think, *It's not my fault.* But you won't succeed either.

So you have a choice. You can choose to settle for mediocrity, never venturing forth much effort or feeling very much. Or you can commit. If you commit, I guarantee you that, for every pain, you will experience an equal or surpassing pleasure.

But pleasure was a long way off in January of 1997. No one believed in us, not even my husband, R.B. My husband is a banker, so he has a natural tendency toward pessimism. But R.B. was as subdued as I had ever seen him. He has a very analytical, numerically oriented mind. That evening he stared at the schedule, and he said to me, "We won't win twenty games."

Well, that did it. I was furious.

"Let me tell you something," I said. "I am *not* waiting 'til next year. Do you understand me? I don't care what we have to do. We're going to win twenty games this year. I don't know how, but we will."

The discussion escalated from there until, finally, Tyler told us to quit fussing at each other.

Two months later, we were national champions.

Whenever I am asked to explain that remarkable accomplishment, I point to a placard posted in the most central place in our locker room. It says, THE DEFINITE DOZEN. The Definite Dozen is a set of commandments. It is Tennessee's most basic set of rules. It is a blueprint for winning.

But the Definite Dozen is more than just a formula for success. It is a set of principles that has evolved over my twenty-four years at Tennessee. You don't often hear ethics discussed in the same breath as success. But to me they are inseparable. A lot of people can win once. They get lucky, or follow their intuition, or strike on a good short-term formula. But very few people know how to repeat success on a consistent basis. They lose sight of their priorities, grow content, and abandon their principles.

Long-term, repetitive success is a matter of building a principled system and sticking to it. Principles are anchors; without them you will drift.

● ● ●

During that first meeting with our 1998 team, I thought about the long, hard road traveled by our 1997 team.

I gazed at our new group of players. I didn't know them very well yet. And they didn't know me either, 'cause I was still being nice to them. Hanging over them were pictures of dozens of past All Americans, and the ten Olympians we have produced at Tennessee—more than double any other school. Among them were Nikki McCray, Carla McGhee, Bridgette Gordon, Daedra Charles. These players had all been undergraduates once—drilled relentlessly in the Definite Dozen and yelled at by me at one time or another. But they were also like daughters, each with her own compartment in my heart.

The 1998 newcomers, I knew, saw similarly glorious visions for themselves: medals, awards, publicity, pro contracts, more titles. They were thinking big.

But the Definite Dozen is made up of small things.

"Your focus better not be on a three-peat," I warned them. "Because mine is not. Your focus better be on getting down in a defensive stance and posting up."

Then, as I have with every team at Tennessee in my recent years there, I introduced them to the Definite Dozen, one by one.

1. Respect Yourself and Others

2. Take Full Responsibility

3. Develop and Demonstrate Loyalty

4. Learn to Be a Great Communicator

5. Discipline Yourself So No One Else Has To

6. Make Hard Work Your Passion

7. Don't Just Work Hard, Work Smart

8. Put the Team Before Yourself

9. Make Winning an Attitude

10. Be a Competitor

11. Change Is a Must

12. Handle Success Like You Handle Failure

"Believe me, you'll work," I told them. "No one's died of it. I don't remember anyone passing out, either."

I paused.

"Although some came close."

And that's how we begin.

Q & A *Abby Conklin*

Forward, 1996–97 national championship team; Atlanta Glory, ABL

Q: Exactly what happened between you and Pat?
ABBY CONKLIN: *I disrespected her. She told me I'd hurt her more than any other player ever had. She wanted to know why I didn't respect her. And she said she wasn't gonna accept my apology. She said maybe she'd accept my apology by the end of the year. And then she threw this cup of water across the room. I just stood there in shock. I was like: She just hit me with water. The thing is, I had tremendous respect for her. But she kept pushing me and pushing me.*

Q: Were you afraid of her?
ABBY CONKLIN: *Well, I mean, it was difficult. I struggled with that.*

Q: Would you play for her again?
ABBY CONKLIN: *My mom asked me the same question, because she saw what a hard time I had at Tennessee. I said, "Yeah, if I had to do it again I'd be back there." She said, "After everything you went through?" But I would. And I'd send my daughter there in a heartbeat.*

Q: Why?
ABBY CONKLIN: *Because she makes you better. And she cares about you. I mean it's genuine. I love her to death. As hard as she is on you when you're on the court, she cares. She teaches more than basketball. She teaches you the things that are going to get you through the rest of your life.*

Respect Yourself
and Others

Sometimes I ask myself, "Could I play for me?" The answer's not always yes.

Back in 1974, no way could I have played for me. I was a twenty-two-year-old head coach, and I had four players who were twenty-one. I was hard on them and myself and everyone around me. I thought I had to be. I thought that's how you commanded respect.

My first day on the job, I stood in front of a packed room of Tennessee undergrads who came to open tryouts for the team. I decided I was going to set the tone right then and there. I was going to let everyone know how in charge I was. I gave a long speech about how demanding it would be to play for the Lady Volunteers.

Well, after that meeting at least thirty kids never came back.

You could say I already had a style.

The opening day of practice was pretty funny, too. I worked those prospects up and down the court, at full speed, for two solid hours. At the end of *that*, I ordered them to run a bunch of conditioning drills. I ran 'em in suicide drill after suicide drill.

A group of four young ladies were running together. When they got to the end of the line, they just kept on running. They ran out the door and up the steps, and I never saw them again.

My ideas about how to command respect have changed since then. I've learned you can't demand it, or whack it out of people with a two-by-four. You have to cultivate it, in yourself and those around you.

There is no such thing as self-respect without respect for others. It sounds like a riddle, doesn't it? But it's not. I don't know anyone who has succeeded all alone. Individual success is a myth. We are all dependent on those around us. This is a fundamental truth you learn growing up on a farm. It applies elsewhere, too. Especially in our locker room.

Respect is essential to building group cohesion. People who do not respect others will not make good team members, and they probably lack self-esteem themselves. You don't have to like each other. But you do have to respect your colleagues' opinions and decisions, because your personal success depends on commitment to the overall plan and doing your part to make it work.

Chances are, you have a "moody" colleague. My question is, what right does he have to inflict his moods on others? Is this colleague more valuable than others? Of course not. Moody people are rude people. They may even be a liability, if they are unreliable and pull other people down. So if you're a moody person, get out of business, fast. Pray for an inheritance.

Rule No. 1 in our program is to respect others, no matter what their place on the team (or in society), because respect is the first step toward team building: Treat people the way you'd like to be treated. It sounds simple enough. But you'd be surprised at the ill manners some full-grown people can display, and how it can interfere with group solidarity.

There are some simple ways to build mutual respect in a group.

The foremost thing we require from our players, before anything else, is that they make good eye contact. To me, eye contact is a sign of both self-respect and mutual respect—it demonstrates that you are confident enough to look at the person who is speaking and that you will give her your full attention. I am known for my eye contact. My former point guard, Michelle Marciniak, says I "look way down" into her eyes. She claims our players don't dare look away or break that contact. Well, that's good.

I'll never forget the afternoon that Chamique Holdsclaw and her grandmother came to our home in Knoxville on a recruiting visit. The team was laying around in the den, watching something on TV, and I brought Chamique's grandmother into the room to introduce her. Nobody moved. They barely looked up from the TV. Worse, no one got up to offer her a chair.

I had to tell a nineteen-year-old to get up and move so Chamique's grandmother could sit down.

Well, after they had gone, I called the team together and let them have it. "I don't ever want to see that happen again," I said. They took a lesson from me, right then and there, in how to stand up when someone enters a room, and how to introduce themselves.

Another simple matter of respect is being on time. Think about it. Why should you be on time? So other people don't have to wait on you, that's why. Lateness sends a message that you're either too sloppy, too careless, or too special to be on time. If your teammates or colleagues always have to wait on you, rancor builds and egos clash. We have enough trouble putting twelve big egos together as it is.

●　●　●

Early on, the '97 Tennessee team had some issues with respect. That was a part of our problem. One of our centers, Tiffani Johnson, had no respect for our curfew. I was forced to suspend her. (More on that later.) Everybody had *too* much respect for Chamique Holdsclaw as a player. They all stood around, assuming Chamique would win games by herself. And then the player I needed to step up and be an example, Abby Conklin, our senior leader, decided to challenge my authority in front of the team.

It happened the day after we were beaten by Stanford at home.

There was one thing I knew we had to do against Stanford: defend the high post and keep the ball out of the middle of the floor. And that was Abby Conklin's job. Well, she didn't do it.

Abby is a complicated, mild-mannered, 6-foot-3 young woman from Charlestown, Indiana. She has a very calm temperament that can be mistaken for impassive or uncaring. She might be one of the sweetest-natured players I've ever had. But she is also one of the most stubborn. She was an enigma to me for much of her career, and I wasn't always sure in my handling of her. I felt like she didn't respect me. She felt like I didn't respect her, because I was always getting on her in front of the team. It turned into an epic war of wills.

Abby had other ideas about how to defend against Stanford. She did what *she* thought was best. I asked her to deny the ball to the high post, but instead she decided, all on her own, to play containment. The truth was that she was afraid she wasn't quick enough to defend aggressively against the Cardinal, which she admitted later. The first time she played hard denial, Stanford drove right past her and scored. That was the real deal.

She lacked respect for her own abilities.

But it showed itself as a lack of respect for me and our game plan, and in that, she made a big mistake.

The next day, in our team meeting before practice, I told Abby straight out that she had played terribly. I said, "What was the one thing I begged you to do?" She just looked at me stubbornly. I told her that she had given up the middle of the floor and that they had killed us from the middle. Now, I knew what I was talking about. I had been up until 4 A.M. watching that tape, throwing stuff at the television. But Abby just gave me her own peculiar, intractable gaze.

"I don't agree with you," she said.

Abby said later that it looked like my head had swiveled around like in that scene from *The Exorcist*.

"You what?" I snapped.

It was Abby's turn to look like something out of *The Exorcist*. She turned green. You know how something can fly out of your mouth, and you wish you could suck it right back in? That's how she looked, like she was trying to suck the words back out of the air. But the damage was done. Here we were, having our toughest season in a decade, and Abby was going to argue with me in front of the team.

Ironically, one of my complaints against Abby was that she was too quiet. She wasn't very vocal or animated, like good leaders have to be. Great, I thought. This was the most animated she had been all season — in trying to take me on.

The thing was, I counted heavily on Abby. Our leaders are our floor coaches, they are the players I am most dependent on and hardest on. They are also the players I frequently think the most of, and they are often the players I become closest to in the end. I can't wear a uniform and go out there on the floor, so I need them to be an extension of me. Abby's most critical responsibility as a leader was to back me up, no matter what. If she wasn't going to respect our game plan, no one else was.

When you lose the support of your leader in front of the whole team, you might lose the team altogether. By taking me on like that, Abby jeopardized everything we were working toward.

Unfortunately, HBO was following us for their women's basketball documentary, and I was miked. They were filming the whole thing — my center, and my so-called leader, challenging my strategy in front of the world. I don't really remember what I said. I was just trying to hold my temper in front of the camera. I dissolved the meeting pretty quickly, and we started off to practice. But I should have gone ahead and let her have it, instead of bottling it up, in light of what happened next.

As we were walking out to the court, I drew up beside Abby. "You know, you're more stubborn than you are smart," I said. "And you aren't gonna win this one."

My anger continued to build. After practice, Abby knew how much trouble she was in. She went into the coach's changing room, off the main locker room, to talk to our assistants, Mickie and Holly, about it. I came into the room. Abby started to apologize.

Well, I told her I wasn't ready to entertain her apology yet. I might not be ready until July. I was sipping from a cup of water, one of those little paper Gatorade cups. But it wasn't cooling me down any.

I threw it across the room.

It hit the wall and showered her. It got Mickie and Holly pretty wet, too, I have to confess. Abby just gaped at me. Finally, I had her full attention. I hollered at her, "I cannot believe you would do that." I told her I was hurt. And I told her we were in real trouble if she didn't have more respect for me than that.

I also told her she was benched.

The next night, Abby came off the bench against Texas Tech and scored a career-high twenty-six points. After the game, she told the press that she was trying to win back my regard. "I was afraid Pat would stop believing in me," she said.

I was still mad at Abby, though. She had punched my buttons good. But then, my buttons are punched just about all the time. They tend to stay about halfway in.

I shouldn't have thrown the water, of course. It was hardly an example of mutual respect. But I felt that I had to do something to impress on her the seriousness of the situation.

It didn't help the team that there was tension between Abby and me. And it began to pervade the whole squad. A few games later, we had to play at St. Joseph's, a tough game in a tough gym. And we were falling apart, right there in front of my eyes. We trailed St. Joe's by fourteen points with about seven minutes to go. I mean, normally Tennessee doesn't trail *anybody* by double digits. So I called a time-out, and the players came to the bench and sat down. I started to talk to them when I noticed Abby and our other senior, Pashen Thompson, kind of scuffling. I looked closer, and Pashen was *hitting* Abby in the leg. Abby was pulling on Pashen's towel.

They were fighting.

Over a towel.

I thought I had seen everything. Obviously, I was not getting the concept of mutual respect across to them.

"What in the world are ya'll doin'?" I said incredulously.

"She took my towel," Pashen said.

"It's my towel," Abby said.

Well, that was it. "Abby, just get outta here," I said disgustedly.

I benched her again.

Like I say. It was a long year.

Abby and I would come full circle. That night, after the St. Joseph's game, Abby and I met in the lobby of the hotel and talked for more than two hours. We put aside our resentments and really communicated with each other for the first time. We'll get into that in another chapter. But the end result was that Abby and I did an about-face. She played the best basketball of her life in the second half of '97.

In the end, I would respect her and her teammates as much as any players who have ever come through Tennessee.

Self-respect sustained us when nobody else believed in us.

● ● ●

If we're going to spend all this time together, me talking and you reading, you need to know me better. How are you supposed to respect my opinions and my system for success, if you don't know anything about me? The first thing you need to understand is that I've *lived* these ideas.

My ideas about respect are severe. But then, they were formed by a severe man, my father, who whipped them into me. When I'm tough on a player, like I was on Abby Conklin, everybody back in Henrietta says, "There's the Richard in her." They say I'm a lot like him. But frankly, I hope I'm not too much like him. While I loved and respected my father, I also feared him.

My father could go for days on end without saying a word, and when he did speak, his voice sounded like it came up out of the bottom of a well. He was fearsome looking, too—at 6-foot-5. As soon as he walked into a room, it fell quiet. The whole house tensed up. Even today, some members of my family, especially my younger nephews and nieces, won't drink or smoke or cuss around my parents, out of that combination of fear and respect.

I think some of my father's silence when I was a child was a result of pure exhaustion. He built up his own dairy and tobacco farm out of nothing in Montgomery County, Tennessee. It's a region of rolling green hills and dense backwoods cleaved by one-lane blacktop roads, where the barns and sheds and lean-tos outnumber the houses. He and my mother,

Hazel Head, started out working a small plot of leased land for just forty dollars a month. When I tell you they worked, I mean they *worked*, back-breakingly hard.

On the weekends my father would drive into Nashville and peddle chickens.

For a dollar apiece.

That's how he saved up one hundred dollars to buy his first milk cow.

When I was a baby we lived in a two-room log cabin. It's gone now, which is too bad, because legend had it that the cornerstone of that cabin was laid by Jesse James. But as you can imagine, my father was less concerned with antique cornerstones than he was with making a living and feeding five kids. The only inheritance farm people pass on are the family clocks, the silver, and acreage.

Over the years my dad steadily built up a thousand-acre farm. At one point we had sixty-four milk cows. Then he bought a general store and opened a hardware store, a feed mill, a gas pump, and a laundry. He got into the construction business, too. Today it's hard to find a brick house in Henrietta that the Heads didn't build.

So when I talk to you about self-respect, it comes from someone who belongs to a family of self-made overachievers.

My older brothers, Tommy, Charles, and Kenneth, all work their own acreage around Henrietta or in neighboring Oak Plains, as does my sister, Linda, and her husband, Wesley. Everyone in the family is an over-achiever. Tommy is a member of the state legislature, and Charles fought with the Big Red One in Vietnam. Linda works as hard as any of us, and still manages to have the best sense of humor, too. She is raising two wonderful daughters who just might be future players. She also runs the family laundry, helps me with my annual summer basketball camp, and hosts all the family dinners and reunions.

Not too long ago, a television reporter told me it was hard for him to believe I'd ever had my hands dirty. He meant it as a compliment, but I'm proud for you to know that I come from a hardscrabble farming family. Hard work breeds self-respect. I wasn't any older than ten when I started driving a tractor, setting tobacco, and raking and baling hay.

If you look at my father's hands, they are as cracked and brown-stained as a pair of old loafers. My dad still works in the fields and in a tobacco warehouse. He and my mother have worn out their bodies from laboring all those years to build their business. My dad has had two knee replacements. My mother has had ankle surgery. She ruined her feet. They are so painfully misshapen she can only wear the sneakers I send her, and even those sometimes hurt her.

On our farm no job was too big or too small. Everybody had to do their part. Ask my father how hard he made us kids work, and he says, "They didn't work hard. They just worked." To which I always say, "All day. We worked all day." We didn't get praised for it, either. It was just expected of us. We didn't hear anything about it if we just did our jobs.

We lived from crop to crop. There was always plenty on the table: heaping bowls of fresh corn cut off the cob, creamed potatoes, butter beans, platters of biscuits, and huge jugs of sweet tea. But we were cash poor, except when the tobacco came in.

Tobacco is a beautiful crop, I think. If you've never seen it, I'll describe it for you. It has a large, teardrop-shaped leaf of near tropical lushness. There are two kinds of tobacco, dark and burley. Burley tobacco is yellow, but dark tobacco is a deep lustrous green that from a distance has a slightly blue tinge. In late summer the fields of Henrietta are covered in bright yellow and dark green-blue, alternating with rows of gold-brushed cornstalks. Surrounding the fields are pastures and hollows full of fat, indolent livestock and thickets of elms, poplars, and sycamores, along with the occasional pomegranate and wild apple. Willows and cattails wave, and the cicadas whine, and smoke seeps out from clapboard barns where the tobacco has been put up to cure.

Here's how you cure tobacco: What you do is, hang the chopped tobacco leaves up in the rafters and then lay sawdust and slabs of wood on the floor and light it. It's called firing a barn. The haze that drifts from the barns gives the air of Henrietta a sweet smoldering smell.

If you were to drive over to Henrietta today you'd see a fairly prosperous-looking place; most of the tobacco gets sold to the big companies, like Phillip Morris or American Brands. But when I was growing up, a lot of the roads were still unpaved. If I wanted to go anywhere I traveled there on a brown-and-white spotted pony named Billy.

All we did with our days was go to school, go to our Methodist church, and work the fields. We had to make up our own fun—what little my father permitted. Once, my best friend Jane and I water-skied the Cumberland River from the Cheatham Dam near our farm all the way to the Bordeaux Bridge in Nashville—a distance of several miles. We skied until every muscle in our bodies trembled. Why? Because it was something to do.

Let me put it this way. A really big night out was when we climbed the town water tower and painted it black—something I have never admitted to until today, for fear that my father, the town water commissioner, would kill me.

My father demanded respect with his belt. We got regular whippings—hard ones. I'll give you a painful example. Once, when I couldn't have been more than five years old, my brothers thought it would be funny to teach me an off-color song about beans and bodily functions. If you've got kids, you've probably heard it before. It's ever-popular with them. Anyway, that night at dinner I dished up a spoonful of beans and sang my new song for the table. "Beans, beans, good for the heart, the more you eat, the more you . . ." I piped.

As I finished the song, my father wordlessly dropped his spoon to the table with a clatter. Then he raised his hand and backhanded me out of my chair. He hit me so hard my mother burst into tears. I did a backflip and landed on the floor.

So I'm not going to tell you I have an untroubled relationship with the man.

But the thing you need to understand is that my father, to a great extent, made me who I am. His peculiar combination of love and discipline was hard to take, but in the end I was grateful for it. He gave me strength. If you saw the two of us together today, you would see two people who have reached a peace. We finally understand each other. He is a man with a buried sense of humor and a fierce devotion to his family. This is the same man who built a basketball court in the top of a hayloft for his kids. He put up an old iron rim, and strung lights so we could play up there at night. We'd climb up the twenty-foot barn ladder and have heated contests of two-on-two in the rafters. My oldest brother, Tommy, would play with me, the smallest, against the middle boys, Charles and Kenneth.

I'm not saying my father is easy to figure out. He doesn't want to be. For instance, he never told me he loved me. He wouldn't show overt affection. His way of showing it was to make a sacrifice. When I got to be high school age, my father moved the entire family across the county line, six miles down the road, just so I could have a chance to play basketball. The high school I was assigned to in Clarksville, Tennessee, didn't have a team for girls. So my dad bought a drafty old place on the main street of Henrietta, a white clapboard house with rumors of a ghost, just so I would be able to play for the neighboring high school in Ashland City.

I was forty-three years old before my father hugged me for the first time. It's become sort of a famous story in Tennessee, that he embraced me for the first time in 1996, on the night we won our fourth NCAA Championship. I had said publicly over the years that he was a forbidding man, and that I'd never been able to win his approval. I guess he got tired of hearing about it. So after we beat Georgia to win our fourth title, I climbed up into the stands to see my parents, like I always do. He put his arms around me, and in his own awkward way, hugged me and kissed me. A few days later, he said grudgingly, "Now I don't want to hear any more about how I never hug you or tell you how proud I am." That was his way of telling me he was proud.

●　●　●

The best, most valuable thing my father gave me was an equal opportunity. Nobody in the family seemed to regard me as a girl when it came to work or playing basketball. I fought hard and played hard, and I was expected to hold my own with my brothers, whether we were in the fields or in the hayloft. In most ways I was raised like a fourth son, while my younger sister, Linda, got the role of baby sister.

They cut me no slack. Let me tell you, competing with three brothers could be life-threatening.

For fun, my brother Kenneth liked to load me in a forklift. He'd raise me up, and then hit the drop switch. I would speed downward, and hit the ground with a huge *whang*. Then he would raise the forklift up again, and *whang*, send me to the ground again. He kept it up, *whang*ing and clang- ing that heavy machinery, while I held on for dear life, until I cried.

One time Kenneth threw a butcher knife at me. We were in the kitchen one afternoon, and he came after me. I bolted from the room, and he hurled that knife right at my head. It stuck in the door frame, vibrating.

The obvious question was, what had I done to provoke him?

I think I hit him with a baseball bat.

I was a force to be reckoned with. Once, I remember, Charles locked himself in our parents' bedroom so he could use the phone to talk to his girlfriend. I wanted to use the phone too. I got so mad, I told him I was going to kick in the door. And I did. I kicked it so hard, for so long, I put a three-foot hole in it.

Another night the boys and I had a pillow fight. It raged pretty good for a while, until we heard my father's feet hit the floor. I jumped behind the window curtains and hid, just before Dad came through the door with his belt flying. I stood there trembling behind the curtain and listened to him whip each one of my brothers, while they screamed. They kept trying to tell on me, but he was whipping them so hard they couldn't get it out. Finally, when my father was done, he turned out the lights and closed the door.

I dove headfirst through that window.

It was about a five-foot drop to the ground. But I was more afraid of Richard Head's belt than I was of breaking any bones.

As I got older, I understood that women had to fight for respect in more ways than one. It seemed to me that my mother worked as hard or harder than my father and my brothers. One impression has stayed with me all these years, and it's as powerful as any left by my father's whippings.

At the dinner table, when my brothers would finish their tea, they'd hold up their empty glasses and rattle them. They wouldn't say a word. They'd just lift their glasses, and shake them, until my mother served them. It was their way of saying, "Come fill my glass." I can still see those hands, holding up their glasses, rattling the ice. My mother waited on them. And I thought, *That isn't right.*

My dad and my brothers wouldn't do any work around the house, whether it was make their beds, or work in the garden, or mow the lawn. They just worked the farm, that was it. But my mother did the cooking and the ironing and the cleaning, and the milking, and worked the garden, and worked in the store, and in the dry cleaners. When my dad got into the house-building business, my mother was the one who painted the houses and laid the carpets. Looking back on it, I don't think anyone in the family worked as hard as my mother or got less credit for it.

As I got close to graduating from high school in 1970, I realized that while my brothers each had athletic scholarships, I wasn't going to get one because they weren't offered to women back then. Tommy and Kenneth both went to nearby Austin Peay on full rides; Tommy was a gifted basketball player, and Kenneth lettered in baseball. I was a good enough player that Cheatham County High School in Ashland City would eventually name the school gym after me. But my parents had to scrape to pay my way to the University of Tennessee-Martin. And I thought, *This needs to change.*

In 1972 I got an invitation to try out for the U.S. national team, and I suddenly realized that I had a chance to be an Olympic athlete. Women's basketball was going to be played for the first time at the '76 Games, and I burned to be on the team. It seemed to me that there was no greater mark of respect than to be an Olympian. But also, I knew I wanted to make a difference for women. So I think that's when I found my real calling.

Sports, it struck me, could be a vital avenue to self-worth for women. It was for me. That shows you what a game can do: It can teach you to explore and broaden your capabilities. That's why the explosion in female athletic participation over the last twenty years has been so important. Think about it. There was actually a time when women were forbidden to run marathons for fear we'd damage our ovaries. Basketball for women was stationary to make sure we didn't swoon. But unfettered play affords the experience of excellence, both physically and mentally. It is too critical for personal development to deny it to half the population.

In my case, it was life-altering.

● ● ●

Ambition can transform you. The starting point of ambition is self-respect.

You can believe me when I tell you this, because I'm self-made. So I don't care how far behind the starting line you may be, or how many shortages or deficiencies there are in your life. Trust me, you can make up for them.

When I arrived on campus at the University of Tennessee-Martin, I was so shy I couldn't tell people my name. All my life I had been teased about how tall and skinny I was. Everybody in Henrietta called me Bone. Naturally, because my last name was Head, there were some who couldn't resist calling me Bonehead. It's funny now. I assure you it wasn't to the sensitive, insecure girl I was then.

Most people back home called me Trish. It came out in a long, slow middle-Tennessee accent. It sounded like, "Treeesh." But my new college teammates and sorority sisters didn't know what to call me, because I was so quiet. Since my full name was Patricia, they assumed I was Pat. I couldn't correct them, because that would mean opening my mouth.

So I essentially became two people. And I still am, really. There is Trish Head, from Henrietta. And there is Pat Summitt, who gives the impression that her hands have never been dirty, and that she is comfortable with her height, and that she has never been shy.

The first time my dad came to see me play for the U.S. Olympic team, he sat up in the stands and yelled, "Trish, Trish," at me. Nobody knew my family name was Trish. I had a teammate named Trish Roberts. She thought that man up in the stands was yelling at her. But I knew exactly who he was yelling at. You've never seen two girls play so hard.

You wouldn't have recognized me then. Trish Head was a farm kid with crooked teeth and all the wrong clothes, who said *ain't* and *reckon* and *yonder.* In the Chi Omega sorority house, they made fun of my blue jumper, and my favorite shirt—one that had turtles printed on it—and they made fun of the fact that the hemlines on my dresses and jumpers were well below my knees. Everybody else wore miniskirts. I was country, and I felt it. I'd always been accepted in athletics, and had confidence on the basketball court. But this was a different world, and I was awkward in it.

You never get a second chance to make a first impression. In those early days at college, I realized that presentation counts. For better or worse, strangers made sweeping judgments based on my appearance and demeanor. So I began the process of self-transformation.

Like any other eighteen-year-old, I badly wanted to fit in. I also knew that I wanted to get off the farm. I wanted to be comfortable in this different, more sophisticated world. Not that I suddenly wanted to join the country club set, or anything. But I wanted to be an Olympian, and I eventually wanted to be a teacher. So it became important to me to at least have the passing respect of people in those circles.

Mainly, though, I didn't want to be made fun of anymore.

I asked two of my best friends and sorority sisters to help me with my grammar. They corrected my *ain't*s and helped me through my English papers and ironed the accent out of my voice. I enrolled in speech classes, and learned how to stand before a roomful of people and speak. You wouldn't know it now, to see me speak to Nabisco or Eastman Kodak or ALCOA, but back then I was white-knuckled and shaking with fear. Still am, sometimes.

I began to pay attention to my clothes. Dressing appropriately for a role can help you play it better. It certainly has helped me, whether as a coach, a mother, a teacher, or a speaker. For years I never wore blue jeans. I spent too much time doing farm work in them, I guess, to ever want to wear them. Also, I felt like that's all I ever had—jeans.

These days, when I coach on the sidelines, I wear tailored suits. In that situation I need to be as authoritative as possible. Now I'm recognized for what I wear. It seems like people are always remarking on my latest sideline garb. They marvel at my ability to find articles of clothing the shade of Tennessee orange.

Occasionally my attempts to set sideline fashion trends can be pretty funny. Like the time I decided to wear clogs, because they were the latest thing.

Well, I got mad about something that happened in the game. When we got to the locker room, I kicked at the floor.

My clog came flying off my foot and hit the ceiling.

It was the last time I wore them.

I care about clothes and other external things because they help form a perception, but I also care about them because I want to know that things are right, whether we're talking about my shoes or my grammar. My quest for self-improvement has never really ended.

When I was twenty-nine, I even got braces.

My teeth weren't awful, they were just slightly crooked. But they bothered me, so I wanted to fix them, because I knew they needed it. We couldn't afford to do it when I was a kid. But shortly after I got married, I decided to do it.

R.B. Summitt and I wed in 1980, after a lengthy courtship. I met him through a roommate of mine, Marcia McGregor. She invited a bunch of her fellow bank examiners over one night, intending to fix me up with one of them, a guy from middle Tennessee. But this other bank examiner, R.B., sort of got in the way, and he stayed around for the next three and a half years. He finally got me to stand still long enough to marry him.

R.B. is as easygoing as I am intense. He is that rarity, a guy who supports what I do for a living, to the point that he used to drive our equipment van on road trips. He is my best, most sympathetic friend. And like me, he believes in getting things right.

When we had been married a year, I asked him what he thought about the idea of me getting braces. I was really worried over what he might think. But he told me to go right ahead.

"I think if it's going to make you feel more comfortable, you should get right on with it," he said.

I wore them for several months. The local media joked that our team was so young even the head coach had to wear braces.

But those braces were a good experience. They did more than straighten my teeth. They taught me to finally stop worrying about being made fun of.

No one had the nerve to remark on them until one night when I was scouting a high school player, and I ran into Mickie DeMoss, an assistant coach from Auburn. I didn't know Mickie well yet, although later she would become my assistant coach and right hand and friend. Mickie is regarded as one of the more comical women in coaching, as I was about to learn. She makes fun of everybody and everything.

We sat up in the high school bleachers, doing our scouting. There wasn't much to eat at the game, except for popcorn. So we watched basketball and chatted and ate popcorn. Finally, Mickie said, grinning sort of wickedly, "You know, you've got popcorn stuck in your braces." She razzed me about it until I started giggling.

I laughed at *myself*. It was a good feeling, too. That's when you know you've got real self-respect.

Laughing at myself is something I've tried to get in the habit of doing ever since, particularly as the Tennessee program has grown into such a power, and the Pat Summitt in me has overtaken the Trish Head. In my opinion, Pat Summitt needs to laugh at herself—a lot. Just to keep herself honest.

Fortunately Trish Head still turns up from time to time. Especially when she goes home to Henrietta to visit, or when the folks come to Knoxville.

You should see the shocked expression on my players' faces the first time they hear my sister or one of my brothers call me "Trish." They think they've got something on me. Every now and then one of them will try to tease me about my country upbringing.

"Treeeesh," they call me.

"Hey, Treeeeesh," I'll hear from across the gym.

I turn around and give them some serious eye contact.

"You don't want to go there with me," I tell them.

Self-respect can be hard won. I know. It's an ongoing process. Take it from me—someone who still wears a retainer at night. But once you attain it, it will bear you up through almost anything, whether you're dealing with a difficult parent, teasing from others, self-doubt, or ordinary work tensions. In critical situations, we all ask ourselves the same silent question: "Do I deserve to succeed?" Under pressure, uncertainty can creep into the subconscious of even the most outwardly confident person—including me. A crafty little sucker sits in your head and whispers in your ear. If you haven't developed self-respect and mutual respect with those around you, the whisper is, "Deep down you know you don't deserve it."

So the next time you ask yourself, "Do I deserve to succeed?" make sure the answer is yes.

Q & A *Nikki McCray*

Forward, All American 1994–95; Olympic Gold Medalist, 1996; Most Valuable Player, Columbus Quest, ABL, 1997

Q: Is it true Pat almost sent you home two weeks after you got to Tennessee?
NIKKI MCCRAY: *Oh, yeah. It was new for me, and an adjustment. I didn't take my responsibilities seriously. I was in my own world, late to class, late to meetings. I thought life was all about basketball. Pat was like, "You need to get serious or you're out of here." I turned it around, though, and everything worked out. I think what happened was, the town I was from, Collierville, was small, and I didn't know anybody. I was intimidated by the staff, the other players. I was afraid, and I didn't know how to deal with it.*

Q: How did you turn it around?
NIKKI MCCRAY: *Trust me, when you play for Pat, you have to figure out who you are and what you can do, and you have to express it with your hard work. We didn't establish a relationship until my junior year. That's when I finally felt comfortable enough to hold a conversation with her. You have to break that fear barrier with her.*

Q: You weren't the only one she almost sent home.
NIKKI MCCRAY: *Bridgette Gordon, her all-time leading scorer, she wanted to send her home, too. Actually, it's kind of an honor to almost be sent home by Pat.*

Take Full Responsibility

If you don't want responsibility, don't sit in the big chair. That's the deal. To be successful, you must accept full responsibility. For everything. Headaches, problems, crises. Even when it doesn't seem fair. And here's part two: The more successful you are, the more responsibility you must assume. Responsibility never ends. It's not a step. Or just a chapter. You don't finish it and then move on to something more fun or interesting. Responsibility is a constant state of being.

You want to talk about never-ending responsibility, let's talk about kids. Better yet, let's talk about my own young prize, Tyler. The other day he pulled out *another* tooth. He decided, after receiving the whopping sum of seven dollars from the tooth fairy, that teeth are a cash crop. It was a pretty timely move, because Halloween was coming. When he smiled, he looked just like a jack-o'-lantern.

I guess setting a precedent of seven dollars for a tooth was not the most responsible thing R.B. and I have ever done as parents. What kind of message did it send?

"Son," I had to tell him, "please don't start pulling out your permanent ones."

I've had to think a lot about responsibility, as both a coach and a parent. I deal with the topic on a variety of levels. It's something I try to instill in our team. It's something I must find a way to teach our son. And responsible is something that I am expected to be, as the head coach of our program. Responsibility is a building block in both personal and team growth.

You really want to talk responsibility, let's talk about being in charge of twelve kids at a time, a dozen young women from all over the country, each with their own varying dispositions, backgrounds, problems, quarrels, and love interests.

Some of them with cars.

You see what I mean. It's a staggering responsibility to have the care and feeding of other people's children for four years. Oftentimes I feel like my heart is on an elevator; it's either lodged in my throat or dropping into my shoes, on their account. So I'm not exaggerating when I tell you they become like daughters to me. It helps that I've got a staff to help me cope, and a supportive husband, and a full-time nanny to watch over my own boy. (Sometimes they all hide things from me. I feel it. They deal with me strictly on a need-to-know basis.)

You only see me at games, standing on the sidelines with my hands on my hips, signaling plays or hollering at someone—I have yet to see a picture of myself with my mouth closed. But that's the least of it. Not too many people realize what the day to dayness of coaching consists of. The tougher, more time-consuming aspect of the job—or any other management job—lies in the constant judgment calls you must make about personnel. In my case, I must make judgment calls about players' health, academic progress, and emotional well-being. And it gets trickier all the time, given issues like alcohol and drug abuse, safe sex, and unwanted pregnancy.

Should I tell Pashen Thompson her grandmother is ill, or hold off and hope she improves? Is Chamique Holdsclaw's new boyfriend a good person, or someone to be concerned about? Who's that guy who's been calling players in their rooms? Can't we do something to help Niya Butts with her shin problems?

It may sound like I take responsibility for some things that are none of my affair. But I guarantee you, if there's a problem with a player, everyone will hold me accountable for it and tell me what I should have done to prevent it. So their personal problems are my problems, too. I assure our recruits and their parents of what to expect at Tennessee: tough love and constant monitoring. For these four years, it's my responsibility to know, within reason, where you are and what you're doing.

When you sit in the big chair, you must make tough, unpopular decisions, because you are responsible for the group and the greater good. It's the absolute worst part of having authority. I'm not going to lie to you about that. If you don't have the stomach for unpleasant tasks, for firing people, fighting battles, or breaking bad news—and doing it forthrightly—you shouldn't be in that position. In a management job, every knock on your door represents a potential problem. Every single one. As a manager you are responsible.

If you don't want to deal with problems, don't accept the job.

Here's another thing about responsibility: It evolves. Example: My most critical responsibility as a coach is to see that our players graduate. But that job gets tougher all the time. In some ways, it was easier to push our players toward degrees before there was an opportunity for women to play professional basketball in this country. Thrilled as I am with the successes of the Women's National Basketball League and the American Basketball League, a lot of complications come with agents and pro contracts. So now I have a new responsibility: to see that players don't jeopardize their eligibility by accepting benefits from agents in violation of NCAA rules. And when they are ready to enter the pros, it's part of my job to see that they get representation.

One hundred percent of the players who have remained at Tennessee for four years have received their degrees.

The statistic I'm almost as proud of, though, is that twenty-four of our former players or staffers have become coaches at the collegiate and high school level. Twelve of them are collegiate head coaches. I'll tell you why

I'm proud of that. Because what it says is that Tennessee doesn't just produce great players. We turn out people who are capable of assuming that kind of responsibility.

• • •

We don't start out responsible, none of us do. It's something that must be taught, and it can be self-taught, too. How do you learn it? There's just one way. By taking on responsibility and forcing yourself to cope with it.

Like you, I don't always feel like being responsible. I've had to learn my own lessons about that. I remember an especially unhappy one on my sixteenth birthday. Again, thanks to my father. What happened was this. A bunch of my friends were planning to throw a birthday party for me that day at a country club over in Ashland City. We were a small group of high school kids who ran around together, and it was my friend Janine's birthday too, so we were all going to get together. But when my dad found out about it, he told me I couldn't go.

He said I had to get the straw in.

It looked like rain, my dad said. We needed to get the straw in.

I spent my birthday sitting on a tractor. There were about one thousand bales of straw that needed loading. We worked all day. I was so furious with my father that I drove that tractor like a crazed person, slamming on the brakes—to the point where I almost threw him off the wagon. He turned around and caught me with that look in his eye. Well, the one person who can outstare me is my dad. He has such an intimidating gaze that most people in Henrietta still call him Mr. Head. That, or Tall Man. Anyway, I straightened up quick.

My father's point was that you can't pick and choose the days that you feel like being responsible. It's not something that disappears when you're tired. On a farm, we had year-round responsibilities. The milking had to be done every single morning and afternoon, no matter what. Milk cows don't take vacations.

What's more, I had to take on new responsibilities all the time, as I got older. If a blade broke while I was mowing hay, he told me to figure out how to change it myself.

In order to grow, you must accept new responsibilities, no matter how uncertain you may feel or how unprepared you are to deal with them. Unless, of course, you want to do the same thing day after day, for the rest of your life. If comfort is what you're seeking, then don't aspire. Ambition is uncomfortable by definition.

You wouldn't believe how unprepared I was to accept the responsibilities that came with being the head coach at Tennessee when I got the job back in 1974. I had to grow up fast—real fast. It was an accident, really. I was supposed to be the assistant coach, but the former head coach left, and suddenly the job was open. So they stuck me in it. I still thought of myself as a player and a student. I was working toward a master's degree in physical education and teaching classes in sports I knew nothing about, like racquetball and self-defense, and I was coaching the team. In my spare time I was a member of the U.S. Pan American team, in training to make the 1976 Olympic squad.

We all get in over our heads sometimes. I was only making part-timer's pay, so I had no money. I bounced checks all over town. Some of those bad checks are probably still floating around Knoxville. Here I was, a kid who couldn't balance her own checkbook, and I was in charge of coaching a basketball team and balancing a budget. I had a lot of responsibilities and very little help.

I was on my own. There I was, twenty-two years old, with four players who were twenty-one. Not one of them was from out of the state. They were all just like me, Tennessee born and bred. What's more, they were all used to playing six-man stationary basketball, because that was the game most young women grew up with in the 1960s and 1970s in Tennessee. You either played offense or defense, but you never crossed the center line. Like I said, back in those days people thought women couldn't run without collapsing with the vapors.

The best way to handle responsibility is to break it down into smaller parts. Take care of one small thing at a time.

I learned that early in my career. But I didn't always know how to make it work. During my second season our starting center, Jane Pemberton, a freshman from Deer Lodge, Tennessee, had never shot the ball. Ever. She had only played defense. So I came up with a plan. I decided that since I had no all-court players, I would give each player one specific responsibility.

I went to Jane Pemberton, and I said, "Jane, don't shoot the ball tonight. I do not want you to shoot the ball. The only thing you have to do is rebound. Do you understand me?"

She said, "Oh, yes, ma'am."

Sometimes I wish they would just tell you: Coach, I don't have a clue what you're talking about.

After I talked to Jane, I went to our point guard, Suzanne Barbre. I looked down at her, all intense, and I said, "Suzanne, I want you to take care of the basketball. That's all. Do you understand me?"

She drawled, "I, I got it, Coach."

Then she looked back up at me, and she said, "Are you nervous?"

"No," I said, trying to seem sure of myself. "Why? Am I acting like it?"

She said, "Well, your neck's all broken out."

And it was. I had red splotches all over. From nerves. It still gets that way, sometimes.

I said hastily, "Let's just go play."

We went out there, and we lost that game by one point. The great thing about basketball is that it gives you instant feedback. There is a final score and a statistics sheet to tell you how you've done. When they handed me the statistics sheet afterward, I looked down and I saw exactly what had happened. The number that jumped right in my face was rebounds.

Jane Pemberton, my center, had exactly one rebound. My little point guard, Suzanne Barbre, had seven.

I looked at Jane and I said, "What was the one thing I asked you to do?"

She kind of scratched her head and thought for a minute, and then she answered, "Rebound?"

"That's right," I said. "You had one rebound, and you're playing center. Suzanne had seven, and she's playing guard. Now, does that tell you anything?"

Jane drawled, "Yes, ma'am. You oughta think about moving me over to guard."

That story is more amusing than it is illustrative, but there is a lesson in it, even so. The smaller and more clearly articulated someone's job is, the easier it is to fulfill. The most complicated plan of action becomes simple if you break it down properly.

But the key is to make people accountable for their piece of the puzzle. The only effective way to teach responsibility to younger people is by making them accountable for the small things, day in and day out. A lot of people like to say "Don't sweat the small stuff." But I do, I sweat the small stuff. Like my father with that hay, I sweat the small things, and I make our players accountable for them, too, because they are habit-forming.

There are no short cuts around this one. Not even for me, the head coach. Especially not for me.

Two things must happen before I can demand responsible behavior from the team at large. (1) I've got to demonstrate to them that I fulfill my own responsibilities. That means that I, too, am accountable. For instance, I'm not the most punctual human being. But the one thing I am never, ever late to is a team meeting or a practice. (2) I must make sure that the responsibilities of our players and staff are clearly delineated and that everyone understands them. That way, when there is a breakdown, we know what happened.

If you do not clearly articulate who is responsible for what, nothing will get done. We've all been in situations where the simplest task has gone unperformed. Why? Because even though Anybody could do it, Everybody thought Somebody Else would do it, and Nobody did it.

Organization is half the battle. Start with yourself, and your own desk.

Our players' responsibilities are clear-cut, and so is the penalty for not fulfilling them.

RULE: If you miss a class, you won't start. It's that simple. Skipping a class means you will be on our bench for tip-off in the next game.

RULE: When you are in class, you must sit in the first three rows, so you will pay attention.

RULE: Our floor leaders must be vocal, because it is their responsibility to communicate our plays.

RULE: Everybody on our team is responsible for a loose ball. Otherwise, I'll sit you in a chair—without a chair.

RULE: No tattoos may show in public. When you play for Tennessee, you are a reflection of the university, not just yourself. Okay, this one, I'll concede, is personal with me. I hate tattoos. I don't allow the players to show them around me privately, either. They have to cover them up in my presence. Chamique Holdsclaw has one down around her ankle, and she has to pull her sock up when she comes to my office, or put a bandage over it. I don't like them because they're trendy, just like body piercing. Which I don't allow either. To me, it's the height of conformity. Why do something just because everybody else does it? We don't want players who follow. We want leaders.

Tennessee has strict rules, I admit. Our competition tries to make something out of that. They say we're too rigid, and call us the Cookie Factory. They say our players act like they came out of cookie cutters. Well, it's true that our players buy into a system and that we demand they be more mature than their peers.

One player for another university told our players she would never play for Tennessee, because she wouldn't have freedom to run the floor and take her shots. Well, she's right. She's a wild shooter. If she came to Tennessee, she'd have to take good shots. Because you don't just take shots for yourself. You take them for the whole team. That's the kind of responsibility we try to instill.

We've had plenty of individualists on our teams. Look at Chamique. She's proof that being a creative, expressive individual is not incompatible with being responsible, as so many people, especially kids, seem to think.

The fact is, we don't have many rules. They're simple and straightforward. The fewer the rules, the fewer that will be broken.

All of our rules have to do with breaking old "baby" habits that some people bring into the program. Like whining. Walking with what I call the "loser's limp." Blaming something/someone else for what's going wrong instead of being accountable for your own actions and part.

But rules and edicts by themselves won't replace a sense of responsibility in the long run. You can't force it on people, or stand watch over them every waking second. You've got to convince them to be responsible to themselves and, most important, to each other.

You may think I sit in my office and issue directives with an "Off with their heads" attitude. But I don't. I consult with the players on most of our rules, so that they take some responsibility for *making them, as well as following them.* I'll ask the team, "What do you think our dress code should be?" Or, "What time do you want to set curfew at?"

When players have input into establishing their own rules, suddenly the rules are "ours" and not mine. And they'll be responsible to each other, rather than solely to me.

I'll give you an example. Right after we had our first meeting with the '97–'98 team, Chamique came by the office. She had a request on behalf of the team. She wanted to know if the curfew could be 11:30 P.M. instead of 11:00 P.M. I said, sure.

Why? Because I liked the fact that Chamique was assuming responsibility for her team, and I wanted to encourage it. Not only did I trust Chamique, because she had proved in the past that she is responsible, I trusted that the others would be accountable to her, and that she would use her influence to keep them in line.

I'd much prefer that the team be accountable to each other than to me. It's a far more powerful method of team-building.

Think about it. The more responsibility they are given, the more committed they will be to a project, and the more they then make it *their* project. When it's theirs, they feel more accountable for its success or failure, and they do whatever it takes to help it succeed. It becomes "our" team instead of "my" team.

And when it's "our" team, it doesn't take second place.

Responsibility equals accountability equals ownership. And a sense of ownership is the most powerful weapon a team or organization can have.

There are a variety of techniques you can use to create a sense of ownership in a group situation. Peer pressure is always effective. Now, I hate peer pressure. I can't stand to see young women succumb to it, especially when the result is tattoos or body piercing.

But I'm not above manipulating it.

At Tennessee we increase our players' responsibilities to each other slowly, incrementally, over four years. By the time our players are seniors, we assign them mentoring roles; they each have the personal charge of an incoming freshman. They are responsible for seeing that their freshman gets to class and eats lunch. They are responsible for calling in the evening to see if she has any questions or problems.

Peer pressure has been especially useful in pushing our players to graduate. We manufactured a little tradition, as an incentive to our players to get their degrees. There's a big white support pillar in the middle of our locker room. We let our seniors scrawl all over it with their signatures. You can see the graffiti autographs of all the former Tennessee greats in magic marker. It's become a ceremonial honor to leave your signature on that pole.

But if you don't get your degree, you can't sign.

No degree, you don't touch that pole.

Over the years, I've employed some pretty inventive methods of cultivating ownership. Some of them were downright diabolical. And some of them were pretty funny, in retrospect.

I evicted our team from their locker room.

It's true. I did.

During the 1990 season I got plain fed up. There is one thing you don't ever want to show me, and that's lack of effort. Well, we were defending national champions that year, and we took winning for granted. We didn't do the things I expected of a Tennessee squad. We had a fun group of young women, and some bona fide greats on that roster, like Carla McGhee and Daedra Charles. But we did not play our brand of disciplined basketball, and we would eventually be upset in the NCAA East Regionals, for that very reason. After a real lackluster road trip through California, I'd had it.

I tossed 'em.

If you saw our locker room you'd understand why I did it. It's no ordinary dressing room. I don't mean to brag, but it's a state-of-the-art facility, with a big overstuffed leather couch, a big-screen TV and sound system, and glass cases full of trophies. The lockers are made of smooth polished wood, with plaques engraved with the names of past greats who have used each cubicle. It's practically a museum.

I looked around that room, and decided the '90 team didn't deserve to live there anymore.

"You haven't paid the rent," I said. "You're outta here."

I made them move down the hall to an auxiliary visitors' locker room.

For a month.

People were kind of shocked by that. It made *USA Today* and ran on the wire services and generally contributed to my reputation as the General George Patton of women's basketball. But I made my point: If you don't fulfill your responsibilities, you will be held accountable. Our locker room is a privilege, a mark of excellence. And they were not being excellent in any way. That auxiliary locker room had nothing on the walls. Nothing at all. Just cinderblocks. It had a water fountain and some cold metal folding chairs. That nothingness made a bigger impression on them than all of our trophies. The message was clear.

Not long ago, someone asked me why I waited a month before I let them back into their own lockers. Did it really take them that long to work their way back into my good graces?

It took *me* that long.

They might be "our" rules and "our" locker room.

It's my temper.

●   ●   ●

Accountability is essential to personal growth, as well as team growth. How can you improve if you're never wrong? If you don't admit a mistake and take responsibility for it, you're bound to make the same one again.

You've noticed by now that not all the stories I tell are about success. A lot of them are about failure, or adverse situations, or downright embarrassments. That's because you learn as much from getting it wrong as you do from getting it right. But you must be willing to take responsibility for failure and be willing to examine it closely no matter how excruciating or embarrassing.

I've been wrong, lots. Just consider the fact that Tennessee did not win its first national championship until 1987. From 1974 to 1986, we reached the Final Four a total of seven times, and lost. We couldn't win the big one. And some of that was my fault. I was wrong when I thought I had to intimidate my players into obeying me. I was wrong when I overcoached. I was wrong in some of my game plans in those early national championship games when I insisted the Lady Vols play a highly structured half-court game. I'm still wrong about plenty.

But I make sure that our teams and our staff remember and learn from our mistakes.

Even if I have to force it on us. In 1988, I made absolutely certain that we remembered the outcome of a big game against Texas. The Lady Longhorns kicked us all over the floor at home, 97–78. It still rankles as one of our most lopsided defeats.

I had the score painted on the training room wall. Huge. Four feet high. In orange.

Every afternoon when our coaches and players got dressed for practice, we had to look at that big ugly orange score.

Also, I made up T-shirts with the score on the front. They had to wear them in practice.

●   ●   ●

At first I thought Nikki McCray was a mistake. I didn't think Nikki could make it at Tennessee. But she is living proof that responsibility and maturity can be taught. Of all the players who have come through Knoxville in the last twenty-four years, Nikki may have traveled the most distance. Even though she was raised in tiny Collierville in West Tennessee, she had a long, long way to go to make it. I wasn't sure she would.

When I first met Nikki, she was one of the most charming and irresponsible kids I'd ever come across. She'll tell you that herself, so I don't mind saying it. The first time Holly Warlick and I went to see her play in Collierville, we arrived at her high school about fifteen minutes before tip-off, only to see her *leaving* the gym. She was just strolling blithely down the street. Mystified, we went inside and asked Nikki's coach where she was going.

"She forgot her uniform," I was told.

She was *sauntering* back home to get it.

Nikki was loaded with talent, and she had a smile like a lamplight. But she was vague. She had no sense of the imperative.

She arrived at Tennessee late, and without a watch.

Nikki had called us from home and told us what day she would be arriving on campus for fall registration. Well, the day came and went, and no Nikki. She didn't show. Holly waited all afternoon for her, and she didn't call.

Finally, at about four o'clock the next afternoon, Nikki turned up. She just hadn't felt like getting to Knoxville any sooner. I explained, not real gently either, that if she intended to play for Tennessee, she was going to have to learn to use a phone.

While I was talking to her, I said, "We've got a team meeting at five."

Nikki said casually, "Oh. What time is it now?"

As I glanced at her, I realized she didn't have a watch on.

There was a big blank spot on her wrist.

Nikki's mother and her aunt had come with her to campus, and they were sitting in on the conversation. They saw me glaring at Nikki's wrist, and their eyes widened.

Before I could say a word, Nikki's aunt unstrapped the watch from her own wrist, and buckled it on to Nikki's wrist.

"Here, take this, take this," she said hastily.

It didn't help. Over the next couple of weeks, Nikki didn't get anywhere on time. When she wasn't late, she flat missed appointments. She had no idea where she was supposed to be, or when. After several days of this, I was convinced I had made a terrible mistake.

"Send McCray home," I ordered Holly and Mickie. "Just send her home. She's never going to make it here."

"Whoa," Holly said. "Hold on."

"Now, Pat," Mickie said. "Don't be hasty. Just wait a minute."

I count on Mickie and Holly to tell me when I'm wrong.

In fact, I'd say that's probably their chief responsibility.

Mickie and Holly convinced me to let Nikki stay. They took personal charge of her. They made her buy an appointment book, and they stood over her while she filled it out. They spoon-fed her and checked up on her for months, until she could be relied on.

Nikki was well-intentioned. It was just a matter of culture shock. The pace and requirements of campus life were new to her. Back in Collierville, nobody had to be much of any place, and certainly not in a hurry. Once she learned some fundamental organization and accountability, the results were stunning.

Nikki went on to graduate with a degree in sports management and then signed up for graduate courses in her final season. She went from being a young lady without a watch, to a graduate student.

Today Nikki is one of the most accomplished women in basketball. She was an Olympian on the '96 gold medal team in Atlanta. She was the Most Valuable Player in the inaugural season of the ABL, and she led her team, the Columbus Quest, to a championship. In the off season she signed a contract with the WNBA, becoming one of the league's most highly paid and highly visible players. And she is on the verge of becoming a full-fledged enterprise. The WNBA intends to make her one of their major corporate presences and spokespersons, along with Rebecca Lobo, Lisa Leslie, and Sheryl Swoopes. Nikki has her own signature sneaker, and a million-dollar contract with an apparel company. She's a beautiful public speaker and a dedicated athlete who deserves every reward she has reaped.

Nikki often comes back to Knoxville for a visit. She is one of the biggest, brightest, loveliest successes we've ever had.

I don't claim responsibility for her. She can do that for herself.

So can you. Ask yourself every day what your responsibilities are, and be accountable for them. When you've fulfilled those, ask for more. Then, ask yourself if you have fulfilled your responsibilities to the other people in your life as well.

And when you turn this page, don't think it's over.

Q & A *Michelle Marciniak*

Guard, Most Valuable Player, NCAA All-Tournament team, 1996; Philadelphia Rage, ABL

Q: *You were one of the first people Pat called when Tyler Summitt was born, right?*

MICHELLE MARCINIAK: *I think if there's one moment you feel like you've kind of bonded with somebody, that would be it. It was like we went through that whole day together, and I couldn't do anything until she had this baby.*

Q: *When did she call?*

MICHELLE MARCINIAK: *I think it was one o'clock or two o'clock in the morning. I had been up the entire time, just thinking about her. I was getting sleepy, but then the phone rang. And she said, "I had the baby." I've never heard her that tired. She said, "I had a little boy, and I just wanted to tell you." She didn't have to call me. She was in pain for how many hours, and she'd just had the baby. She didn't have to call me.*

Q: *She says the team is a family. Would you agree?*

MICHELLE MARCINIAK: *There is no question that we're a family. That comes from Pat, from her creating that atmosphere. She doesn't force it on us. And she's hard on us, too. But that makes us come together. We have our bitching sessions in the locker room. She knows that. But she's like, "If that's what you need to do, go on and get it out. Get it out in the locker room. But it better not leave here."*

Develop and Demonstrate Loyalty

If you think I can be unreasonable when I'm coaching, you should have seen me when I was pregnant.

Being pregnant makes you threaten people.

Right now you're wondering what pregnancy has to do with loyalty, and what loyalty has to do with success. Stay with me here.

One afternoon when I was seven and a half months along with Tyler, Mickie DeMoss and I were driving in my car out on Alcoa Highway on our way home from the airport, when we ran into a terrible traffic jam. We were sitting there, bumper to bumper, when all of a sudden some guy came driving along the median illegally, passing people. Well, he targeted my car as the one he was going to cut in front of. *Wrong.* No way was I going to let him in. He fell in behind me, and he gave me the finger. Then he called me something.

I shoved the car into park. I jumped out, and I marched over to his window.

He was a big old shirtless guy. He had muscles that were jumping with tattoos. But I waddled up and jabbed him right in the chest. I stood there in the middle of the highway, poking him in his pectorals.

I said, "Mister, if you ever do that to me again, I'll whip your butt."

Mickie just sat in the car laughing and urging me on. I heard her hollering, "Go get him, Pat!"

What I'm saying is, I wasn't the most reasonable person when I was pregnant. I asked the people around me to put up with a lot. A whole lot. I made some unusual requests of my staff, and my family, which we will go into later in this chapter. But they stuck by me, and understood me, and remained loyal, which brings me to my point. My staff and my family are one and the same. My staff *is* my family.

It's an unusual way of doing business, I know. And it's not for everyone. But I sincerely believe the "family" model is the most conducive to success.

Here's why.

In pressure situations, you don't wonder how the person next to you will react. You *know*. Isn't it better to work with someone you have a regard for and a relationship with, someone you have shared good and bad with, and have developed some trust in and loyalty to? The single most common reason organizations self-destruct is disloyalty, especially when they are made up of young people who have a tendency to talk behind each other's backs.

In the family model, you can count on each other.

Loyalty is not a prescriptive for success. It is a value, something that is, one hopes, incarnate. I seriously doubt whether it is something that can be "taught." But it *can* be developed, and earned. To build a sound organization you must surround yourself with people who share the same basic values, people who are constant and who will be true to your organization. Creating a family atmosphere is, as far as I'm concerned, the surest way to do that.

Over the years at Tennessee, we have prided ourselves on our relationships with the families of our student athletes. Recently, at the suggestion of our sports psychologist, Dr. Nina Elliott, we held a team meeting in which all of the players and coaches brought in pictures of their families. We sat together and showed our pictures and talked about our parents and brothers and sisters, and described how we grew up. Some of us cried. At the end of that meeting we all knew each other a lot better. We had created a support group.

The next time someone is in a bad mood, or low, or struggling, we'll have a better idea of what the problem might be. We'll know the right question to ask.

For the same reason, I insist on being just "Pat" to our players and staff. I like the way it sounds when I hear it. It sounds like you can come into my office and talk to me. You might not feel comfortable talking to Coach, or Head Coach, or Mrs. Summitt. I wouldn't confide in someone I called "Coach." But I would in "Pat."

I depend on my assistants, Mickie, Holly, and Al. They are more than colleagues to me. We work together, we travel together, and to an extent, we live together. We recruit, practice, or travel in each other's company three hundred days a year, if not more.

Everyone wonders how we've managed to keep our staff intact for so many years. Mickie and Holly have been with me since 1985. Both of them are as qualified as I am to run their own programs. In fact, Mickie is one of the most sought-after coaches in the country. She has turned down four head coaching offers, including overtures from Southern California, Arizona State, and the pros, too.

How do I keep my staff?

My reply to that question is, how do you keep your family?

I'll tell you how. You take care of your family, and you protect your family. The next obvious question is, "How do I do that?" Paying people well is a start. That's why I've got the highest-paid nanny in Knoxville. It's why you must fight for every available raise for the staffers you value. You must find a way to show that you appreciate them. Even with a simple gesture like buying them lunch. I'll let you in on a secret about my business. It's up to the head coach to decide how much to pay their assistants. You'd be shocked at the paltry salaries of some assistants I know. There is just no excuse for underpaying them that way.

If you want to develop loyalty, the first thing you have to do is demonstrate it. Too many people use the term unilaterally. Especially bosses. They demand loyalty, without reciprocating. They ask, "Staff, have you been loyal to me?" But what about the manager's loyalty to the staff?

Mickie is the single greatest recruiter of young players I have ever known—thanks to her sincerity, caring, and unflagging humor. Year after year, we sign great players. In 1997 we signed four freshmen who have been described as the greatest collection of high school talent ever. So I'd *better* pay her commensurately.

You win with people. I don't care how good you are. I don't care what kind of a genius you may be. If you don't have a good, loyal staff, you will not succeed. Your chief asset is the array of personalities you work with.

That's why, whenever I am asked how we've won so many championships at Tennessee in the last ten years, I point straight to Mickie and Holly. Life changed dramatically at Tennessee when I hired them in the spring of 1985. By 1987, the Lady Vols started winning the big games instead of losing them. Of course, prior to '87 we weren't any slouches either. We went to the Final Four seven times, thanks in large part to our first great assistant, Nancy Darsch, who is currently head coach of the New York Liberty of the WNBA. Nancy was, and is, as good a floor coach as any in the country.

But since Mickie and Holly arrived, we've won five titles in ten years. It's a pretty remarkable swing, wouldn't you say?

Holly is a native Tennessean who was an All-American guard for us from 1976 to 1980. She finished her career by making the Olympic team in '80. She had floppy blond hair that would get so sweat-soaked it would stick, dark and flat, to her head. She was possibly the most crowd-pleasing player in the history of the program, and she would have given her last breath on the court. She played for me in those brutal early years, and I was as tough on her as I've ever been on anyone. I have a bad habit of forgetting that she's not a player anymore. But as an adult she's become a close friend.

Which brings me to Mickie.

She's little, about the size of something you could hang from your rearview mirror, and she has a way of being feisty and funny at the same time. She played point guard for Louisiana Tech and was a real prodigy as a coach. She was named head coach at Florida when she was just twenty-three, but it wasn't a very happy experience for her. She hasn't tried it since. Instead she has turned her talents to building relationships with players. She is the person who argues with me the longest and hardest, and she tells me when I am absolutely dead wrong.

Two years ago we added a third full-time assistant, Al Brown. Al is a gray-haired, methodical man who was a noted coach in the men's game until he crossed the tracks. He worked at four different schools, including Purdue and Minnesota, before he landed at Tennessee as a member of former head coach Wade Houston's staff. He was living in Knoxville and coaching at Lenoir City High School when I asked him if he would be interested in working with us. He is the first coach, male or female, to coach in both a men's and women's Final Four.

Looking back on it, Tennessee basketball, when I arrived in 1974, could have been compared to a "start-up" organization. We had no budget to speak of. But we developed a good program despite our limitations, thanks to people like Nancy Darsch, who was integral to laying the foundation. But in 1985, after nearly ten years, we wanted to get to the next level.

In those years, Tennessee had a stigma. We were the perennial bridesmaid, never the bride. At that point, in 1985, we'd been to the Final Four six times. And we'd never won. Boy, I wanted it. I couldn't stand it. I mean, do you go to the grocery store six times and forget the same thing every time? No. Do you come home empty-handed? No.

After a while it really starts to get at you. And after a while you think, I've got to win the big one.

I knew if I could hire Mickie we could win a championship. I felt Tennessee was just one great player away from winning; we had gone as far as we could on homegrown talent and now we needed some national-caliber players. And I wasn't bringing them in. I consider myself a persuasive person, but I knew I was running second in that department to someone else. As an assistant at Auburn, Mickie had a reputation as both a strategist and a great recruiter. I knew how good she was at her job from trying to recruit against her.

I asked Mickie to spend two days interviewing with us at Tennessee and observing our program. I said, "I'd like to consider hiring you."

Why did I want Mickie so badly? Because she was *better* than I was.

Ask yourself if you've ever hired someone who was better than you. If the answer is no, then go find that person and hire him or her. Now.

A lot of people won't do it. They're intimidated.

But if you are secure in your own abilities, you should have no fear of surrounding yourself with people who are better than you. Why, in any endeavor, would you want people who are not of the same or superior quality as yourself?

At the end of Mickie's visit, I said, "Do you think you can bring in the players to help us get over that hump, to take us to the next level so we can win a national championship? Can you get us the players to do that?"

Mickie looked me right in the eye, and she said, kind of feisty, *"That's not the question. I'll get you the players. I have to ask you the question. Do you think you have what it takes as a head coach to win it?"*

What would you do if someone said that to you?

I thought about putting her on an airplane right back to Auburn.

Instead, I hired her immediately.

But first I glared at her and said, "Oh, I have what it takes."

The next thing Mickie said to me was, "You tell me what player you need to win a championship, and I'll go get her for you." Now, have you ever had anyone in your corporation say, "Just tell me the person I have to hire to improve sales, and I'll go get her"? That's a pretty confident statement, is it not?

That summer, I went to an AAU tournament and watched several hundred young ladies play basketball for one week in Hartford, Connecticut. I selected the one person I thought we needed to win a title. Her name was Tonya Edwards, and she was a point guard. She was from Flint, Michigan, and she didn't know where Knoxville, Tennessee, was.

She didn't want to know, either.

But I said to Mickie, "If you get her, along with our other players, I know we can win it all."

We went after her. Mickie persuaded her, and Holly worked on her, too, and they signed her. And that next April we won our first championship.

Tonya Edwards, our freshman point guard, was the Most Valuable Player of the Final Four tournament.

The moral of that story is, Mickie was someone who met me on equal ground. She was as strong as I, and she went out and recruited other strong people to join us. If you are both strong and selective, if you seek out quality people and convince them to be loyal to your organization, then you will succeed, and you will eliminate a lot of trouble, mistakes, and wasted energy along the way.

But you must be willing to acknowledge their talents and let them do their jobs.

When I say surround yourself with loyal people, I don't mean yes people. I want to make that clear. In fact, it's a crucial distinction. In a family-model organization, you have to allow for differences and entertain the opinions of others, without accusing them of disloyalty. People who say yes to you all the time are, in my opinion, insulting you. They assume you are either too immature or unstable or egotistical to handle the truth.

I know for a fact that Mickie and Holly and Al would run this team differently than I do. I know, because they've told me so.

Behind closed doors, we've had some real shouting matches. I mean, we've gotten into some absolute howlers. We argue over how I handle a player, or what offense I'm running. Or we argue about some new and unusual way I've found to overreact to a situation. However, I have absolute faith that in the end, no matter what happens, we're going to support each other.

I'll give you an example of a typical situation in our business. Let's say a player is unhappy with her role. She goes to an assistant coach and confides how unhappy she is about sitting on the bench. The assistant coach says, "You know, if I was the head coach, you'd be playing more." That's exactly the kind of backstabbing that can tear away at a team.

Mickie and Holly and Al have never done that to me. Instead, they follow in my wake, sweeping up after me, shoring up damaged egos and comforting hurt feelings, while still remaining loyal to the overall plan. We have a complementary chemistry. When I'm forceful, they're compassionate; when I'm punishing, they're soothing. They have patience when I'm out of it, humor when I need it, and good judgment when I lack it.

No matter how bitterly we argue behind a closed door, when that door opens, we face the world as a unified front. The reason we are able to do so is because we leave any lingering resentments or wounded egos behind in that room. We have come to appreciate the merit of a good argument, and we have learned how to move on. And we trust that the argument arises from good intentions.

The absolute heart of loyalty is to value those people who tell you the truth, not just those people who tell you what you want to hear. In fact, you should value them most. Because they have paid you the compliment of leveling with you and assuming you can handle it.

●　　●　　●

You could say my pregnancy forced our staff to become a family. I didn't intend for it to turn out that way. But Tyler's birth was complicated and dramatic, and I couldn't have done it alone. I needed help. In the end, it seemed like everyone got into the act.

I thought the worst pain I'd ever had was when I tore my anterior cruciate ligament in 1974. I blew out my knee my senior year in college, in an early regular season game for UT-Martin. My doctor told me that the only thing he had heard of that was more painful than a torn ACL was having a baby.

I just looked at him and said, "I think I'll be adopting all my kids."

Well, he was right. Nothing rivaled the delivery of Ross Tyler Summitt for sheer wracking pain.

Looking back on it, I think my labor pains started the night before Tyler was born. I was up and down all night long; I couldn't sleep, because my back was hurting. That should have told me something right there. But I did my usual deal. I said, "I can handle it."

I got up the next morning, and I started off on a three-mile walk. It was my habit to walk every morning. I walked five miles, every day, seven days a week, right up until the last three weeks of my pregnancy. After that I cut back. So I really didn't gain much weight. It was all baby. People said, "You don't *look* pregnant." The walk was important to me, because it was time I could spend alone, thinking and talking to the baby. I talked to him every morning while I walked.

I set off on my walk, despite the pain in my back. I was determined to get through the day, because it was an important one. A critical one, even. Mickie and I were scheduled to go to Macungie, Pennsylvania, for the afternoon on a recruiting visit. We were trying to sign Michelle Marciniak, a top point guard prospect. Michelle was a brilliant young player who we knew could make a real impact on the team—if we could convince her not to go to Notre Dame.

R.B. wasn't crazy about the idea of me traveling. And rightly so. I was traveling too much in those last weeks of my pregnancy, chasing recruits. But the thing you have to understand about recruiting is that it only happens once a year; the NCAA gives you a small window of time in which to visit young women at home and convince them to attend your school. Winning over recruits is a key to winning games. But R.B. was concerned. He said, "You can't do this anymore." I promised him I'd slow down after I went to see Michelle. The University of Tennessee women's athletic director, Joan Cronan, was also concerned, and insisted that I charter the school plane.

That morning I walked, and I talked to Tyler. We knew he was a boy and had already named him. I wondered aloud if we needed to make the trip to see Michelle. My back was hurting so badly that I only walked two and a half miles. I don't often quit on something, but I just wasn't feeling up to it.

I came back to our house, and I went out on the back porch and sat down. Our house hangs on a lovely wooded bank overlooking the brown, slow-moving water of the Little River. I rested for a minute and watched the river coursing by, and I said, "You know, Tyler, I don't know about this trip today, buddy. I'm not real sure we need to go." I sat there a minute more, and I drank some water. Then I said, "I'm going to be all right.

Mom will be all right, so let's get ourselves dressed." And that's what I did. I know exactly what I put on. It's weird, but I remember that orange-and-black outfit. Like I say, clothes are important to me.

I went to the office and worked for a while, and then Mickie and I drove to the airport. The UT plane is a comfortable eight-seat King Air, but as soon as we took off, I started feeling uncomfortable again. For the whole two-hour trip I shifted around, hoping my back would stop hurting. Finally, right as we were about to land, Mickie looked at me and said, "What's wrong with you?"

I said, "Mickie, I think maybe my water just broke."

She stared at me. She said carefully, "What does that mean?"

I said, "That means I'm getting ready to have Tyler."

You should have seen her eyes. Mickie has dark eyes as big as half dollars anyway, but now they took up her whole face. She was speechless.

I said, "I'm okay. I'm fine."

We got off the plane, and I called my obstetrician, Dr. Leonard Brabson. I explained everything. He said, "Well, do you still want to make the visit?"

I said, "I really do. I flew all the way up here. I'm okay, maybe it's my imagination."

I didn't want to overreact. I'd heard all those stories about women going to the hospital thinking they were in labor, and being sent home. They'd go to the hospital, they'd go back home, they'd go to the hospital, they'd go back home. Anyhow, the doctor told me he thought I would be all right; it didn't sound like the baby was imminent. And I really wanted to sign Marciniak. We had been following her progress since she was a young girl, and we knew her family, and we thought it was going to be an awfully close call between us and Notre Dame. We had been twitching for our chance to make a presentation to her. I was going to make it, unless I just physically couldn't move.

So we went on to Marciniak's house. Michelle's mother, Betsy, came out and met us at the front door. She gave me a big hug.

She said, "How are you doing, Pat?"

I said, "I'm in labor."

Betsy looked at me and said, "What are you doing in my house?"

I said, "I'm okay, really. Just don't tell Michelle."

I didn't want Michelle to be distracted. I was still trying to sign the kid. I wanted to close the deal.

Michelle and her dad came into the living room, and we started the presentation. Actually, Mickie did a speed-reading version of it. We had brought a big book with pictures of our facilities and programs, and Mickie flipped through it at about sixty miles an hour. She was talking a mile a minute, and I was trying to contribute, but my back was killing me. I was sitting way forward on the edge of the couch, fidgeting and trying not to show that I was in pain. I excused myself and went into the bathroom a couple of times, trying to get my breath.

By now I was having full contractions. The problem was, they were in my back, so I was confused. I had never heard of back labor.

I came back and sat down again. But I got right back up and excused myself again and went back to the bathroom, for the third time in twenty-five minutes. Then I borrowed the phone and called Dr. Brabson again. This time he said, "Why don't you just come on home." He did some calculating. He figured it would take us thirty minutes to get in the air and a little over two hours to get back. "It's a first child, so you've got some time," he said. Then he added, kind of uncertainly, "I think you're fine."

I came back into the living room. By now Michelle was one poor confused child. But she was about to figure things out. She had watched me getting up and down and had overheard me on the phone saying the word *Doctor*. She thought, *Bathroom . . . doctor . . . nervous . . . baby!* And she knew the baby must be on the way.

I stood there in the living room, and I said, "Mickie, we've got to go."

Mickie just looked at me.

"Now!" I said.

"Michelle," I added, "I'm in labor."

Everybody panicked. Mickie slammed the book shut and started babbling. She was so undone she couldn't remember how to get back to the airport. Michelle and her brother, Steve, had to lead the way in their car, while we followed them. They drove about ninety miles an hour, weaving in and out of traffic.

Well, we got lost. Michelle and Steve couldn't find the right terminal.

Mickie started driving the wrong way down one-way streets. She was in ditches, running lights, driving on sidewalks.

Michelle said later that she had looked through the back window of her car and had seen Mickie driving like a lunatic, and me in the passenger seat next to her, my feet up on the dashboard, my head thrown all the way back, moaning with contractions.

Finally we found the right place. We pulled on to the runway. I called R.B. quickly. Meanwhile, Mickie was so flustered that she got on the wrong plane.

She did. She started up the gangway of somebody else's plane. When she got to the top, a pilot said, "Can I help you?" Finally she realized she was on the wrong plane. I was standing on the tarmac, and as Mickie climbed back down, I asked the pilot if he had any wine on board. I had read in one of my pregnancy books that a glass of wine could slow down contractions.

The pilot said, "No, but I've got a bottle of bourbon."

"Well, give me that," I said.

He brought a plastic cup full of bourbon to me. But I took one sip of it and knew I couldn't possibly drink it.

I handed the bourbon to Mickie.

"Here," I said. "You're going to need this."

Well, she bolted it.

Ordinarily Mickie is not a drinker. But she tossed that bourbon right off.

This time we climbed into the right plane. Our pilots asked the tower for an emergency takeoff, and got permission to go. Our pilots were good. Flying us home were Steve Rogers, head of the university's flight operations, and Dave Currie, his copilot. Dave had actually helped deliver two of his own children with a midwife, but he never told us that.

After we got up in the air, I reached into my purse and pulled out a pamphlet on having a baby, and I handed it to Mickie. She took it with a look of stark terror in her eyes. She sat there, clenching her pamphlet on how to have a baby in one hand and her bourbon glass in the other.

As we flew, my contractions got so bad that I couldn't sit in the seat anymore. I crawled to the back of the plane and knelt there on all fours, moaning. Mickie tried to rub my back, and she started babbling about Ruthie Bolton, the great Olympic player from Auburn, and her sister Maeola, who come from a family of twenty-one children.

"Just think about Mrs. Bolton," Mickie said. "If she could have twenty-one, Pat, you can have one."

"Mickie," I said, "you have got to calm down."

Steve and Dave were flying as fast as they could, but they were growing concerned as they heard me wailing with contractions. So they radioed ahead to the nearest airport, in Roanoke, Virginia, and requested an emergency landing and an ambulance. Then Steve came back and whispered to Mickie that they wanted to put the plane down in Roanoke and get me to a hospital.

Now, you have to understand three things about what I did next. First, R.B. has missed a lot of big moments with me over the years. What with me dashing all over the place, we haven't celebrated a whole lot of momentous occasions together. He has sat through game after game, loyally, and then has had to work at the bank when it came time to celebrate. For most of our seventeen anniversaries, I have been off recruiting or giving a speech or coaching.

So he was going to see the birth of his son. If I had anything to say about it. Which I wasn't sure I did at this point.

The second thing you have to understand is that I have never lived or worked in any place but Tennessee. And I've never cared to be in much of any place but Tennessee.

The third thing you have to understand is that year we had been beaten in overtime in the NCAA East Regional championship and hadn't made it to the Final Four, which was held in Knoxville. You can guess who beat us.

Virginia.

I said, between clenched teeth, "Mickie, you go tell those pilots that if they land this plane any place but Tennessee, they're going to have a *madwoman* on their hands."

And that's what she told them.

Well, those pilots in the cockpit hit the gas. They ran that plane as fast as they could, at the lowest safe altitude they could find. They burned nine hundred pounds of fuel an hour, and turned a two-and-a-half-hour flight into two hours.

When we landed, the plane had black streaks down both sides. From fuel exhaust.

An ambulance and R.B. were waiting for me when I landed. They loaded me, and R.B. climbed in.

There was one more small drama. As R.B. and I got into the ambulance, the driver announced that he didn't know how to get to St. Mary's Hospital.

It was the most upset I'd ever seen R.B. I had called him from the airport to tell him I was in labor and was flying home. He had drawled, calm as could be, "Well, do you need anything?" And I had said, "You need to pack a suitcase for me." I hadn't even packed yet. And he had said, still calm, "Well, okay then. I guess I'll see you there."

But when he got into the ambulance with me, and the driver called on the radio to get directions, I thought R.B. would have his head. All I could say was, "It's okay, R.B., calm down, calm down."

We got to the hospital at 7:37 P.M. I checked in under the name Patricia Smith, for privacy. But they had put it out over the police scanner that the UT jet was landing and Coach Summitt needed an ambulance. So it was all over Knoxville, of course. When I got to my room we turned on the TV, and on the nightly news they actually had a picture of me and said I was in labor at St. Mary's.

It took about five more hours for Tyler to arrive, because his head was turned. He would most likely have been born on the plane, otherwise. The doctor didn't want to do a C-section if he could help it, and I sure didn't want one either. We felt that if we could be patient with the process, we could avoid it. Now, patience is not my strong suit.

Mickie and Holly were with us almost the entire time, which I will always be glad for. The hospital had asked if any of my family or staff wanted to be in there. Mickie and Holly, aside from R.B., were the only ones who said yes. But with all the confusion, I didn't know if they would be able to get there. After we landed, Mickie went home to change clothes and calm down. But she finally collected herself enough to come over.

R.B. and I were in my room shortly after we got to the hospital, when we heard a voice out in the hall. Somebody was hollering and causing a big commotion. It was Holly, who was outside looking for me. The hospital staff wouldn't tell her what room I was in.

Holly said to the nurse, "Well I *will* find her!"

Then she came charging up the steps and down the hall, yelling, "Pat? Pat Summitt? Where's Pat?"

She hollered "Pat!" and raced down hallways and fought off the hospital staff until R.B. went out and found her and brought her into the room. It's funny but I remember exactly what she was wearing. She had on jeans and a green shirt, and she was carrying a bottle of champagne under her arm.

Holly ended up watching every second of Tyler's birth, along with R.B. I mean, everything. She was fascinated. Afterward, she told me it was more exciting than any championship we had won. But Mickie was different. She was still shaken from the whole plane ride. And she wasn't used to seeing me in pain. She had never known me to cry out like that or to say I couldn't take it anymore. She just stood across the room staring out of the window for most of the time.

It was real special to have them both there. You can see how they're like sisters to me. My mom couldn't be there, and my sister, Linda, couldn't be there, and I'm not sure they would have watched anyway. But Mickie and Holly saw the whole thing, and they've also helped care for Tyler ever since.

It took a while longer for Tyler to be born, and it was a struggle. When we realized it was going to be a problem because his head was turned, I told Dr. Brabson, "I have to have an epidural." I was through being brave. So he sent in a guy, an anesthesiologist with a long needle, who said, "This is going to hurt."

I said, "Just hurry up and hurt me."

I wanted him to hurt me as quickly as possible. I thought, *Nothing is ever going to hurt again after this.*

After the epidural, I settled down a bit and watched TV and visited with everybody. The nurses all came in and out. Holly and Mickie got on Dr. Brabson, because he was sitting over in a chair not doing anything, while the nurses fussed over me. They said, "You're just like Pat at practice. She sits and watches while we do all the work."

But every so often, Dr. Brabson would get up and stroll out of the room to deliver other babies. He delivered three babies while I was lying there. He'd go out and bring somebody else's baby into the world. Then he'd come back in and say, "Another boy."

The third time, I just glared at him. "Don't you leave this room again," I said. "We're having this baby *now*."

And we did. He was born just after midnight, at 12:32 A.M.

When the clock passed midnight, it was September 21. I knew that it was the birthday of someone else in our family, but I was too groggy to remember whose. I called my sister, Linda, to tell her Tyler had arrived. Linda was thrilled. I suddenly remembered that it was the birthday of her eldest daughter, my niece, Lindsey.

I called my mother, and then R.B.'s mother. And then I called Michelle Marciniak and her folks. Even though it was well after 1 A.M., I wanted to talk to them. I had a funny feeling that they might like to know how everything turned out. So I sat up and reached for the phone and dialed the number.

Michelle picked up on the first ring. She had been waiting up, hoping to hear something. I told her Tyler had arrived, and everything was fine. "I had a little boy," I said, "and I just wanted to tell you." She said she was happy for me, and we hung up. We didn't speak for very long. But neither of us would forget that call.

Not too long after that, I went to sleep. The last thing I remember about that night is Tyler sleeping with his hand curled around my finger.

The next morning, when the players got to the track to run their sprints at 6:30, they found out Tyler had been born. So as soon as they finished running, they all changed and came over. And I remember Lisa Harrison, our All-American forward, sitting on the end of the bed with Tyler in her arms. She was the first one of the players to hold him.

Joan Cronan, our athletic director, came by that morning, too. She bent over Tyler, while the nurse was changing him. Wouldn't you know, he wet all over her. She had on a red dress, and Tyler completely covered the front of it. So he started right off pulling tricks on people.

The thing was, after all that, we actually lost Marciniak. She went on and signed with Notre Dame. It was a childhood dream of hers to be part of the Golden Dome. I understood the pull of Notre Dame, so I had to wish her well. But I had a hard time believing she really preferred their program to ours. In the long run, it turned out I was right. We had put our hooks into each other. Thanks to Tyler. Throughout Michelle's freshman year in South Bend, she kept thinking about Tennessee. She felt, because of what had happened with Tyler, that she really belonged more with us.

At the end of that year, she transferred to Tennessee.

As Tyler has grown up, he has become part of the fabric of the team. R.B. and I worry sometimes that he has too many "aunts" and "sisters." But then we see how much love and attention he gets, and how many wonderful relationships he is developing, and we feel all right about it. For his first birthday, his Aunt Mickie gave him the pilot's crumpled flight plan from that fateful trip. There are times when we're on the road that Tyler insists on sleeping in Mickie's or Holly's room, instead of mine.

It seems like there is a Tyler story for every one of our championships. Like in 1997, when he kept the team loose all during those tense NCAA tournament games by doing his imitation of Elvis Presley. He did it at an NCAA banquet before we faced top-ranked Connecticut, our archrivals, in the Midwest Regional Final. We went out and scored the biggest upset of the season, 91–81. He did it again in the hotel suite before the championship game against Old Dominion. Our little Elvis bounced up and down on the bed, wailing.

You said you was-a high class
But that was just a lie. . . .

Now, I'm not suggesting you should run out and have a baby in front of your staff. I'm just saying that shared personal experiences, whether they are shared arguments, laughs, weddings, funerals, births, wins, or losses, are the only way I know to build genuine long-term loyalties.

Loyalty is not something you can demand or enforce. You can't "make" someone loyal to you. In fact, I'd say that that's a pretty good way to prevent loyalty.

If you consider the things or people you are loyal to, nearly all of them are longtime associations. You are loyal to institutions and individuals that you have come to trust and understand over time, like your college, or your oldest friend. Usually you have endured some adversity with them, or through them. That's why I've never viewed adversity as a negative. It can be tremendously reinforcing, handled in the right way.

Loyalty is not a bargain, or an exchange. It's something that must be tended to on a daily basis, and it will be sorely tried on occasion. In any family, in any organization, jealousies arise. Relationships get stale. Some people want to move up. Others want to clean house. Not everyone to whom you feel loyal is automatically loyal back. It's not an "I'll do this for you, if you'll do this for me," deal.

Loyalty is a selfless proposition.

You won't ever have it unless you're willing to give it away first.

Q & A *Abby Conklin*

Forward, 1996–97 national championship teams

Q: Why did you and Pat have such a hard time talking to each other?

ABBY CONKLIN: You know, Pat and I didn't really get a good relationship probably 'til halfway through the year. And that was my fault, just because I wasn't a good communicator with her. I never really gave her the chance to get to know me. She was waiting for me to come to her and talk to her. And I was the type of person, like, if she wants to talk to me, she'll come to me.

Q: Did it just go on that way?

ABBY CONKLIN: I mean, I really wouldn't even talk to her unless we actually ran into each other, you know. It wasn't because I didn't like her. I just . . . I don't know.

Q: When did you start to understand her better?

ABBY CONKLIN: I talked to Michelle Marciniak about it. I told Michelle, "She's always yelling at me, and in front of my teammates. She never gives me an inch. Nothing I do makes that woman happy." And Michelle basically said, "Look, in Pat's eyes, that's how she shows she has confidence in you. By yelling at you. When she ignores you, that's when you're in trouble."

IV

Learn to Be a Great Communicator

There is a lot more to communicating than just plain talking. Take it from someone who spends half her life hoarse.

Talking is the least of it. If you really want to get something across, body language, facial expression, eye contact, and listening are all necessary parts of communicating. Sometimes so is yelling.

I'm a firm believer in going off. I admit it. You never know when I'm going to go off. It just depends. If I tell someone five times to post up, and they don't do it, I might just run out of patience. Now, I'm not a chair thrower. But I've thrown the ball into the stands, and I've kicked it. Just as an attention grabber.

There are also times when all I have to do is *look* at somebody to make her hear me. Niya Butts says about me, "She has that stare. I don't know how she can stare at you for so long without blinking. She must have had surgery."

My point is, there is a whole spectrum of communication available to you. There are oratories, sonnets, tantrums, codes, tirades, signals, and just plain declarative sentences. Each form has its uses.

By communicate effectively, what I mean is, how can you best command the attention of those you are speaking to? Should you employ high decibels or low? Are you talking to your boss or your employee? Would a touch of humor help? Decide what you are trying to accomplish, whether you are trying to motivate, elicit a confession, ask for a raise, or instill confidence. Be clear on what you want to say, and say it in a way that is appropriate to your surroundings.

Each situation requires a different tone. We all know people who yell at every opportunity. They yell in the office, at home, in a restaurant. After a while, we tune them out. Too much of one thing tends to dull your listener's sensibilities. If all you ever do is yell, then you will be heard less and less. That's why, sometimes, saying nothing at all can be just as powerful.

I'll show you what I mean.

Back in the 1977 season, I got word that our team had been out late drinking one night. They had had a big old party and had stayed up until 4 A.M., even though we had an early practice scheduled for the following morning. They had violated just about every one of our team policies. I was one upset coach, and I was ready and waiting for them when they arrived at the gym.

They were a sorry, hungover lot. You could practically smell the beer coming from their pores.

I considered laying into them verbally. I could have lined them up and started hollering like a drill sergeant, like I usually did. But I didn't think one more lecture from me would make my point effectively enough.

Instead I decided not to say a word.

I dragged four plastic trash cans into the gym, and I placed them at the four corners of the court.

Just in case anybody felt, at any time, like throwing up.

Then I made them practice—for four hours. We practiced straight through the Tennessee-Vanderbilt football game. Well, they used the garbage cans. Every so often another young lady would limp over to the sideline and do some business.

At the end of four hours, just to be sure those trash cans were thoroughly used, I made the team run suicide drills. A suicide drill is a sprint in which you have to run from the baseline to the free throw line and back, then to half court and back, then to the far free throw line, and so on. Enough of them can leave the most fit athlete bent double.

I made them run sixteen straight. By the time they were done, every can was in use. I think a couple of them even butted heads. They gave new meaning to the term "four-corner offense."

See, I made my point. And I never had to open my mouth.

●　　●　　●

Why is communicating important? Because you can't do anything without it. Communication is necessary in order to avoid confusion. It's vital to any successful organization to be clear. When you communicate, you eliminate mistakes. Everybody understands the system and understands his responsibilities within the system, so that he can carry them out.

Communication is paramount in a game or pressure situation. A perfect example of this is a time-out.

A time-out lasts ninety seconds. Ninety fleeting seconds. But consider all of the things a team must do in that short amount of time.

First, you have to *signal* the time-out and get five people over to the bench.

Then you have to sit them down in an organized fashion.

Next, you have to be sure they're listening.

You must consult with your assistant coaches and decide what adjustments to make.

You must impart that information to the team clearly and quickly—despite the fact that ten thousand people are screaming all around you, and a band is playing fast in your ear.

Finally, you must tell the players what to do in such a way that they *believe it will work.*

No wonder you never see a picture of me with my mouth closed. All I do is stand on the sideline with my mouth wide open, telling people where to go and what to do. I look like a cross between a traffic cop and an orchestra conductor. And in some ways, that's what I am.

It makes some people uncomfortable to see me snarl at our players from the sideline. I know my reputation: I'm that lady who's so mean to those poor young women. But I'm not concerned with that, or with hurting our players' feelings. They know me. Sure, my volume can be off the charts. But it has to be — in that game-day situation.

Off the court is an entirely different matter. You have to see the inside of our team structure and understand our relationships to understand why I speak to them the way I do and how they transfer it.

I employ three completely different modes of communication as a coach. Off the court I am a confidante and substitute mother. In that situation, my chief role is to listen, advise, and comfort. In practice I speak as a teacher who sometimes needs to employ severe methods to maintain the attention of the students. In a game I issue blunt commands and motivate our players to endure adverse situations. It's a competitive situation with no time for politeness or misunderstanding.

My different tones, taken out of context, would be counterproductive or even downright offensive in any other situation. For instance, sometimes we have "guest coaches," in our locker room, benefactors of the program who observe us at halftime. Once, I threw an eraser across the room to get our players' attention. I could tell that the guest coach was shocked. The gentleman decided not to ride back on the team bus with me.

But I wouldn't speak to a player in my office the same way I would on the court. Circumstances dictate how you need to speak, or whether you need to just shut up and listen. You don't holler at a golf tournament. And you don't whisper at a forest fire.

In order to communicate most effectively in a pressure situation, you need to do some groundwork first. Most of your real communicating should be done before you ever take the floor.

A clear understanding of what's expected of each person is crucial. At Tennessee it starts with our playbook, a binder containing breakdowns of everything from our practice calendar to our offenses and defenses to our scouting reports. Paper trails are healthy; they document your plan and leave no room for misapprehension.

We require our players to write everything down. Everything. For instance, if I want to install a new in-bounds play, I don't just *give* them the play. They must diagram the play themselves in their notebooks. The reason for this is twofold. They'll have better recall if they write it down themselves, and they will understand everyone else's position and role as well as their own.

Understanding each other's roles helps you execute. And so does understanding each others' personalities. The better you know your staff, the better you know how to work with and motivate each other. For instance, when we are trying to decide who should take our last-second shot, we need to know who *wants* the ball.

I know Chamique Holdsclaw wants the ball.

I know because she told me.

During her freshman year, she actually interrupted me during a game. I was having a sideline conversation with our assistant coaches in a time-out against Vanderbilt. I was standing there, talking to Mickie, Holly, and Al, when I felt somebody tugging on my jacket. She was yanking on my sleeve. I turned around and there was Chamique, with an urgent look in her eye.

"Give me the ball," she said. "Give me the *ball.*"

In front of fifteen thousand people, she wanted the ball.

I said, "Okay, okay."

I gave her the ball. Then I sat down, and I smiled, and I thought, *Four more years of this. I love it.*

I meet four times a year with each player on our team, individually. We look eyeball to eyeball and talk about everything from her fears to her ambitions. I spell out what her role is and what's expected of her, but more important, I ask what *she* wants. After those talks, I feel more in tune with her. I know what she needs to hear to help her performance. And I have heard *her.*

You have to listen to develop effective, meaningful relationships with people. Especially seventeen-year-olds. As a coach, I need to know a lot about them, and a lot about their families, their goals, and their dreams.

You can't do that by talking. You do that by listening. What I have learned is, coaching is not all about me going into a locker room and telling them everything I know about basketball. It's a matter of knowing how they think and feel and what they want and what's important in their lives. Listening has allowed me to be a better coach.

I also believe that our players should communicate among themselves, without me. I insist on it to the point that we bring in a sports psychologist to teach them how to conduct team meetings without coaches present. There is tension in any group, particularly one made up of talented performers. Dr. Nina Elliott teaches them how to have discussions and confront issues in a constructive way, instead of backbiting. When something unpleasant happens between two members of our team, I don't believe in burying it. I ask the two players to confront each other and settle it. If that doesn't work, we get it out in front of the whole team.

Typically, a young player will start a discussion by saying to someone, "That's wrong," or "You're crazy." We teach them to modulate their tones, and instead, say, "I feel," or "I believe. . . ." It's pretty simple stuff. But it makes a difference out on the floor, because they have developed some interpersonal and stress-management skills.

We require our players to be as communicative on the floor as they are off it. One afternoon I kicked Jody Adams, one of our point guards, out of practice for not being vocal. The next day Jody came back and she had VOCAL written all over her body. She wrote in on her wristbands, her socks, even on her shoe tops.

Some of the players I have been hardest on over the years are point guards, like Holly Warlick and Michelle Marciniak; usually it was because they were being uncommunicative. It is unacceptable for our point guard to be inhibited. The point guard is the quarterback of the entire system; if she doesn't speak up, no one will know where to go or what to do. That's why an exhibitionist personality like Michelle, the point guard on our 1996 NCAA championship team, was so valuable. Even though she gave me fits at times. The quality that made Michelle a good communicator also made her difficult at times.

Michelle was so outgoing, she even chatted up President Clinton when we visited the White House in 1996. As we posed for our team picture, Michelle threw her arm around the president's shoulders. That tells you all you need to know about Michelle.

One day in practice, during Michelle's senior year, she and Pashen Thompson weren't vocal enough to suit me. So I told the managers, "Go get two chairs, please." I set them up at half-court. I told Michelle and Pashen to sit. I made them sit there at half-court, right on the sideline, while we practiced in front of them for about twenty minutes.

I didn't want to kick them out. Normally I would, but in their cases I knew how much they liked to practice, especially Michelle. And I knew how embarrassing it was for two upperclassmen to sit in chairs like children. It was my way of making them understand the importance of communicating with their teammates. But Michelle says it was just my way of making them suffer.

After a few minutes I turned around, and I saw them whispering to each other. I couldn't believe my eyes. I snapped, "You guys have a lot of nerve. I sat you down there because you won't talk on the floor, and now you sit there and talk! Separate!" I made them pick up their chairs, and scoot down the sidelines. Like a couple of grade-schoolers.

There is more to being vocal than simply being audible. Especially if you are in a leadership role. You communicate with gestures and body language all the time without realizing it. How you sit in a meeting may send a message. Which chair you choose to sit in might send one also. You can unconsciously project confidence or uncertainty.

Generally I don't sit on the sidelines. I stand because I feel closer to the game and in a better position to communicate with our players. Also I am aware that my body sends a message from ninety feet away. Good eye contact, straight posture, and a thumbs-up can impart conviction.

Or, if they jack up a bad shot, I stand there and stare a hole through the middle of them.

After a while, they get it.

It's not enough to say "I'm confident." You can say the words one hundred times over, and no one will buy it if your shoulders are slumped and your voice cracks. You have to project it, particularly when it comes time to persuade others. An instance of this was the Lady Vols' victory in the 1991 NCAA championship game against Virginia. We were down by five points with 1:25 to go.

In a huddle during a time-out, I said, "We got this one. We're *going* to win."

But we were still trailing by two points with about fifteen seconds to go, when our guard, Dena Head, was fouled. She went to the free throw line in a one-and-one situation. She could put the game into overtime. Or, if she missed, we would lose.

Time-out.

I knew that what I said to them wouldn't be nearly as important as *how* I said it. Whatever came out of my mouth, it needed to be spoken with conviction, so that our team would believe it.

It's a general rule of speaking that the first and last thing you say will be what they remember most. Everything in between will probably go in one ear and out the other. So those first and last things must send a strong message.

The team gathered around.

"Okay," I said, "now when Dena makes these two free throws . . ."

I went through everyone else's role. And at the end of the time-out, I said again, "So remember, when Dena makes the free throws . . ."

I made sure that the first and last things she heard were absolutely positive, a dead certainty.

Of course, after she ran back on to the floor, I grabbed our two post players. "If she misses the front end, you better get the rebound," I said.

Dena made the free throws. And we won in overtime.

A pressure situation—whether a game or a business presentation—is not unlike a performance. It requires a lot of rehearsal. Clear communication on what will occur instills confidence in the performers before the lights ever come up.

When you get ready for that last-second shot, you should already know, for the most part, what to do. Those ninety seconds are not the time for questions, doubts, or new information.

●　●　●

When is it appropriate to use harsh words? Only you can be the judge of that. But I'll say this: They must be used in combination with praise. What I don't condone is berating players. Negative reinforcement must be used sparingly.

My father taught me that.

My father could communicate just by entering a room. When he arrived at the dinner table, everyone stopped talking. My brothers and I would be telling stories and throwing the dinner rolls. Then he'd walk in and we'd fall silent, and the whole house would close in on itself. You could practically feel the floorboards seizing up. If my father chose to talk, it was about farming, or sports, or what we hadn't done right. But I don't recall any lively sit-down repartee with him at the dinner table.

As a result, I wasn't always a very good communicator. I was pretty hopeless, in fact. Before I left for college, I tried to tell my parents I loved them. I kissed my mother, and I said, "I love you." I could barely choke out the words. Her eyes filled up with tears, and she couldn't even say it back. Now I can say it. It comes right out, especially with Tyler. But it took years of practice.

I tried to tell my father I loved him, too, but less successfully. When I left home to join the World University Games team in 1973, for a tour that would take me all the way to Moscow, I wanted to say something to him. I thought it was important to make an effort because I was going such a long way away. I'd never flown on an airplane before, and I wanted to say it aloud to him. I opened my mouth. But I couldn't get the words out.

I tried to hug him. But I couldn't do that either.

I remember crying on the plane because I hadn't been able to tell him I loved him. It was ironic, because almost as soon as we got to Moscow, I got my jaw dislocated. In our first game, I took an elbow right in the mouth. My jaw is still crooked to this day. I came home fifteen pounds lighter, unable to eat solid food or talk much.

Now, you can't shut me up. It's a change I'm proud to have made, and it's the way in which I've grown most as a coach. I always cared about our players. I just couldn't tell them. They were important to me, but I didn't know how to show it. Now, I do.

My son is the one who finally taught me how to be freer with my feelings. I talked to Tyler every day when I was pregnant. When I took those daily walks, I chatted out loud to him the whole way. I'd talk about what we were going to do with our day, and how I couldn't wait until he got here. I'd tell him I thought he was probably going to be a redheaded little boy with a temper, because there's a lot of redheads in our family, with tempers. Things like that.

A wonderful thing happened when Tyler was born. As soon as the doctor laid him up on me, I said softly, "Hey, buddy." When he heard my voice, his eyes rolled up and he turned his head right toward me. It was incredible. He knew exactly who I was. From that day on, I have told him I loved him, and I have held him, and kissed him every single day.

Something I learned from my father was how bad you can crave a compliment if you've never gotten one. There is this to be said for negative reinforcement: It will motivate you. I know, when I ride my players, how deeply they ache for a good word.

And I use it. I'll tell you that straight out. I use it against them, to bring out the competitor in them. They want to show me I'm wrong, prove they're better than that.

But the trick to using negative reinforcement is to always phrase it as a challenge.

There's not much I won't say to challenge our team.

Tiffani Johnson, can you not guard Kara Wolters? Do we need to put someone else on her?

Is there anybody in this room who can guard Saudia Roundtree? Latina Davis, would you like to try again? She only got twenty-five off you in the first half.

In December of 1994 we played a memorable game at Colorado. Our players hate playing in Boulder because of the elevation. It's impossible to catch your breath. When you go to the free throw line, you see, stenciled on the floor, what the altitude is. It's a clever little reminder for the opposition. Anyway, Colorado was tough. At halftime we were only up by two or three points, and our players were absolutely dying. We had extra canisters of oxygen wheeled in. Abby Conklin was practically passed out on the bench. As we wheezed into the locker room, I knew I needed to say something to get them through the second half.

A tirade wasn't going to do it. They were too tired and breathing too hard. If I started in, they wouldn't even hear me.

"Ladies, I just don't know if we can handle this altitude," I said, concerned.

They all stared at me, openmouthed.

"It's just too tough," I said, in my best den mother tone. "I don't see how we're going to do it. We're not tough enough. So I tell you what. All I'm asking is that you keep it close. Forget about winning. Just don't embarrass yourselves and the program."

They practically broke the door down trying to get back out there.

If you come to Tennessee, I'm going to challenge you. There will be times when you're going to have a love-hate relationship with me. You're going to look at me and say, "I don't know why this woman is always on me, I can never please her." That's all right, as long as we're getting positive results. But once a player or an individual starts to slide in a downward direction, then it's time to examine my methods. And I've had to examine them on occasion.

I'll tell you a story I have mixed feelings about. In 1989, a Lady Volunteer team led by Bridgette Gordon was playing Auburn for the NCAA championship. We had a big lead for much of the game, but in the second half Auburn, led by the great Ruthie Bolton, made a run at us and cut it to six. I called a time-out.

The team came over, and I started talking. But I could see Bridgette was only half-listening to me. She was glazed. She wasn't getting what I was saying at all.

Bridgette had taken an elbow to her front teeth, and she was in pain. A lot of it. But I didn't know it. She had her hand over her mouth. But in that moment, on the floor, in all that noise and excitement with the game on the line, all I knew was that I had to find a way to reach her. She was our leading scorer, our go-to player, our answer to Bolton. We needed her to take the game over.

I got about three inches from her nose and started jawing right in her face.

"Bridgette, are you listening to me?" I demanded.

She kind of nodded. I got even closer to her, ignoring the other four players.

"Bridgette Gordon, what's wrong with you?" I snapped.

She just shook her head.

"You can't tell me Ruthie Bolton wants this more than you," I said.

Bridgette just shook her head again, wordlessly, with her hand over her mouth.

I pulled her hand away.

"Get your hand away from your mouth," I said, my voice rising, "and get back in there and *do* something. You mean to tell me you're not going to step up and make a play here? Don't you hide. You can't hide."

Bridgette nodded. She still wasn't exactly there, but she understood the message.

After the time-out, Bridgette, dazed as she was, went back on the floor and sank four straight shots. By the time she was done, we were up by eighteen points. She just looked over at me, with a hard look in her eye that said, "Is *this* what you mean?"

After the game, we got Bridgette to a dentist. That's when I realized her tooth had been knocked loose. As it turned out, she needed a root canal to save it.

I felt awful. Every ounce of compassion I had put on hold during the game came flooding back.

Did I say the right thing, or the wrong thing?

I still don't know. But I had to trust that Bridgette and I understood each other.

The only reason I could speak to Bridgette that way and still maintain a relationship with her was because we had done so much communicating over the years. As it happens, I was as close to her as I have been with any Lady Vol. Bridgette was one of just two players who ever came home with me to Henrietta. After she graduated, she asked to see my hometown. She was curious about it. So we drove over there together, and she spent a day with me and my whole family.

A lot of conversations had led up to that moment against Auburn. Bridgette and I had sat in my office any number of times, talking about her aspirations. We discussed game-ending situations, and pressure, and how we wanted to handle it. I knew how hard Bridgette had worked, and how bad she wanted a championship. I told her, "You're going to be the hero or the goat when the game's on the line. You're going to stick your neck out. Whether you succeed or fail, I'll never criticize you for that." We didn't fail much with Bridgette.

The problem with using negative motivational techniques is that they can backfire. You take a big risk in playing with someone's emotions that way. Challenging a player might be a good strategy, or then again, it might be a confidence breaker. The goal is to motivate, not to demoralize.

An unfortunate example of the latter was the way I handled Michelle Marciniak during the 1995 NCAA championship game against Connecticut, which we lost. I used the in-your-face approach with Michelle, and it was the wrong one. Michelle was playing out of control; she was trying too hard, pressing and playing on too much emotion. I called her to the bench and tried to shake her up, matching her emotion with my own. I got up close and told her, "You're trying to do it all. You're forcing it. You've got to play with the team." And then I benched her. Well, that pushed Michelle further into the tank. After I stalked away, Michelle just sat there, staring off into space, not moving. Mickie DeMoss looked down the bench and knew we'd lost her.

All she needed me to say was, "Calm down."

I had to go back to Michelle in the off season and tell her how much I valued her. "If I could choose any player in the country, I'd choose you," I said. "There's no one else I'd rather have run this team. I don't want any other player. I want you on my side."

After that, Michelle and I understood each other better. The next year, when we were in another tight NCAA tournament game against Connecticut, I knew what *not* to say to Michelle. We hadn't beaten Connecticut in three tries. But we were up by three with just seconds remaining.

Then Michelle overran the ball on defense.

It gave the Huskies' Nykesha Sales a shot at a three-pointer, and she sank it, with four seconds to go, to send the game into overtime.

During the time-out, my instinct was to go straight at Michelle and overreact again. But I didn't say a word to her. I talked to the team calmly, and I let Michelle regain her composure—and we pulled the game out, 88–83 in overtime. A day later we beat Georgia for the title.

Frequently, knowing what to say to someone is all about time and location. You don't always make the right call. There's a judgment involved. You have to ask yourself, "What does this person need today?" And you have to watch his or her body language. You may need to say, "You're better than this!" just to inspire him and let him know you believe in him.

Sometimes I'd tell Abby Conklin, "That team won't stop you. You can stretch the defense out, you've got to be aggressive." Whereas there were other times I would tell her, "Anybody can guard you." So, it's a matter of situation. Are you getting ready to open your season? Are you coming off a loss? Does she need a kick in the rear or does she need a pat on the back?

I may want to just rip into a player. But if what the team needs at that moment is something else, I have to be able to hold my tongue. I will say, or not say, whatever I need to in the moment, if it means the difference between winning and losing.

It's important to strike the right balance between commending and criticizing. Take benching players. Typically, if you've sat them down for making a mistake, you want to put them back in before the game is over. You don't just berate them and bench them with no chance of redeeming themselves.

The trick to communicating with a group is to maintain the credibility of both praise and criticism. Too much praise loses effectiveness—just as too much criticism does.

You don't compliment people for driving the speed limit or stopping at a stop sign. I'm not going to rah-rah every time you sprint down the floor, because you're *supposed* to sprint. If you make six passes, set four screens, and make five cuts, I can't possibly compliment you for doing all those things. That would clog the gym with inane chatter.

The best way to maintain the credibility of compliments and criticisms is to use them meaningfully. Don't overuse them.

At Tennessee, we use a system called Rebound and Two Points.

We came up with it in 1984, and we have used it ever since. The reason we invented it was because we had players on that team who were very sensitive to criticism, no matter how constructive. They felt I was too negative. And maybe I was. It seemed like whatever I said crushed them. It's often been said that people tend to hear negatives more than positives. Well, this team was especially attuned to the negative.

I had another dilemma, as well. I was to coach the Olympic team in the Los Angeles games that summer. The Olympic team was made up of players who were not accustomed to my aggressive verbal style. I needed a way to soften my tone.

R.B. is the one who really came up with the system. He minored in psychology at Tennessee, and he likes to fiddle with motivational techniques. We were sitting at the kitchen table one night, trying to figure this out, and he said: "Look, let's come up with a way that the players have to verbalize and recognize both negatives and positives, because people tend to only hear negatives. Is there a way that you can emphasize it when you're giving positives, so they are aware of it?"

We decided to play with the terms *rebound* and *two points*. Anytime a Lady Vol got a compliment from me, she had to say, "Two points." If I criticized her, she had to yell out, "Rebound!" It forced her to keep score in her mind, to count compliments.

In the process, we were also teaching them to communicate on the floor—to be vocal, so everyone can hear. It was interesting as I watched the players, because it seemed that they were much more comfortable saying "Two points" than "Rebound." That "Rebound" stuck in their throats.

I chose the word *rebound* because of what it connotes. When you make a mistake, you have to find a way to move on. Otherwise, dwelling on it will just cause you to make another mistake. When our players say "Rebound," that's exactly what I want them to do. I want them to rebound the ball, get back up off the floor from this negative situation.

Even since then, it's taken over the program. Maybe a player will drop by the office and I'll say, "That's a cute outfit." She'll say, "Two points." It's become our communication system, on and off the court.

At around that time, I also began writing letters to our players. I've always written personal notes to our recruits. But I hadn't really done it with players. I decided that, as much as we stress writing things down at

Tennessee, it would be a good idea to put my own thoughts down on paper.

I write a lot of handwritten notes to our recruits. I didn't want them to feel that when they got to school they stopped getting mail from me.

I sent Michelle, in particular, a lot of notes. I let her know when I was proud of her, or worried about her, or wanted to encourage her.

One day I realized that the players kept them. They would stick them in their wallets and carry them around. Or pin them in their lockers. Words on paper, it struck me, have more meaning than something spoken aloud. They have permanence. I could say something twenty-five times, but when they read it once, it seemed to make a difference.

Now, when I go off on a player, I jot a note afterward. Usually, the notes say the same thing. They say, "Don't let me break your spirit. I'm only trying to help you. I care about you, I want your best. Please, don't take it personally."

●   ●   ●

Lack of communication was the problem between Abby Conklin and me. I did not convey to her what I wanted out of a team leader. And she was not the type of personality who was going to come and talk to me about our problems. She spent most of the '97 season thinking, *If Pat wants to talk to me, she'll come to me.*

Well, some of it was my fault. I never gave her the opportunity to really get to know me. But she didn't give me the opportunity, either. She wasn't the sort who would just wander into my office and talk, and I wasn't the type to go over and sit down next to her and say, "Hey, Abby, what's going on?"

Abby and I wrangled throughout her career, because we were so different. I'm intense; she's laid back. I'm aggressive; she's passive. I sat her down on the bench I don't know how many times. I'd just be like: "Conklin, go sit down." So she'd go sit down in her chair, and we'd ignore each other.

After a while, I'd hear Abby whisper, "Holly! Holly! Can I come back in now?"

Holly would look at me. I'd be standing right there, twenty feet away, ignoring Abby.

Holly would say, "Pat, can Abby come back in?"

I'd turn around and I'd say to Holly, "You tell Abby that she can come back in whenever she wants to start hustling and putting forth some effort."

Holly would just look at Abby and shrug, and say, "You heard her."

That was the story of our relationship. Until that day early in the '97 season when she tried to contradict me in front of the team. After that, I not only benched her.

I stopped talking to her altogether.

Abby did everything she could to make up with me. That's why she came off the bench against Texas Tech in the next game to score twenty-six points. Still, I wouldn't speak to her. I was too angry with her, and I knew I would just make things worse if I lost my temper again. I decided to just leave things as they were rather than have another ugly confrontation.

I didn't speak to her for almost three weeks, outside of practice. It wasn't entirely intentional. Abby wasn't my only, or even my main concern. I was dealing with other problems on the team, like how to save the season.

Then we went to St. Joseph's for that terrible game, when we trailed by fourteen points, and I benched Abby again. We managed to come back and win the game, but it was obvious to everybody that we had a serious problem.

Afterward, Mickie came to me and flat out told me I was wrong. A cooling-off period was one thing. But now I was being stubborn. She said, "Pat, you have to talk to Abby. This can't go on. You need to confront this. You're the adult, so you're the one who has to do it."

It was one of those occasions when Mickie told me something I needed to hear. She said Abby and I needed to let go of the past, and that I should find out what was on Abby's mind. Abby aimed to please. And my riding her so hard wasn't helping, Mickie said.

I knew I was putting a lot of pressure on Abby. She wasn't a natural floor general. The problem was, one of our point guards, Kellie Jolly, was out with torn knee ligaments. Our other point guard, Laurie Milligan, lacked experience. That left Abby and Pashen, our two seniors, as our leaders. Pashen was a leader by example, but she was deeply shy. With Pashen I had to communicate much more softly than with other members of the team. Every now and then players will accuse me of favoritism. They say I get on some players too hard, while I leave others alone more. Well, it's true. The reason is, everybody is different. I don't communicate with them the same way, because they aren't the same people.

It's a question of personalities and finding the most effective language to use with a player. Some people, you can rip their heads off, and they still won't give you their full attention. Others will break at a single word. That's why I handled Pashen in a totally different way than I handled, say, Michelle Marciniak.

Michelle was the most headstrong member of our 1996 national championship team. Like I say, she had a strong personality and a tendency toward freelancing. Michelle, I yelled at. She needed curbing. I could rebuke Michelle and not worry about her feelings; in fact, sometimes she only heard me when I let her have it. But Pashen was a shy young woman from Mississippi who wasn't accustomed to that tone. If I yelled at Pashen, I had to be sure to tell her in the next breath that I still had confidence in her. She was extremely sensitive to my voice.

But I needed help in getting through to Abby. Nothing between us was working.

That night after the St. Joe's game, I asked Abby to meet with me. We sat in the hotel lobby for two hours, talking.

I told Abby we had to resolve the feelings of resentment between the two of us. I said I needed her support, and I needed her to be able to handle criticism as well as praise. We laid all our cards on the table.

I told her it seemed to me that at times she didn't care what happened to the team. I said the reason I pressured her so much was because I counted on her, and when she didn't come through, it bewildered me. And it made me fly into her.

I said, "I need you to lead this team."

She said, "I'm not sure I know how to."

For the first time, I understood. Abby wanted to lead, she accepted that responsibility. But she needed to learn how. She basically said to me, "You know, I need some help here."

I asked her if she would like to talk to Michelle Marciniak. She said she would. On that note, we called it a night. The next day we flew to Connecticut. While we were there, Michelle and I talked, and I asked her to call Abby.

I had an idea that it might help if Abby could talk to someone else about her struggles. She sure wasn't talking to me. I had stayed in touch with Michelle. I asked Michelle what she thought about the situation between Abby and me.

Michelle said, "Let me talk to her. I've been there. Nobody knows better than me."

They talked. At the time, I didn't know exactly what they said to each other and I didn't *want* to know—it was privileged communication. Any time a player talks to someone else—whether to a sports psychologist, or an assistant, or a former player—I don't go back and say: "Now, what happened?" I want them to be able to have that conversation privately. But later, they told me about it.

Michelle said to Abby, "You've got to go to Pat. Whether you want to or not—no matter how bad the game's been, or how great the game's been, you still need to go to Pat every day and say, 'Pat, what do we need today?' "

But Abby would only talk to me if we actually bumped into each other. It wasn't that we didn't like each other. It was just awkward, like when someone always seems to interrupt you, or you both start talking at once, and then stop at once. That's how it was with Abby and me.

When I would get on her, she acted completely indifferent. Her facial expression, her body language, seemed unfeeling. It was like she was saying, "You're not hurting me." When, actually, I was.

Abby vented all of her resentment as she was talking to Michelle. "Nothing's ever good enough for that woman," Abby told Michelle. "She's not satisfied with anything I do. I can't get an inch. It's like I can't do anything right."

Abby told Michelle how much it bothered her that I would yell at her and use her as an example in front of the whole team. Abby's main frustration was that she felt I undermined her leadership in front of her teammates. "I'm trying to be a leader, I'm trying to have leadership qualities," she said. "But Pat yells at me in front of my teammates, and what does that make them think? How can they have confidence in me, when Pat's always yelling at me?"

Now, Michelle had lived that way for four years. It's hard to name a player I chewed out more. What Michelle explained to Abby was that my yelling didn't mean lack of confidence. In fact, it meant the opposite. I tend to yell at those players I expect the most of. In fact, I target them. More on that in another chapter.

Michelle told Abby, "The thing you have to understand is, that's how Pat shows that she has confidence in you. By yelling. When she *doesn't* talk to you, that's when you know something is wrong."

I can't tell you how many times I came up to Michelle, or another player, and said, "When I'm quiet, if I don't say anything to you, that's when you better worry."

Michelle instinctively knew that. She got the message. She was a pugnacious kid from Macungie, Pennsylvania, the kind of person who would stop by the office no matter how rough I was on her in practice. She never backed away from me. She always knocked on my door, even when she knew I was mad at her. That made me raise an eyebrow. And I think I liked it.

Once Abby and I understood each other, it changed our whole relationship. We weren't always at loggerheads anymore. We cooperated. Of course, we still had our moments. The progress of the '97 team was never smooth. But Abby and I were easier in each other's company, and the rest of the team sensed it.

At a certain point toward the end of that season, it was time for me to stop talking. I was gravel-voiced from trying to urge them on. In the end, I found that a meaningful silence was more effective than an overwrought locker room speech.

We got killed by Louisiana Tech in our last regular season game. It was long past the point when we should have been struggling. The Southeastern Conference tournament was coming up, and we lacked confidence. Here we were, with nine losses, thinking our chances of getting to the NCAA Final Four in Cincinnati were slim to none. I felt for the team. But I didn't want to pity them.

Our media relations director, Debby Jennings, asked me who we should send to the press. It's not a popular job after a loss. Usually, the reporters want Chamique Holdsclaw. But I said, "Chamique's going to the shower. She's not going to do press, because she gave a good effort. Abby Conklin and Tiffani Johnson can go in there and do the explaining. Because personally, I don't understand it. And Kellie Jolly can do the radio back home to Tennessee." Then I gave my own press conference. I used it to send a message to the team. "That performance was an embarrassment," I said. "And I *promise* you, it will never happen again."

Afterward, rather than yell and scream directly at the team, I ignored them. I said: "I'm not talking to 'em." They didn't need to hear another negative speech from me. They were feeling humiliated enough. We were setting all those records for losing. We were seeing it, and we were hearing about it, on every newsstand and TV channel. The press was after us bad; we were the only Tennessee team in twenty-three years to have back-to-back home losses.

Typically, fifteen years earlier, I would have gone off on the team just so *I'd* feel better. But it wasn't about me—it was about trying to figure out how to get this team to come around and respond. I wanted them to figure it out for themselves. I didn't want to call another exhausting meeting, and *give* them all the answers, or try to pull the answers out of them. We had done that. They needed to talk amongst themselves and come up with their own answers.

I made us leave real early the next morning, and I sat over in a corner of the team bus, not saying a word to anyone. Somebody came over and said, "Abby wants to know if we can open up the gym tonight and practice." And I said: "No. We won't be practicing today. But when I do call practice, you tell 'em they better be *ready* to practice." And we all took a day off.

Why? Because in recent years I've tried to understand that more is not better. You don't beat a dead dog. Sometimes you step back, create some space and silence, and let things solve themselves. I needed to cool off; I needed to let Abby and the team think.

We had one more crisis to experience. Once again it was up to Abby and me to resolve it. We got upset in the semifinals of the Southeastern Conference tournament, losing a heartbreaker to Auburn on March 2.

What happened between Abby and me after the game that night may have won us the national championship.

I like telling this story, because it proves I have my softer moments. And it shows that a simple gesture can be worth a thousand words.

Abby played horribly in the SEC tournament. She was in a shooting slump. She made just seven of forty-eight shots. I mean, she could not have thrown a BB in the ocean. Well, she was torn up. Just sick about her performance. She couldn't talk to me; she couldn't even look at me. She felt the loss was completely her fault.

Again, I didn't say very much after the game. I just let them go back to the hotel. A short while later, I was walking down a hallway, and here came Abby. Now, seeing me at that moment was Abby's worst nightmare. She absolutely dreaded hearing what I might say to her. She froze.

I walked right up to her. She stood there, trying to look impassive. But really, she was stricken.

I said, very quietly, "Abby, we're going to get you through this slump. I promise."

She couldn't believe it.

I said, "We're gonna go back, and we're gonna shoot, until we fix it."

She started crying. Abby had never cried in front of me like that before. She was usually so emotionless. I put my arms around her, and gave her a big hug. "We gotta have you," I said. "Don't worry. We'll fix it and we gotta have you."

And fix it is what we did. I gave the team three days off. When we did reconvene, I asked them what they wanted. We needed to get our intentions straight, because we were out of time. After the SEC tournament came the NCAA tournament and the road to the Final Four in Cincinnati. I looked right at Abby. And she spoke up.

"We want to go to Cincinnati," she said.

"Okay then," I said. "But we've got a lot of work to do."

Abby didn't cure her slump overnight. She just worked, and we worked with her, and one week later she pulled herself out of it.

In the NCAA championship game against Old Dominion, we shot 59.3 percent as a team. It was an NCAA record for the title game.

●　　●　　●

How many of us go through a day without saying a word? None of us. But maybe we ought to try it.

Communicating is not just about giving great speeches. It's about allowing others to express themselves. Often a strong, dominant leader is the worst listener. He or she is too busy telling everyone else what to do and what to think. The more I have listened to our players, the better I have known them and understood them. And the easier it has been to know the right thing to say to them.

While you are listening to someone, don't just take in the words. Study the speaker. Be aware of the speaker's voice and mannerisms. Notice what his effect is on you. Become aware of your own voice and body language, too. Are you dismissive of someone without realizing it? Do you project vulnerability or a loser's limp?

You've probably worked with a group that just wouldn't listen. They look at you, and as you are talking, you just know they aren't getting the message. I've had teams like that. When I know a team is tuning out, I play a trick on them.

I'll say, "Today we're going to cancel practice."

That gets their attention right off. Those are the most popular words in a coach's vocabulary.

Then I say, "Before you leave, there's a banker who wants to give the first one of you who gets to his office a cash prize. Now, here's the directions."

Then I start talking faster.

"You take a left on Neyland Drive. You go to the business loop and make a right, go two and a half miles to the foot of the hill, go left, three lights, make a right, three more lights, up the hill half a mile, make a left . . ."

I stop and smile at how closely they're listening. Finally, they realize I'm putting them on.

While I still have their undivided attention, I tell them, "Just imagine if, every day, you listened this closely. What do you think would happen?"

You'd win a national championship. That's what.

Q & A *Michelle Marciniak*

Guard, Most Valuable Player, All-Tournament team, 1996

Q: *What happened in that Louisiana Tech game, when Pat grabbed your jersey and it made all the papers?*
MICHELLE MARCINIAK: *It was the last game of my sophomore year, in the NCAA Sweet Sixteen. I hit a three-pointer, and I was all excited. But I got beat on defense. I didn't get back to the other end of the floor. So she grabs me by my jersey and starts yelling at me on national television.*

Q: *What did she say to you?*
MICHELLE MARCINIAK: *Basically, she said, "You do that again, your butt's going to be on the bench."*

Q: *How did you take it?*
MICHELLE MARCINIAK: *You know, in a warped kind of way it probably made me have the year that I had my junior year. I put a picture of her yelling at me in a frame on my dashboard. I can't really put my finger on why I did it, either. Here I've got this lady yelling in my face, and I looked at it every single morning when I got in my car. I kept it there the whole year. Like I say, it was kind of warped.*

V

Discipline Yourself So No One Else Has To

I don't like this subject. It makes me bite my lip. I warn you right now that my warmest, friendliest side doesn't show up in these pages. By the time you're done, you'll think I'm one tough lady, and you may even like me a little less. That's okay, as long as you respect me and believe in what I tell you. Because that's what discipline is really about. It's about belief.

You don't want to try to put something over on me. I'll find out about it. "Pat knows," our players say. "Whatever it is, Pat always knows."

I practice preemptive discipline. Preemptive discipline is what happens when the mere thought of the consequences—like, say, facing *me*, right up close—is enough to prevent a problem from occurring in the first place. You can see how it would be pretty effective in getting people to do what you want them to do.

Our players suppose I can practically see through the walls of their dormitory rooms. They half believe that, from my glassed-in office in Thompson-Boling Arena, their every move is visible. Well, good. That's exactly what I want them to think. I want them to wonder just how I know so much. That way, they'll learn to discipline themselves, which is my aim. The ultimate goal of discipline is to teach *self*-discipline.

Discipline is about more than just punishment. Discipline is the internal structure that supports your organization. Used properly, it can help you maintain order without ever having to actually do the unpleasant work of punishing people. It is the basis of leadership. But most important, discipline fosters achievement and self-confidence. Discipline is the only sure way I know to convince people to believe in themselves.

Discipline is the internal mechanism that self-motivates you. It gets you out of bed in the morning. It gets you to work on time, and it tells you when you need to work late. It *drives* you. It is essential to success, whether individually or in a group.

So if the Lady Vols believe I am all-knowing, I see no reason to correct them. A touch of belief, I've found, can go a long way toward building success.

I probably shouldn't admit this, because I'll be shattering my own myth. But I really don't know everything.

I know a lot, though.

How do I know? People tell me things, that's how. Knoxville is not a big town. After twenty-four years of living there, I've met just about everybody. And after five national championships, an awful lot of the citizenry have an interest in the program. If our players are out and about, chances are I'll get a friendly call from a concerned supporter telling me where they've been and what they've been up to.

I tend to perpetuate the idea that "Pat knows," because it's an effective way of imposing order on, and demanding high standards from, a set of spirited performers, our players—who without it would be a real handful. As their head coach, I have to lead them. I must somehow convince them to do what I say.

I ask them to believe in me, and I ask them to trust me. The best way to persuade them to do that is to prove that I *mean* what I say.

The truth is, I hate punishing our players. I hate punishing my son, too. I try to avoid it at all costs, because it's wrenching. If only they knew.

That's why I bite my lip. I have a knot inside my lower lip from biting it. I bite it from worry. I bite it from agonizing over whether I'm being too tough, or too soft.

And I bite it when I'm trying not to laugh.

There are some matters I have to treat seriously, even when it's hard to keep a straight face. Like the time I took Tyler over to visit Holly Warlick at her place out in the country, and he punched all of the door locks from the inside.

While I don't want our players or my son to be afraid of me, I do want them to have a healthy respect for the consequences if they cross me. Recognition of the consequences is the surest way to instill discipline. When you are about to do something potentially foolish, take a moment. Is there a consequence, and does it give you pause? Too many people don't think about consequences, or if they do, they don't care. My whole philosophy of discipline is that if you learn to think about consequences, and more than that, actually see and feel the repercussions of your actions ahead of time, you just might prevent yourself from doing something stupid.

In order to teach that, sometimes I have to play the role of disciplinarian. Our Tennessee players have to think that just about anything is better than facing me.

There is a particularly funny story along these lines, involving, who else, my perpetual antagonist, Abby Conklin. She loves to tell this one on me. Some of it even happens to be true.

During Abby's freshman year, in one of our early season games, she had a bad habit of allowing the ball to get knocked out of her hands. She was scoring and rebounding well, but she couldn't hold on to the ball. She would let some little guard slap it away from her.

At halftime we went into the locker room, and the team sat down in their regular places. I went storming by them. They were all thinking, "Where's she going?" I motored past everybody back into the equipment room and started rummaging around. I was going to make sure that Abby was more disciplined in how she held the ball.

Abby was sitting there, unsuspecting, when all of a sudden, I jammed a baskeball into her midsection. Her eyes got as big as plates. I came around in her face, and I said, "I am so sick of seeing you being weak with the ball! You get offensive rebounds, and you get 'em slapped out of your hands. Do you know how weak that makes you look?"

Abby just looked at me meekly.

But I wasn't satisfied.

How do you correct a bad habit? Repetition is the only sure way I know of. You have to discipline yourself to do something the right way until it's second nature. Just plain practice is the answer.

So I used an age-old coach's method on Abby. I said, "You're going to take that ball and you're going to hold it. You're going to hold it the rest of halftime. When we go back out on the court, you're going to take that ball out there and sit on the bench and hold it there, too. And then you're going take it home with you tonight and hold it."

I left Abby sitting there with the ball and got on with our halftime business. At the end of the intermission, Abby went off to the bathroom to gather herself.

She carried the ball into the stall with her and held it.

When we took the floor for the second half, Abby sat on the bench with her ball. The game progressed to my satisfaction for only a few minutes — until Dana Johnson got two balls knocked away from her. Well, I leaned around the bench and started reaming Abby all over again. "You see how weak that looks?!" I said. "See how ridiculous that looks when you get the balls knocked away from you like that?!"

No sooner did I finish talking than it happened again. "Conklin," I barked, "you watching this?" I turned to our staff. "Get Dana out of there," I said. "I'm tired of watching her get balls knocked away from her."

Dana came over to the bench and sat down.

After a moment, Abby said, smart-alecky, "Do want me to give her my ball?"

I glared at her. "Yeah, you do that," I said.

After the game, I told Abby that I wanted her to carry a basketball all over campus.

Abby told me later that when she got home that night after the game, she sat on her bed with her ball in her lap. She just sat there, all alone, crying, and clutching the ball.

After a while, Abby's roommate, Amy Livsey, came in. Amy was an athlete, too, a golfer, and Abby's best friend. Amy took one look at Abby sitting there and said, "Abby, what in the world are you doing?"

"I'm holding my basketball," Abby said.

"Why?" Amy demanded.

Abby said, "Because Pat Summitt told me I couldn't put it down."

"Abby," Amy said patiently, "we're in the dorm room. You can put it down."

"She'll find out," Abby said. "She will. If I put it down she'll know."

So Abby took the ball to class the next day. She took it everywhere she went. We had to leave for a road trip that afternoon. Abby carried the ball until we left for the airport. As we were getting on the plane, someone told me that Abby had carried that ball everywhere.

Well, normally I don't torture our players unless it's for a good reason. But this time I couldn't resist.

"Conklin, where's your basketball?" I said, biting my lip.

Abby froze.

"Didn't I tell you not to put it down?" I said.

But then I couldn't help it. I burst out laughing.

Abby was so sure that I'd find out about whatever she was up to that she finally made Amy paranoid, too. Over their whole freshman year, they obeyed all the rules. And Amy didn't even play for us. They were both perfect little angels. They never missed class, never touched alcohol.

But at the end of the year, after they took their last final exam, Abby and Amy decided to have their first drinks. Since they were freshmen, they didn't know what to buy. They went out to a market and picked up two four-packs of wine coolers.

They were so paranoid after they bought them that they buried them in their backpacks and stuffed clothes all around them, so they wouldn't jingle when they walked across campus.

When they got back to their apartment, they turned the blinds down. Even though they were on the fourth floor.

They sat up there on the fourth floor of the dorm, worried about who might see them in their window, behind closed blinds, as they had the first wine coolers of their young lives.

When they got done, they put them in the trash can and went to bed. But at some point in the night, their paranoia came creeping back in. When Abby woke up the next morning, she saw Amy sitting on her bed, wrapping each one of the wine-cooler bottles in newspaper, and taping them up. Abby watched, while Amy wrapped and taped, and wrapped and taped.

"Amy, what are you doing?" Abby asked.

"I'm wrapping these things up," Amy said. "Because when we put them in the trash, I don't want them to clink. If they clink, someone will think they're alcohol bottles, and find them. And then they'll dig through our trash and link the evidence to us."

Abby helped her wrap.

There's actually a point to that story. Discipline is infectious.

● ● ●

To accomplish anything of real quality requires discipline. Think about it. Good cooking. Gardening. Parenting. These are all things that cannot be rushed or done slapdash. They require a certain order, and a thoroughness. They have to be done correctly to turn out well.

Nine-tenths of discipline is having the patience to do things right. There is no better example of this than shot selection. You don't just jack up the ball. You work in an organized way to create the best chance to score. You don't shoot a three off the dribble when you can get a layup.

The same is true of any job. You don't just freelance and hope your talent will make up for lack of discipline. Not letting an unforeseen bad break, an official's call, or some obnoxious crowd take you out of your game plan is another form of discipline. And it takes discipline to understand that it's a forty-minute game, and that you must do the things that will allow you to win all game long, not just in the closing seconds. It takes discipline not to panic in the stretch. Discipline is what helps you finish a job when you're tired and ready to go home.

The purpose of discipline in any field is to produce a unified, consistent effort toward a common goal. That's why I don't like to discuss discipline in terms of punishment. Punishment will only work as form of temporary behavioral control. Discipline is much broader than punishment. It's a form of training, in which you drill or exercise repetitively, in the interest of improvement. Otherwise, you're misusing it.

You can apply all of the above to your own life. Although I spend most of my time building discipline in a group, I use the same techniques on myself. Self-discipline is a matter of how hard you are willing to work when no one is watching.

I am known as a disciplinarian. But really, the entire aim of our policies at Tennessee is to get our players to discipline each other—and through discipline, to achieve maturity. We've been pretty good at it. We have evolved a system in which, by the end of four years, I don't have to do a whole lot in the way of punishing, or penalizing, or pushing them. Our upperclassmen become the disciplinarians of our team instead of me.

In order to get to that point, however, we need a set of rules. And some players are going to break them and have to suffer the consequences en route to learning self-discipline.

A situation came up just recently with the '97–'98 team. I got word that five of our younger players, four freshmen and a sophomore, missed a scheduled appointment with a tutor. In reply, we made the entire team, all twelve players, attend a mandatory two-hour study hall. Why? Because it is the responsibility of our upperclassmen to teach the younger players the importance of making every appointment and attending every class. If they don't discipline our younger players, I'm going to discipline *them*.

Some of our upperclassmen have become excellent team mothers. Melissa McCray, a guard at Tennessee from 1985 to 1989, was so much the conscience of our team her last two years at Tennessee that she got the nickname "Emma." They said it was the name of somebody's grandmother.

During a game in Hawaii, I explained to Melissa what I was after. One of our forwards, Kathy Spinks, was in danger of fouling out. Now, some coaches would have pulled Kathy and sat her on the bench, to keep from getting that last crucial foul. But I left her in the game.

Melissa said to me, "Aren't you going to take her out?"

I said, "Nope."

"Why not?" Melissa asked.

"I want to see how much self-discipline she has," I said.

It was up to Kathy to learn how to play under control.

At the very first team meeting of every year, I issue a challenge to the Lady Vols. I tell our team, "Each year, we have had at least one disciplinary problem. Why don't you be the first Tennessee team to go through an entire season without one?"

We're still waiting for that first. But by and large, we have few serious problems. Discipline is the signature of the Tennessee program, and I don't apologize for that. We are disciplined in the way we dress, in the way we run our offense, and in the way we play defense. We could change uniforms and come out on the floor in purple, and you'd still be able to pick us out—just look for the more disciplined team.

Tennessee discipline has acquired a certain mystique on a national level. That's both good and bad. It scares off some prospective recruits, which is unfortunate. But it also makes opponents respect us. Whenever our players are on national teams in the summers, women from other programs barrage them with questions. "What is it like?" they ask, awed. Actually, it's a compliment.

As a leader, you cannot develop discipline if you don't have self-discipline. It starts at the top. You have to demonstrate that no staff member, no employee, no star player, is above the rules. I don't ask anything of our players that I haven't asked of myself, as you'll see at the end of this chapter.

The truth is, Tennessee is not boot camp. The program is demanding but not impossible. If you keep yourself fit, behave responsibly, and maintain your grades, you won't have a problem with me. But if you don't do these things, you and I are going to tangle. And I'm going to win. It's just that simple.

I have dismissed some players from the team. Some key players. Everyone knows it. It's not easy to do. I don't take pleasure in it. It's hard to know what the right disciplinary action is. You don't want a first offense to cost anyone her career. But there is a point at which dismissal is the only recourse, if you feel the values and credibility of the entire organization are at stake.

Once you have made dismissal a possibility, once you threaten some-one with it, and there is a repeat offense, you have to follow through. You can't cry wolf and maintain overall discipline and the respect of people in your organization.

That was the case in the summer of '97, when I had to dismiss our senior post player. It was a tough decision, but a necessary one. Tiffani Johnson, a 6-foot-4 center from Charlotte, North Carolina, had been an integral part of our back-to-back titles. Tiffani made the NCAA all-tournament team in 1996, and she was one of two returning seniors. I was, and am, fond of her. She probably would have been Tennessee's starting center in '98. The job was hers to lose.

But Tiffani, or T.J., as we call her, violated team policy. She had a habit of missing curfew, and I had warned that I couldn't tolerate any more broken rules. We set a curfew of 11 P.M. from Monday through Thursday during the season. That may sound rigid to you, but the fact is, we didn't need a curfew at all until we started having a problem with players staying out too late and not showing up for class, or being sluggish at practice the next day.

Rules should not be arbitrary. Every one of them is in response to a problem. If we didn't have the problem, we wouldn't need the rule. There's a word for that. It's called accountability, and it is the backbone of discipline. You can't have one without the other.

The way I look at it is, I treat our people like adults—unless they act like children. As long as you behave like an adult, I'm pretty flexible. But as soon as you don't, I can be as tough as anybody you've ever met. I'll give you some rope and hope you can handle it. If you don't, I'll be all over you.

In the summer of '97, I discovered that Tiffani was violating our team housing policy. The policy states that you must be a junior with a 2.5 grade point average or better and have the coach's permission to live off-campus. I had no choice. I call on our seniors to be the most disciplined, responsible members of the team. Especially with four freshmen coming in who would look to them as an example. Not to mention the fact that everyone else on the team was living up to their responsibilities, and it wouldn't have been fair to them to have a separate standard for T.J.

On a July afternoon during our summer camp, I told T.J. she was off the team. It was a terrible day, made even worse by the fact that I am crazy about her mother and grandmother, and I knew how upset they'd be. They're good people with high hopes for Tiffani. But I couldn't in good conscience give her another chance. Much as it hurt to cut her, it would have hurt the team more to keep her.

Tiffani has accepted the consequences and gone on. I wish her all the best, and I hope she's going to be a great pro player. I also feel sure she will get her degree.

I had penalized other players for similar violations. Like Latina Davis, a guard, who drew my ire for violating our class attendance policy during her senior year in 1996. We were in the midst of a national championship run that year, on our way to the Final Four and an eventual victory over Georgia in the title game. But I made Latina stay home and go to class while we went on a road trip to a tournament in Hawaii and got to lay on the beach for two days.

Latina joined us late and played a key role in helping us in a tournament in Kona. We were playing Penn State in a real battle. Latina took over the game. It was a great example of how our players understand and respond to discipline. She accepted her punishment and moved on. She had the maturity to put it behind her, step on to the floor, and take care of business.

Discipline is all about structure. It is the bare-bones architecture of your organization, the beams and joists that hold everything together. Maintaining the integrity of your interior philosophy is crucial. Even if it costs you a valued member of the team. Otherwise, your structure will collapse.

It's important to remember that discipline is not something you wield on others for your own personal empowerment. And it's not something that should be inflicted capriciously, either. In the right hands, discipline is simply a tool for fostering organizational success. It provides conviction to a philosophy.

Really, discipline is just a way of getting people to cooperate with each other. You agree to obey a set of predetermined regulations so that you can all work together toward success.

●   ●   ●

There are three things to remember about discipline.

Discipline should be fair, firm, and consistent.

The key to using discipline so that it is conducive to success is to find out what's important to people. Once you find out what they care about, then you know what to reward them with or take away from them. It's an exchange, a form of currency. In the case of our players, it may be starting time, or freedom from requirements. In the case of children, it might be toys. In the case of employees, it may be a bonus.

This can be applied on a personal level as well. You discipline yourself with rewards and penalties. A natural system of self-incentives will evolve. You can keep yourself on the right track by alternating self-congratulation with self-restraint.

You have to decide what's important to you—you have to set goals. And that is a daily process. An overall goal can seem intimidating, or too distant. For instance, if we set a goal of winning a national championship every year, it would seem inconceivable, and even ridiculous. But if we set a reasonable short-term goal, like winning twenty games this season and getting to the NCAA tournament, our chances of achieving it are a whole lot better, and we will be naturally more inclined to work for it. Taking on too much can be a morale breaker, and when morale breaks down, so does self-discipline.

You have to have a daily goal, and you have to make a daily commitment to the goal. Once you have set that reachable goal for the day, set up a reward-and-penalty system. Take something away from yourself if you don't reach the goal. In my own case, when I was in training I would set a distance I needed to run. If I should have run five miles, but only ran three, I forced myself to make it up the very next morning. I'd run two extra miles.

I did the same with eating. If I ate too much, I'd make myself do a second workout. Or, if I did a great job all week with eating healthy foods,

I'd give myself a milk shake. I'd go to Baskin Robbins and get a chocolate shake made with French vanilla ice cream. That was important.

Here's an example of group incentives we use with our Tennessee teams. In our practices, we set a statistical goal. It comes with a small reward or punishment attached. Let's say the goal is to cut down on our turnovers. If they meet it, they get a reward: They get to shoot at the end of practice, instead of run. If they don't meet it, they run what we call "Big Three" sprint drills.

Shoot or run. It's up to them.

Another example: Clothes are important to our team. They really prize our gear. So in 1989–90, the same season I evicted the team from their locker room, I also took away their selection of practice gear. They got to keep one set of gear and one set of sneakers, and that was it. I made them wear the same plain stuff, day after day. My reasoning was that taking away their garments was a fair, fitting exchange for the undisciplined way they were behaving. They were coming off an NCAA title and too complacent for my liking.

The message was perfectly simple: If you don't fulfill our requirements, you won't fill our jerseys and shorts, either.

Be firm: You have to be willing to set a precedent. It's no good just announcing a set of rules. Trust me, whether you are dealing with colleagues, or your own child, or yourself, the best way to discourage anarchy is to be uncompromising in enforcing the regulations. A stiff, nonnegotiable penalty the first time out will prevent a repeat offense.

In 1988, when Daedra Charles was a freshman, she cut a class. Actually, she only half-cut it. It was a long three-hour class, and when the midway break came, she decided to just leave. She thought it didn't matter much, as long as she got her work done. But it mattered to me. Daedra was a terrific young recruit, a 6-foot-3 young lady from Detroit, Michigan, with a soft, easy grin, who would become one of our finest centers. But she was also academically ineligible as a freshman. She needed to apply herself. The professor dialed me up and told me Daedra had skipped out on the class.

I called her into the office. I was on the phone when she got there. I smiled pleasantly, waved her to a chair, and said, "Sit down." So she sat down. But as soon as I got off the phone, I started yelling. "What gives you the right to skip class?" I said.

Daedra just sat there, stunned. I could literally see those words pass through her mind, *How does she know?*

Daedra said, "I figured I'm in college now and long as I did the work, no big problem."

I said, "I don't care what happens, you don't skip class."

I made her run five miles, at 5 A.M. It was all hills. That may sound excessive. But Daedra never skipped class again. She graduated in four years with a degree in Child and Family Studies. Her team won two national championships in three years, while she became a two-time All American, received the Wade Trophy awarded to the best player in college basketball, and became an Olympian in 1992.

Daedra became the team's disciplinarian. I never had to say two boos to Daedra's teams. Whatever the problem was, Daedra took care of it. I remember one day in practice—toward the end of the 1991 season, Daedra's senior year—when I got on our freshman center Peggy Evans. I thought Peggy was not putting out enough effort, and we were about to go to the Final Four in New Orleans. So I started tearing into her. Which only seemed to make her move slower. "We're going with or without you," I told Peggy. "I'll leave your butt behind if I have to."

Daedra came running across the floor. "Pat, let me handle this," Daedra said.

"Okay, Dae," I said. "But you better straighten it out."

She did. She talked to Peggy and brought her around. Peggy turned out to be instrumental for us in the Final Four, and she helped Tennessee bring home another title.

There were plenty of times that Daedra came into my office, shut the door, and told me about a disciplinary problem that needed my attention. I would be completely unaware of it. She would say, "I'm going to tell you something, just between you and me. This is what's going on, and this is what you need to do about it." Usually, I did what she told me.

Be fair: The fewer rules you have, the fewer rules will be broken. Establishing discipline will be a lot easier if you don't burden people with a lot of silly minor regulations. All you need is a handful of fair ones that you are prepared to enforce. And when people participate in setting their own goals, standards, and regulations, they tend to be more cooperative.

If all you ever do is crack down on people, they won't stay in your program, or your business. They'll leave. Why would you stay someplace if all it offered was punishment? Answer: You wouldn't. Similarly, if all you do is punish yourself, chances are you won't maintain your training regimen or work regimen. You'll quit on it. If you are fair with yourself, you stand a better chance of maintaining your self-discipline.

Take our cap rule. I'm not crazy about our players wearing caps. The only time I like them is when we win a championship.

I like them then.

But I know kids like to wear them all the time, so I have to compromise. Recently, it got back to me, via a phone call from a professor, that some of our players were wearing their peaked caps to class and using them to nap under. So I made a new rule: No caps to class. Well, the players complained that they needed to wear their caps on bad-hair days. If I was going to insist that they attend every single class, they needed some slack on the cap issue, they said. They wanted to be able to roll out of bed and stick a cap on, instead of worrying about their hair.

I'm not an unreasonable person. Not entirely, anyway. And it's important to let them win some battles.

I give them one bad-hair day a week.

Be consistent: The implied content of any rule is, "This is a priority. This is important enough to make it a rule; and this is the reward if you adhere to it, this is the penalty if you don't."

Don't mess with your exchange rate. Make sure the focus of your sanctions remains clear and consistent: If you do X, the consequences will be Y. When you suddenly change the rule, so that a consequence disappears, everyone will be confused. And a lot less likely to take her commitments seriously. You will lose sight of what's important.

Coaching, parenting, and working in an office are all alike in that respect. To be credible, you must be consistent. Any sign of inconsistency, and you lose credibility instantly. Especially in dealing with children. I don't know about your kids, but mine has a hawk's eye. He watches me for the slightest sign that my deeds are inconsistent with my words.

I don't normally spank Tyler. But I do have to discipline him. He's a good child, generally. But he is just that, a child. Children aren't, by nature, self-disciplined.

They are mercenaries.

When Tyler was about three, we had a meaningful stare-down over toys. We were playing together in the living room, when he dumped an entire box of blocks out on the floor. There must have been thirty of those little alphabet blocks scattered all over.

"Well, okay," I said. "But you're going to have to put those away later."

We continued playing together. But when we finished, I told him we had to put those blocks away, like I said.

He wanted me to do it for him.

No way, I said. I explained that I would be happy to help him, but that he was *going* to put them away.

So we made a deal. I would put one away, I said, for every one that he put away.

It worked pretty well. Until we got to the last toy.

It just sat there.

He wouldn't touch it.

I wouldn't either.

My son and I are both stubborn. We sat there, our chins stuck out at each other, for about thirty minutes. It must have been pretty funny-looking. Me, the most notorious disciplinarian in coaching, in a Mexican standoff with a three-year-old.

R.B. sat in a corner watching the whole thing. *Good Lord*, he thought. *Now there's two of them.*

At one point, I considered dumping the whole box out and making Tyler start all over. I also considered yelling at him, or just putting that block away myself.

By far the easier thing in the short run would have been to put it away for him. But I knew that if I did that, I'd spend the rest of my life picking up after him. If I wanted him to learn self-discipline, I was going to have to show him what I meant by it.

Finally, after a half hour, Tyler reached out and picked that block up. He wasn't happy about it, but he did it.

Sometimes I think he's been making me pay for it ever since.

The older Tyler gets, the more ingenious he becomes at getting what he wants. And the more thoughtful I have to be in my dealings with him. I don't always win. After twenty-four years in this business, I have finally encountered a strategist who might be better than me. My own son.

Not too long ago, we were traveling through the Atlanta airport, when we passed a Disney store full of toys. Naturally, he wanted me to buy him one.

I said no. Well, Tyler started pouting. He pouted all the way from Concourse A to Concourse B. That didn't go over big with me.

The problem with buying Tyler a toy is that it's an easy way to placate him, and would spoil him in the end. Discipline is not about the easy solution. It's supposed to be thoughtful and appropriate, not knee-jerk. Remember, the purpose is train people (and yourself) into good habits and out of bad ones.

The problem is, you don't always have the time and energy to be a disciplinarian. Especially if you're a working mother. Chances are, you're tired and distracted and at the end of your rope. In my case, I was bone-weary and pulling a suitcase, in addition to my seven-year-old boy, behind me. We only had a short layover in Atlanta, and I had to shop for a couple of birthday presents and make a bunch of phone calls while we were there. What I really wanted to do was flop down in a chair at the gate. But somehow, I had to figure out a way to deal with Tyler.

"Okay, here's what we're going to do," I said to Tyler. "We're going to open your backpack and count how many toys you have in there."

Tyler emptied his backpack on the floor and started counting. He had a grand total of twenty-five toys in there. Big ones, little ones, toys of all description. It was like the circus car with all the midgets piling out. They just kept on coming.

He started negotiating with me.

"That one's not a toy," he said.

"Okay, twenty-four," I said. "Now, explain to me why you need another toy."

He couldn't, of course. So I won that round. But it was a short-lived victory. In the end we made a bargain. We agreed that he could earn the money to buy a new toy by doing chores around the house.

Well, as soon as we got home, he went into R.B.'s closet and straightened all the shoes.

"Fine," I said. "How much do you think that was worth?"

He stared at me shrewdly.

"Seven dollars," he announced.

I bit my lip.

●　　●　　●

Disciplined people finish the job.

The furniture that is most valuable or worthwhile is beautifully finished. That last coat of varnish is what makes a thing shine.

Back in 1980, I wanted to teach our team a lesson about the importance of playing from start to finish. The '80 squad was a great one, led by Holly Warlick. But in a midseason game down at South Carolina, we stunk. We were just awful. The hostile crowd got to us, and so did the opposing band. It was so loud, we had to take our time-outs at the foul line instead of on the bench. We were totally disorganized, and we panicked.

Let me put it this way: The band played better than we did.

In the locker room after the game, I told our players not to turn in their uniforms. Normally, they would hand them over to the team managers to be laundered. But on this occasion, I said, "I want you to keep your uniforms. And when we get back to the hotel, I want you to lay them out on a chair in your rooms."

Jerseys, shorts, socks, and all.

They grew stiff and cold overnight.

The next morning, as we were packing to go to the airport, I told them, "Now I want you to pack your own uniforms, and I want you pack them so they're easy to get to."

They packed up apprehensively. We flew home. When we landed, a van was waiting for us at the airport. I told the driver to take us directly to our gym, Stokely Athletics Center.

When we got there, I told our players, "You're not going to your dorms. You're going straight to the locker room. We're practicing."

We walked downstairs into the locker room. I said, "Okay, now I want you to unpack your uniforms. And put them back on."

They stared at me, openmouthed.

"You're going to play forty minutes in those uniforms," I said. "You didn't do it yesterday, so you're going to do it today."

They pulled their smelly, cold uniforms on, and I made them practice in them for an hour. People would walk through the gym and say, "You guys got a game tonight?"

My message was clear and simple. Those uniforms weren't ready to be washed yet. They hadn't played enough minutes in them to get them dirty.

A task has not been done properly until it has been done completely. Take shooting a basketball. It is not enough to score. It's part of the scorer's responsibility to finish the job by getting back to the other end of the floor on defense, too. If you're going to stand around while the other team scores in reply, what good is that? It's a job half done.

One of my more famous public displays of temper came over just that sort of thing. It made all the papers and highlight shows. *USA Today* ran a picture of it on the front of the sports section. It was a real Kodak moment.

I guess it was what you would call an incident.

What happened was, I grabbed Michelle Marciniak by the jersey and hollered at her on national television. It happened late in an NCAA Mideast Regional Semifinal against Louisiana Tech, the last game of her sophomore year, in 1994. Michelle hit a big three-pointer for us. A beautiful arcing shot. And then she just stood there admiring her handiwork, and gave up a layup.

Louisiana Tech breezed right by her and scored. Now, a shooter who hits a three has no excuse for not getting back on defense, because she is already in great position to defend. We're not in this game to trade baskets.

After she gave up the layup, Michelle tried to breeze by me. She was running down the sideline, trying not to look at me.

I grabbed her. I shot my arm out and clutched at her jersey, and hauled her to the sideline. Then I hollered right in her face. "The next time you do that," I said, "you're going to be sitting over here with me, and I *mean* that. I *promise* you. Your butt's going to be on this bench with *me*. Don't *do* it *again*."

The pictures made it look even worse than it actually was. It looked like I was screaming at her. But, frankly, sometimes that's what it took to get Michelle to focus, if you knew her.

When I saw it in the paper, I was horrified. I said to myself, "This doesn't look good." So I called Michelle's mother, Betsy.

"Betsy," I said, "I'm not abusing your child, I promise."

I love Michelle, and I love her family. But Michelle and I needed to have that type of communication on occasion. I had to force some structure on her. She was untamed. She was a freelancer, a 5-foot-9 young lady with a touch of glamour and a mane of blond hair that flew all over the place unless she tied it back. Trying to refine her game was a real challenge—and sometimes a battle.

When you have that style of play, and you've been successful with it, it's difficult to accept change. I had to force Michelle into accepting a more disciplined team concept. Michelle was unselfish, and she wanted to win as much as anyone, but she would say, "That's me, that's my style." She'd think, *What are you doing to me, Coach?* My job was to convince her that she was going to be a better basketball player and enjoy more overall success within the team structure.

Michelle struggled to play within the system and not according to her own agenda. She needed an incentive. Two days after that Louisiana Tech game I had called Michelle up and asked her to come by the house to have a talk. We sat in the living room, and I asked her if she thought she could be our starting point guard. I wanted to give her the opportunity. We had a terrific guard already in Tiffany Woosley, but I felt Tiffany might be more effective as a shooting guard. Michelle showed potential greatness at point guard, but she would need to be disciplined. I told her, "It's up to you to win the spot. You've got this summer to prove yourself. In the fall when you show up for practice, we'll see."

One of the things I always used to tell Michelle was to slow down. "Slow your butt down, you're going too fast," I'd say. "I can't even watch you."

After Michelle graduated and went on to the pros, she came back to Knoxville and asked me to help her with her shooting. She needed to figure out a way to play full-out transition basketball yet still be in control on her shot. So we went into the gym to work on it. I talked to her about four things: footwork, body control, focus, and follow through.

During her visit back to campus, my staff and I took her to play golf with us. On the golf course, in a very calm setting, Michelle would approach the golf ball, get properly set up, and swing. I noticed that she had a good, methodical pre-swing ritual. Her approach was the same every time. I said, "Now, why don't you think that way when you're shooting the basketball? Just slow down, get done what you need to get done."

In the summers, our players have an optional workout schedule. We send them off with a sheet recommending a regimen, but they don't have to do it. A lot of them don't even bother to fill it out. But Michelle got after it. She worked when no one was there to watch her.

The next fall Michelle won the point guard spot.

● ● ●

Self-discipline is entirely up to you. You can make or break your own habits. No excuses.

People who exercise self-discipline have an effect on everyone around them. They are tremendously influential in motivating their co-workers and colleagues. Conversely, undisciplined people can have a lousy influence.

Take it from me, someone who lost twenty-seven pounds in less than a year. I learned a lot about self-discipline and about how to influence others while trying to make the Olympic team in 1976. I was struggling with my knee injury. It required surgery—leaving a twelve-inch scar that still curls along the inside of my knee—and in those days we didn't know as much about rehab. I gained a lot of weight and couldn't move very well. My chances didn't look good. I was basically told by Bill Wall, executive director of the Amateur Basketball Association of the USA, and Billie Moore, the head coach, that I didn't have a chance.

They said it to challenge me, and it worked. I spent the better part of a year in the gym. I gave up red meat. I worked out for close to six hours a day. As the saying goes, I played through pain.

It's a phrase most often used for athletes, "playing through pain." But it's a descriptive one that can apply to all of us. We all have to do it, in one way or another. Maybe you have a small child, and you have to juggle parenthood and career on no sleep. Maybe you get migraines on the job. Maybe you travel a lot and struggle with jet lag. Maybe you're trying to recover from a divorce. Maybe you are coping with the death of a family member.

There are days you just don't feel like taking on the world. We all have them. That's when positive self-talk works. You can talk yourself into or out of anything. All it takes is discipline. Discipline is what pulls us through those days. It's what you hope takes over when you switch to automatic pilot.

Sometimes, that crafty little sucker gets in your head and tells you how much you don't want to go to work. He whispers in your ear that you'd much rather take the day off, or that you don't like your job, or your co-workers, or that you just can't face it. That's when you have to counter with positive self-talk.

Attitude is a choice.

You have to force yourself to concentrate on the positives. Every champion and high achiever I've ever known had the discipline to substitute good attitude for bad attitude.

Visualization is a good aid. See yourself at the *end* of the long day. If I can visualize it, that helps me push myself. I used to see myself being in great shape during Olympic try outs. Call up a mental picture of where you will be on vacation. Say to yourself, "I'm going to get through this, and after I'm done, I'm going to play golf."

I struggled with my attitude at times, in that year before the Olympics. When I wasn't working out or coaching, I sat on the bench for the '75 Pan Am team that went to Mexico City. I never got to play, unless it was a blowout. If we had a twenty-point lead, I might get into the game. I was still overweight, and my knee wasn't really 100 percent. I remember wearing a size 16 dress, two sizes larger than I am today. But I learned a lot about discipline sitting on that bench.

My attitude had to be good because even though I was on the bench, I was one of the oldest members of the team, and I was the head coach at the University of Tennessee. Everybody was watching me at the end of that bench. Nancy Lieberman-Cline was one of the youngest players on that team, and she sat down at the end of the bench with me. We were among the oldest and the youngest players there, and we both ached to play. We hated sitting down there.

The end of the bench is where complaining starts. Players can feel uninvolved and disaffected. It's an ego bruiser. That's why our coaches at Tennessee fan out all along the bench. On most teams the coaches sit at the head of the bench with the players lined up along the sideline. How many times have you seen the players at the end of the bench looking bored, or resentful, or distracted? The best players jog off and take their marquee seats near the head coach, and the role players sit at the end, out of the sight line of the coaches.

Not on our team.

I sit right smack in the middle of the bench. Our assistants are on either side of me. The reason I sit among our players is that I want to be able to get at 'em. I want to be able to see them and communicate with them. Second, I don't want players sitting at the end of the bench, complaining and inattentive. I hate the effect it has, and I hate the way it looks.

When I sat at the end of that bench in 1975, I had too many opportunities to have a pity party for myself and to create dissension on the team. But I knew I wanted to be a responsible leader and positive influence on the younger players.

One afternoon, we got a big lead over Cuba, and it was time for all the starters to come out. The game was out of reach, so the subs were supposed to go in and mop up. Nancy was humiliated.

She said, "I'm not going in."

I said, "Why?"

She said she was embarrassed, because it was obvious to everybody that we only got in if the game was out of reach. She felt insulted.

I said to myself, "What am I going to do? How am I going to handle this?"

Nancy said again, "I'm not going in."

I said, "Oh, yes, you are."

"No, I'm not," she said.

"Yes, you are," I said. "And I tell you one thing, you'd better not pass me the ball. Because if you do, you'll never get it back. I'm going to shoot it every time I get it."

Nancy practically chased me into the game. I had spoken to the performer in her. Like she always does to this day, once she was out there she gave her all. She really wasn't capable of doing anything else. But she needed someone else to set a disciplined example. When it was there, she followed it.

The most difficult part of self-discipline is convincing yourself that it's in your own best interest. Being disciplined doesn't always feel good. In fact, it can feel awful. It makes your knees hurt, and your ego suffer. It's easy to say to yourself, "I really should take a break, give myself a rest."

But I'll tell you what. I got a spot on the Olympic team. I became a starter and co-captain. And we won the silver medal in '76. It still ranks as one of the most satisfying achievements of my life.

Self-discipline is not the path to instant gratification. The reward is much farther down the road, and not always obvious. But in the end, it is a much deeper form of gratification. The real reward is self-respect and long-term success.

As a coach and a parent, one of the hardest things to do is to convince young people that self-discipline is in their best interest. Unfortunately a lot of them don't fully understand or appreciate Tennessee discipline until they leave. And that bothers me. But I felt the same way about the discipline in my own childhood. Today, however, I appreciate it.

The reason I find the patience and stamina to cope with Tyler, even when I am exhausted, is because I know that he won't always have me there to teach him. Self-discipline is one of the most important things I can leave him, more important than inheritance money or farmland. It's among the most crucial qualities I have to give him as his mother. It's also the hardest, least enjoyable part of our relationship.

The same is true of my relationships with our players. As more Tennessee players go to the pro leagues, I've been hearing from some of them that they struggle with the lack of structure. Our program was so structured that they always knew what was expected of them, and what the penalties were. As it turns out, all that discipline gave them a sense of security. One player, who graduated recently, told me that she felt adrift on her pro team. On the first day of conditioning workouts, she didn't know if she was supposed to be on the court, or on the track, or in the weight room. As she was driving to the arena, she caught herself thinking: *This would not be happening at Tennessee. I'd know where I'm supposed to be.*

But the problem is, she's not at Tennessee, and she won't be ever again. Life lacks structure. You have to provide it for yourself—and that means learning self-discipline.

Q & A *Holly Warlick*

Guard, 1978–80; Member, 1980 Olympic team (boycott); Assistant Coach, 1985–present

Q: *What was Pat like as a player?*
HOLLY WARLICK: We got a tape of her, once. Mickie and I did. Pat was always saying, "Back when I played, we crashed the boards, and we didn't throw hook passes, we threw the correct pass." One day we told the kids, "We've got one more tape for you to watch." And it was of her. Pat had no clue. We put it in, and there she was, throwing hook passes and the last one down the floor. The camera would follow the team down the court, and we were like, "Well, where's Pat?" All of sudden you could see her, coming into the bottom of the screen. Everybody else was waiting on her to get down the floor. And when she jumped, you could just about slip a credit card under her sneakers.

Q: *How hard did she work those early teams?*
HOLLY WARLICK: Well, she'd put thirty minutes up on the clock, and we would run one continuous fast break drill. I can remember walking out of the gym thinking, "What have I done? My God, this woman is crazy. I literally cannot do what she wants me to. I'm not going to make it."

Q: *She says, "Holly hated me at least once a day."*
HOLLY WARLICK: Yeah. You know, she'd get in my face, and I'd look at her like I was agreeing with her, but really inside I was thinking, You need to get out of my face because I'm about over you. I was going to show her. I'd go out and correct whatever I did wrong, and then I'd just kind of look at her. She knew it. That's how she would get to me. I would not even be in the play, and yet somehow, she could twist it around and bring me into the picture.

Q: *Why did she do that to you?*

HOLLY WARLICK: *She knew I could take it. And I think she wanted everybody else to see how I handled it. How I handled it, that's how the rest of the team would handle it. See, that's what motivated me, and she figured that out early. I mean, I was competitive. But man, she just about put me over the edge. It was like she punched every button in me. But she was like a mother to me, too. And now she's become a great friend. I wouldn't change a day of what I went through.*

VI

Make Hard Work Your Passion

Here's how I'm going to beat you.

I'm going to outwork you.

That's it. That's all there is to it.

You've just learned my most valuable secret. It's not that exciting, I know. You were hoping for some mystery, or witchcraft. The problem is, there is no great intangible quality to success. It's not a gift people are born with, or a touch, or a talent, or a knack. It's a simple matter of putting your back into it.

I don't pretend to be a reasonable person on this subject. Between 1994 and 1997 we had a point guard from Tigard, Oregon, named Laurie Milligan, and I never saw her when she wasn't covered with sweat from giving so much effort. She loved to work. That right there tells you why she was at Tennessee. But when we recruited her, I had to wonder why anybody would come from Tigard, Oregon, to Knoxville, Tennessee.

It wasn't easy to convince her. It came down to us and a beautiful school out west in the Pacific-10 Conference. Laurie decided she wanted to win championships.

She told the coach of the Pac-10 school, "Coach, I've made up my mind and I'm going to Tennessee."

The other coach couldn't believe it. She said to Laurie, straight out, "Pat Summitt is crazy."

Laurie said, "Why do you think she's crazy?"

The coach said, "She works *all* the time. She's a workaholic. If you go to Tennessee, you won't believe how hard you'll work. She'll make you practice at two o'clock in the morning."

Laurie just listened. When that coach was done talking, Laurie said, "Well, if that's what she thinks we need to do, I'm willing to do it. I'll just practice at two A.M."

Then Laurie called me up and told me the story. When she was finished, I said, "So, that didn't bother you?"

"No, m'am," Laurie said.

"You're still coming to Tennessee?" I asked.

"I'm coming," Laurie said.

"Well, good," I said.

We went on to other things. But then, just as we were about to hang up, Laurie paused.

"Can I ask you one thing?" she said.

I knew what was coming.

"Go ahead," I said.

"Have you ever practiced at two A.M.?" she asked.

"No," I said. "Of course not."

"What's the earliest you've ever practiced?" she asked.

"Four A.M.," I said.

I only did it once. I swear. It was several years ago, back in the days when I thought terrorizing a team was the same thing as coaching it. We had lost a game to Vanderbilt on the road, thanks to a lackadaisical effort on our part and an outstanding one on theirs. If there is one thing I cannot abide, it's lack of effort. We went right back to campus in our team bus. R.B. was with us, and as he got on the bus, he said, "Where are we going to eat dinner?"

I said, "Are you kidding me? We're not eating. We'd choke on it."

We drove straight through dinnertime. We pulled into campus at about 1 A.M. I made the team go right to my office to watch film. We graded the film that very night. Every time someone on our team didn't run the floor, we marked down another sprint. When we were done, we went into the gym, and our players did all the sprinting they hadn't done against Vanderbilt. By the time we got done it was 4 A.M. Naturally, I told them to sleep the rest of the day—after they went to class. It turns out someone saw the lights on in the gym that night, and it made the papers, which only contributed to my reputation as the Great Dictator.

Like I said, I don't pretend to be reasonable. I'm pretty intense about my work. If I'm awake at 6 A.M., I think the rest of the world is, too. I'm not suggesting you copy my personal style.

But I can tell you this: The harder you work, the harder it is to surrender. Tennessee wins because, in the end, our players feel they have worked too hard not to.

A lot of people said to me when I set out to write this book, "Aren't you afraid of giving away your all secrets?" The answer is just plain no. I could throw open the door of our locker room and show you all the inner workings of our program, and you still wouldn't beat us, if you weren't willing to outwork us.

If we have won more games and more championships at Tennessee than most people in the profession—and we have, with twenty-two straight seasons of twenty wins or more—it's because there is a direct correlation between our record and our work ethic. I often hear that we make winning look easy, or that we're lucky. But if you could see how hard our players work, and how hard our staff works—if you had any idea—you might ask me, "Is it really worth it?"

The work never ends. We never finish. We are constantly trying to be more thorough, more fit, and more knowledgeable. Our staff knows they're expected to outwork everybody in college basketball, and our players take pride in knowing they can outlast their opponents.

I'm a firm believer that unless you are willing to work daily, you will underachieve. Some people think they can just turn it on when the lights come on and the popcorn starts to pop. Well, very few players in my career were actually able to do that. The real achievers were those who formed work habits.

It's important to surround yourself with people who have the same work ethic you have. The fact that you bought this book in the first place suggests that you have an extremely strong work ethic; you are so interested in achievement that you are willing to work at it even in your leisure time, by reading this when you could be reading a paperback novel. It tells me you will work long past the point of reasonable behavior.

That's why you should seek out others with the same commitment. Otherwise you will spend a lot of your days frustrated.

When we recruit players to Tennessee, we make no secret of what a commitment it is to play for us. There's no point in disguising what we do in Knoxville, or how we do it. Mine is not the most elegant, sweet-talking recruiting pitch you'll ever hear. We are not the kinds of recruiters who try to sell you on the good times you can have on our campus. We don't make our program sound like a resort or country club. We talk about the sweat.

Now, I'm not saying I can't be as convincing as the next recruiter. I have gone to some ridiculous lengths to persuade a talented young woman to come to Tennessee. In 1984 I recruited a 6-foot-4 young woman named Sheila Frost from Pulaski, Tennessee. I ate an entire half of a pumpkin pie, just because Sheila's mother had made it for me.

"I made something special for you," she said.

I hate pumpkin pie with every fiber of my being.

"You like pumpkin pie, don't you?" she said.

"Oh, I love it," I said.

"You want some now, or later?" she asked.

I choked it down. A huge wedge of it.

We talk about the good times and the positives at Tennessee, too. We talk about all the laughs we have—and we have a few. But we also talk about the day to dayness of it, the part where you roll up your sleeves and go to work. I don't want to mislead or misinform somebody who's interested in being part of our program. And I don't want her to mislead me, either, when it comes to how hard she's willing to work.

The fact is, I've had some players who rival me for workaholic status. Take Kellie Jolly, our current point guard. All you have to do is say something once to Kellie, and she does it. Last year she tore her anterior cruciate ligament before our first practice. It should have been a season-ending injury. A normal recuperation takes about four months. But Kellie worked at her rehab like a maniac. I had to tell her to slow down. She was back with the team after just two months, in time for the last few games of the regular season.

Well, then Kellie tore the ligaments in her ankle in the first-round game of the NCAA tournament. The trainers told her she would most likely be out for at least a week or two. But Kellie refused to accept the prognosis. She *slept* in the training room. For forty-eight hours. Our staff would come in, and she'd be napping on the couch or having her ankle worked on.

She was back in two days. It was actually embarrassing, because I had announced to the entire country that we had lost one of our point guards to an injury. Then, at 5:30 P.M. on the night of our second-round game against Oregon, our trainer, Jenny Moshak, told me Kellie was good to go. Kellie went on to figure prominently in our title run.

After the season ended, Kellie would require surgery on that ankle. She spent all summer rehabbing. She couldn't really work on her total game too much. So, instead, she just shot the ball. Endlessly, every day, she worked on her perimeter shooting. When she arrived back on campus in the fall of '97 she had a whole new facet to her game: She was a sharpshooter from three-point range. On the night of Midnight Madness, the annual opening of college basketball practice across the country, Kellie represented us in a co-ed shooting contest with the Tennessee men's basketball team. She drained seven of ten from three-point range on national television.

People like Kellie can influence a whole team or organization. What happens is, people start believing in her. If Kellie says something is going to take two weeks instead of four, that's what happens.

Similarly, one lazy team member can sap the entire team of their motivation and faith. No matter how talented a person is, if her work habits don't match those of your organization, she will be a disadvantage. Sometimes the more talented she is, the more challenging she can be to work with. All too frequently people think talent is a substitute for application.

Every fall we bring in new players, and every four years the cast of characters changes. Any first-class organization will struggle to maintain its work ethic as personnel changes. So we have to make sure the players we bring in basically share our work ethic and values. The people in your organization have to be willing to commit to an agreed-on minimum standard of work. Otherwise we would fight amongst ourselves all the time. There are few things more destructive to the morale of an organization than deadweight. Nobody likes a goldbricker with an attitude. For instance, you probably know someone in your office who comes in late, hangs her coat on her chair, and then disappears. She goes off to get coffee or gossip, while everyone around her has started the day. If you ask her why she's late, she'll say something like, "I'm not a morning person."

You can affect the mood of everyone else with your habits and attitude. It's not a matter of being a "morning person" or not. "Morning people" don't exist. It's not a legitimate state of being or a physical complaint. It's just an excuse for dogging.

How many times have you heard someone say, "Don't talk to me 'til ten A.M.?" What gives him the right to decide what time he will start the workday, when his colleagues have to take up the slack?

We don't have lazy people in our organization. They either leave, or I run them off.

People wonder how I get our players to work so hard. They hear tall tales about me and marvel that I don't have a player revolt. But the truth is, our players *want* to put out that effort. It's not a forced march. They do it because they aspire, and they understand the value of work.

I always say you've got to come watch us practice if you want to understand us. You have to see our intensity level to believe it. We challenge people to be the best they can be—every day. In practice, I expect the team to perform at a certain level, and it bothers me when they don't give effort, because we're only talking two and a half hours a day. When they step off the floor, I don't jam basketball down their throats. I leave them alone, to live their college lives. But when they're there, I expect concentration and effort. So if you are selfish or you are lazy, you won't make it with me.

Not everybody is meant to work in a demanding organization. You're not going to convince 100 percent of the people in your office to commit to working at that level. And that's fine. Not everyone wants to achieve.

But those players don't need to come here to Tennessee. Because that's what we're all about. Players have left our program for different reasons. Over the years a number have departed prior to graduation. Some transferred because they didn't like it. Some left because they wanted more playing time. Two or three got married. And a handful were asked to leave by me for disciplinary reasons. I do have a demanding style—I'm not ashamed of that.

But I firmly believe that, in general, kids today want to achieve. They just don't know how. They want someone to help them when they need a push or a pull. They want someone to believe in them, to teach them, and to lead them. All they need is to be shown how to work in an organized fashion.

A lot of kids think Tennessee is tougher than maybe it is. They don't want the competition, or they don't see themselves playing for us because they're intimidated. But truthfully all we expect is this: that they maintain a minimum 2.5 grade point average, that they be committed to refining their basketball skills, that they be good citizens, and that they be well-conditioned athletes. We determine conditioning with the help of a first-rate staff: our trainer, Jenny Moshak, and our strength coach, Jeff Dahoda. We don't press the boundaries to the point of unhealthiness. We have certain standards based on muscle mass. We expect our guards to be in a certain range, our forwards in a certain range, and our post players in another range. So, if you are a worker, you'll probably make it with us.

I'll give you an example of our kind of work ethic. Our players are allowed to pull themselves out of a game to take breathers. If they're winded, they come to the sideline. It's a trust that we have developed from working together and sharing the same standards. I'm not one of those coaches who says, "I'll tell you when you're tired." If they're tired, they come out. I call time, or I get a sub in. They so much as grab their jersey, and I know they need a breather.

Why? Because when they're in there, they go all out. I've said to our players time and again, "If you're tired, I want you to pull yourself out, because I'd rather see you play five minutes all out than ten minutes where you are basically pacing yourself." So all Chamique Holdsclaw has to do if she needs a break is hold up her fist.

I might try to squeeze a little more out of you in the big game, though. I can remember Bridgette Gordon, a couple of times, getting really tired. She'd wave. I'd wave back at her, like, "Hey, Bridge. Hang in there!"

At the start of the year, I give our players a sheet of paper and ask them to list their values. The sheet is blank, with the numbers one through ten. I ask them to list their values in order. I tell them they don't have to list all ten. I just want to know a few of the things that are important to them.

We sit down together, and I give them my list, and they give me theirs. We swap lists. Almost invariably, they put hard work somewhere on their list.

There is an unspoken understanding that develops between like-minded people who share a goal. The understanding is, "Only you know and I know how hard we are willing to work on each other's behalf."

Our players understand that all I'm trying to do is help them. They want to go to a Final Four. They want to win a national championship. Well, I'm going to do everything I can to see to it. They know that I'll work as hard at it as they do, and they know that I *love* my work. I'd better. I've been coaching longer than they've been living.

In the end, the hard work is what makes our team have so much faith in itself. I tell our players, "All you've got to do is work. I'm here for you. I don't *have* to coach. I'm here because I want to be. Let me help you."

●   ●   ●

A lot of people say, "I want to be the very best," or, "I want to win a national championship." Everybody says it. Who doesn't?

It's not enough to say it, or even to mean it.

If you want to succeed, you need a plan.

At Tennessee, our ambition every year is to win a national championship. That's obvious. Sure, we *want* to win a championship. But we need a more specific plan than that. We have to recruit the right players. We have to know how to use those players once they get here. We have to devise our strategy. And we have to make individual game plans for every opponent. We have to know what we're doing on a daily basis.

Plan your work, and work your plan.

You have to work toward a goal in an organized fashion. You don't just show up in March and win a championship. You work every day in a systematic fashion. You have a long-range plan. But you also have a short-range plan. Most important, you have to plan your daily activity and know what your goal is.

Personally, I use the Franklin planner system. I have a yearly, a monthly, and a weekly calendar. But I work better day-to-day.

Think big, focus small. That's the way I like to put it. You have to focus small, because attention to everyday, ordinary detail is what will separate you from everyone else.

Check your weekly plan every Sunday night. Think about what you need to do over the course of the next seven days. Every night, look at a plan for the following day.

At Tennessee, our overall plan is the Definite Dozen. It's our system and philosophy. But if our staff and our players tried to fulfill all twelve, every single day, we'd be exhausted and pulled in different directions. You have to take them one at a time.

Taking things one at a time is my own personal struggle. Sometimes the Definite Dozen can get me going in twelve different directions at once. And that's not good. "Make your work your passion" doesn't mean running around like a chicken with its head cut off. Narrowing your priorities is important.

My problem is a tendency to think I can do everything. I can't say no. If I have a choice between doing nothing and doing something, I'm going to do something. And I'm going to make the people around me do something, too. Like flying. I hate sitting on planes doing nothing. So a lot of the time we have study hall.

But I go too far. I have a thousand things to do on any given day: meetings with contractors on remodeling the house, a corporate speech, a United Way campaign appearance. And that's not counting my jobs as mother, wife, daughter, and coach. Sometimes I don't know where to start. I get paralyzed. Or, I try to do them all at once. I sit in my office, and instead of doing one thing at a time, I juggle two, three, four things at once. I sign letters while I'm talking on the phone, with Tyler hanging on my arm, while I'm trying to put on makeup.

A tried-and-true technique for narrowing your focus is to make a list. Most people know that already. But try this. Periodically, condense the list. If your list is three pages, condense it to one page. That will help you prioritize. Say to yourself, "What am I doing *today?*" And if that doesn't work, say to yourself, "What do I need to do this very moment?" Force yourself to be specific.

I'll give you an example of a typical day and night for me. One day not long ago, I got up at 6 A.M. and checked my planner. I had breakfast with Tyler and saw him off to school. I rushed off to speak at a Rotary Club breakfast. I went to my office and did a pile of correspondence and returned phone calls. I met with my staff. We ran a three-hour practice. Then I watched film with some of the team. After that I did more correspondence and returned more calls.

Driving home from work, I was exhausted. In the car, I thought about all the things I had to do once I got home. I had to cook dinner for R.B. and Tyler. (I cook just about every night, unless we have to go out. Also, we entertain a lot.) Then I had to move all the furniture, clothes, and toys back into Tyler's room, which I hadn't done since the remodeling job was completed. After that, I had to call a recruit and try to convince her to come to Tennessee. Then I had to prepare for a speaking engagement and a photo shoot the following day.

I almost pulled off the road and cried. I said to myself, "Just take a deep breath and relax and think about what you're going to do when you get to the house. When you get home, just concentrate on getting dinner on the

table. After that just do what you can." So I went home and concent.
on one small thing at a time.

Narrowing my vision becomes a matter of survival. It's almost an es-
cape. And sometimes that's not so good. But it can be funny, too. I get so
intense, I don't notice anything else going on around me. Mickie and
Holly joke that they have to pack fruit and a snack every day, because I get
going so fast I forget to let them eat.

It's a running joke with my family and staff that I can't even be trusted
to tell you what the weather is like outside. I'll come into the office and
someone will ask me if it's still raining, and I haven't even noticed.

I have to think about whether I turned my car wipers on.

I jog or power walk the same route on campus every day, a three-mile
loop around campus. One afternoon Mickie and I were jogging when I
noticed something different.

"Look, that building burned down," I said to Mickie. "When did *that*
happen?"

"Three months ago," she said, rolling her eyes.

One time I drove home, parked, and walked in the front door, without
ever noticing that a new car was sitting in the driveway.

Another afternoon I strolled into our locker room for a tape session with
my point guard, Michelle Marciniak. Michelle was huddled on the couch
under a blanket. She was wrapped up in a sweater and leg warmers, and
she was wearing gloves.

She stared at me oddly.

"Pat, aren't you freezing?" she asked.

"What do you mean?" I said, looking down at my outfit. I had on a
short-sleeved golf shirt and a pair of light slacks.

"Pat," she said. "There's an ice storm outside."

"You're kidding," I said.

But focus is what makes a job seem doable. I would be overwhelmed if
I thought, at the start of every year, *We have to win a championship*. I
would be overwhelmed every day if I thought, *I have to be a great mother,
wife, coach, and businesswoman*.

In going for a national championship, what we think about is daily
improvement. We say to ourselves, "Let's get better today." It's like writing

thought I had to write 280 pages at one sitting, I'd never
It had to be written one small page at a time.

...hes use that cliché, "It's a forty-minute game." The
...minute game focuses our team on the task at hand, and
... the clock. You're fully aware that it's a forty-minute game. But you have to play well for each of those minutes.

You spend most of the game preparing to win in the final seconds. And that is what separates winners from losers. Everybody wants to win. But very few people are willing to *prepare* to win.

When you are in those final seconds, what allows you to perform well and with confidence is the knowledge that you have worked and prepared up to that point. That's why we practice so hard. We simulate and prepare and train so that the task of winning does not seem daunting. It's what we are *supposed* to do, because we have worked hard all year.

We expect to win because we practice it.

I believe you get what you expect.

We practice game situations daily, so that our team can make decisions and judgments. We rehearse, we put a time up on the clock and a score on the scoreboard, and we let our players make decisions. Then we say, "How do you think you did? Would you do it differently the next time?" And then we do it again and again, until our players are practically hypno-tized into believing they deserve to win.

They are focused on *winning,* and they are focused on *executing.* They focus on completing each play. In a game situation, you focus on what you have to do in each moment. You'd panic if you thought, *Oh my God, I've got to win right now.* You can't win the whole game with one shot. But it's amazing how many people force up a lousy shot in a critical moment. You have forty minutes to win, but you have to do it one possession at a time.

You can apply the forty-minute concept to any kind of work. Let's take sales. If you are making a presentation, you should have done most of your work beforehand. Good preparation allows you to go into the presen-tation relaxed and calmly talk confidently about what you have to offer. The presentation is such that it's informative, professional, personable, and delivered in a way that will gain the trust of the people you are talking to.

You aren't staring at your watch, sweating the time. And you aren't wondering what the competition is doing.

Hard work is about controlling those things that you are capable of controlling. In any situation, there are certain things that are in your control and some that are out of your control. Pretend you are playing for me. Let's say you are sitting on the bench, and you feel you should be getting more playing time.

What is in your control is how hard you work every day in practice to demonstrate to me that you are ready. What's out of your control is *me*. When I'm coaching the game, I'm going to make executive decisions, and everyone has to live with them. But what you can do in the meantime is show me that you are prepared to play, and play hard.

That's why I demand that our players work just as hard without the ball as they do with it. How many times have you watched a game and seen players standing around? In our system there are no peripheral players. Nobody should be easy to guard. It aggravates me. I tell some of our players, "They'll be fighting in the opposing locker room over who gets to guard you. They know they get to rest." That's why we try to improve the movement of every Tennessee player without the ball. You don't want to be the one the opposition wants to guard. You want to be the one on the scouting report that worries them.

Mickie and Holly tease me that I can't stand it when things are going smoothly. They say I look for ways to create work. If things go too well, I like to stir up trouble. And maybe that's true. I'm always looking for another way to prepare to win, I'm always wondering if there's something I've left undone.

One day, I stopped practice and started hollering out of the blue, when everyone was doing a good job. Our post people were running up and down the court and showing effort. Our point guards were being vocal. On the defensive end, everyone was in a stance. All of the things we require in practice, they were doing. But I felt something was missing.

I couldn't stand it anymore. I said, "Hold up." Everybody stopped and gazed at me, including Mickie and Holly. I could tell by the looks on their faces that they were thinking, "What is this crazy woman going on about now?"

I surveyed the group. My eyes fell on our All-American forward, Lisa Harrison.

"Lisa Harrison," I said. "What have you done to *lead* this team today." I made up a reason to be dissatisfied.

Mickie and Holly got on me again the other day, because a friend of ours—Trish Roberts, who played in the Olympics with me in '76 and was our first All American—remarked that I have calmed down a lot in the last few years. She is now a highly regarded coach in her own right. She came by to visit us and watch practice. Afterward she was sitting around in our offices, and she said, "Boy, has Pat mellowed."

Holly and Mickie both cringed. "Don't say that in front of her," Holly said. "She'll come in here and tear the door off."

I'm always looking for something more to do, because it's that last small thing that can make the difference. What the forty-minute concept does is make our players think about the worth of each specific possession and learn to play with a one-possession mentality. They say to themselves, "If we hadn't thrown that one away . . ." You begin to understand the value of each seemingly insignificant moment of extra effort. A loose ball. A free throw.

When you understand that, hard work gets a lot easier.

● ● ●

Work is work. There's no way around it. Like Tom Sawyer said, "Work is something a body is obliged to do. Play is something a body is *not* obliged to do."

How can you make work fun? You can't, at least not entirely. *Fun* is the wrong word for something that makes your back hurt, your hands stiff, and your head ache. There is no nice word for work. There is no pretty way to say it and no pleasant substitute for it. It is drudgery, grind, toil.

But you *can* make your work more satisfying. The first step is to commit to it. Decide to do it well.

I love my job more than anybody I know and I still don't *like* it about a third of the time. Seriously. About one day out of three, I'd just as soon not do it. There are a lot of things I have to really force myself to do. So I use a mental trick on myself. The tasks that I most dislike are the ones I tackle first thing.

Do the things that aren't fun first. And do them well.

Nobody ever got ahead by doing something they didn't like to do poorly, or late. You probably know someone in your office who only works at the things he or she likes. If he doesn't like to do something, he just plain doesn't do it. It goes undone. Or it's badly done. I know people like that, and they shouldn't expect a promotion in our office.

If there's one thing I can't abide it's lack of effort. I don't have much sympathy for people who act like they can't stand their jobs. I spent too many years watching my parents work themselves to the bone, uncomplaining, at things they didn't like to do. If you've never chopped tobacco, let me try to explain it. By the end of the day, it feels like someone has permanently planted a shoe in the small of your back. My mother quit school to go to work in the ninth grade. She worked in a boot factory to make money. She still works at the family-owned dry cleaners most days, out of force of habit. My father still works the family acreage.

My parents are in their seventies, and I can't get them on the phone.

So you won't hear me complaining that I hate paperwork. Now, the truth is, I hate paperwork. Absolutely hate it. My passion is teaching. I love to work with players in practice, and I love to watch film. But I can't stand correspondence and memos and budgets, and the other small, repetitive work that goes into administrating a program.

But it's the first thing I do. There are days when Katie Wynn, my secretary, will come into my office with sixty pieces of mail that need to be dealt with. But we sit down to that pile every morning. And frequently, it's the last chore I do before I leave.

Hard work is hard work. But the results of hard work *are* fun. They're rewarding. People ask our kids all the time, "Why go to Tennessee? It's so hard." The answer is, because the process leads to greater rewards.

Frankly, hard work is a lot like having a baby. It's like being in labor. There's nothing fun about it while it's happening. Nothing at all. But you forget about the pain when you see that child.

You forget about the long practices when you see the championship.

But when I say that work isn't fun, I don't mean you should sentence yourself to a job you despise. I'm not suggesting you place yourself under house arrest.

I'm just saying, figure out what you want to do, and commit to it. Accept that no job is the answer to your entire life; nothing that happens in an office can or should make you thoroughly contented.

Maybe you don't like your job. Here's what you do. Find out if there is anything you could learn to like about it. Accent the positive. Change your attitude about what you don't like. If you don't like the people you're working with, maybe you need to communicate with them better.

See yourself as self-employed. We all essentially work for ourselves, no matter who signs the paycheck. Too often people resent their bosses. They say things like, "Why should I work hard for him?" or "Why should I go out of my way for this company, when they aren't paying me enough?" That kind of thinking is not only negative and immature, it's also false. You work on your own behalf. It's entirely up to you how much time and effort you put in for yourself.

Maybe you will find out that you really *can't* work at your job. But rather than work at something for ten years unhappily, confront it. Get to the root of the problem, and decide whether it's time for a change.

If you don't like what you are doing, then I urge you to find something else. If you can't, then at least do the job before you respectably. There is not much you can control in this life. Freak accidents, good or bad luck, these things are out of our hands. But how hard you work *is* within your control. Rather than complain about bad breaks, or being trapped, make a few breaks of your own.

The best work should have an alive quality. It should be performed with some feeling—even with passion. You may not think your intention is visible, but it is. The intent is obvious in your every action—more so than you may know.

You and I can both tell a heartless, mechanical job from one that was performed with sincerity. So it's up to you. When a job has been done with devotion, the result is palpable. It will elevate off the desk, or the page, or the basketball floor.

I know this about work, too: People always have a little bit more of it in them than they think they do. Again, I learned that coming from my background. We'd work, work, work. At the end of the day, my dad would look up at the sky and say, "We can get another hour in."

I try to squeeze as much as I can into a three-hour practice, or into a twenty-four-hour day. It's like I try to put ten pounds of flour in a five-pound sack. And sometimes, I get into trouble because of it.

But I'm going to put as much in that bag as will go.

Q & A   *Bridgette Gordon*

Forward, 1988 Olympian; All American 1988, 1989; Member, national championship teams, 1987, 1989; Olympic Gold medalist, 1988; Sacramento Monarchs, WNBA

Q: Let's talk about Pat's driving.
BRIDGETTE GORDON: *Oh, my God. You don't want to drive with her. She used to have this 300ZX. You'd buckle up, and she'd say, "Hang on." It was like taking off in a jet. Believe me, you don't ever want to drive with her.*

Q: Does Pat ever relax?
BRIDGETTE GORDON: *She's pretty intense, but then, all of a sudden, she'll be laughing and loose. It was hard to understand at first. After four years you realized that she really cared about you. I mean, she took me in. I was like her child. But my freshman year, I couldn't believe it. I had a problem with rolling my eyes and talking under my breath. She would get on me. At three o'clock in practice she would be screaming at me. But at 3:15 when practice was over, she would want to talk, all nice. "Let's talk," she'd say. "How's school?" I would look at her, like, "Lady, you think I want to talk to you?"*

VII

Don't Just Work Hard, Work Smart

The first time Bridgette Gordon ever saw snow was on a cold white-out of a night in 1985 in South Bend, Indiana. I made sure it was an experience to remember. Bridgette had never witnessed a flurry before, much less such a downfall. She was just a shy freshman from the humid flats of DeLand, Florida, a broody young player who could barely raise her head to meet my eye. But when Bridgette saw those sidewalks blanketed in white and the drifts piling up in the streets, she lifted her chin and stared.

We had just beaten Notre Dame, and we were heading back to Chicago that evening in a caravan of rental cars to catch a flight for home. We pulled over at a strip mall to get ourselves some dinner. We won big so I was in a good mood.

We sat in the restaurant, chatting and giggling, as the snow continued to fall, until pretty soon there must have been at least a foot of it on the ground. Bridgette marveled at the weather. My mood rose, beyond good, and turned into something lighter.

"You've never seen snow before?" I asked Bridgette.

Bridgette shook her head.

I grabbed the car keys.

"Well, come on," I said.

I marched Bridgette, Melissa McCray, and a couple of other players out the door and into the deserted parking lot. Bridgette, at my side, traipsed through the snow, uncertain of what I was up to. Like most freshmen, she was about half afraid of me. I unlocked the car and asked Bridgette and the others to get in.

I started the car and pulled into the middle of the empty lot. We idled there for a moment.

Now, I tend to take life on two wheels. But Bridgette didn't know that about me yet. I turned to look at her in the seat next to me.

"If you've never seen snow, then you've never done a doughnut, have you?" I asked her.

Bridgette said, "No, m'am."

"Hang on," I said.

I gunned the engine and spun the wheel. Then I floored it.

We did a 360.

Bridgette and the others shrieked, delighted.

I grinned, and spun the wheel, and jammed the gas pedal to the floor again. The car fishtailed in another circle in the deserted lot. Next to me, I could hear Bridgette going, "Whooo."

I did it again, and then again, and then again. I did several 360s in that empty lot before I got tired of watching Bridgette Gordon's eyes widen.

"Okay, I think I've seen enough snow now," Bridgette said.

Nobody believes I'm capable of that sort of behavior. Well, I am. But it took me a few years to get to the point where I would show it. It used to be, I was so consumed with work that it was difficult for me to develop relationships with our players—much less have fun with them. You could practically see my gears grinding and the smoke pouring out from under my hood.

But finally, I learned that grinding my gears and spinning my wheels was not the best way to get ahead. Doing 360s is fine for playing around in a snow-covered parking lot, but not for much else. Bridgette was part of the team that helped teach me that. By the time she left Tennessee in 1989, we had won two national championships. In those brief few years, something in me grew.

I learned that hard work wasn't much use without intelligence and understanding.

How bad was I? There was a time when I worked our players so hard that they literally wouldn't get into a car with me. After a road trip we would pile into two vans for the trip back home. It was pretty clear how they felt about me when I would get into one van, and they would all get into the other one. Whatever vehicle I climbed into, they made sure they weren't in it.

I rode alone with the equipment.

Well, that hurt my feelings pretty badly. But I wasn't going to let them see it. I think I even tried to tell myself it was a compliment. Not anymore.

While I preach hard work, I also preach smart work. What do I mean by smart work? I mean the combination of efficiency and effectiveness that will help you succeed without wasted motion, and *with* perspective. Smart work is a matter of sizing up the job that has to be done and deciding on the best way of doing it.

You can't push a piece of string. But you can pull it.

If you do a job in a nonsensical, disorganized way, then no matter how much hard work you apply, you won't get anywhere. You'll just go in circles, like me in that rental car. And have a whole lot less fun doing it.

Abby Conklin said something about me after the 1997 Final Four that I liked, even though it wasn't the most flattering remark I'd ever heard. "Pat turns into a monster in March," Abby said. "But if there is a championship within us, she'll get it out."

It is crucial in the game of basketball, or any other endeavor for that matter, to know how to peak. Peaking is a matter of timely work. It's a matter of knowing when to sweat and when to rest. We spent a lot of years overworking in the stretch and lost a few championship games as a result. It used to be that I would ask our team to do twenty-five things instead of a few things well. But I learned my lesson once and for all at the 1986 Final Four in Lexington, Kentucky.

I learned that less can be more.

On the day before our national semifinal game against Southern California, we practiced in Rupp Arena in front of a huge crowd. This was the first time, in an effort to stir up excitement, that the NCAA opened practice to fans and the press. There was a real charge in the air, and we got caught up in the hyper atmosphere. Because of all the people in the stands, I felt like we had to put on a show.

I ran our team ragged. I wasn't fully conscious of just how hard I was making our players work, until we walked off the court. But it hit me as soon as we left the arena. Our point guard, Dawn Marsh, said, as she limped on to the team bus, "Boy, that was a hard practice." All of a sudden I didn't feel good about it. I knew we had done too much.

It was entirely my fault that we came out flat as a board against Southern Cal. We lost, 83–59. I had been coaching for ten years by then, and I should have known better. It hasn't happened again. And it won't.

It was a whole different story the very next year. When we got back to the Final Four in 1987, something crossed over in me for good. I realized the value of tapering. Our workouts that week in Austin, Texas, were some of the lightest of the whole season. The hard work was all done. We had done the hard work in September and October, when I made them get up at 6 A.M. to run the track. We had installed our offenses and defenses in building block fashion in November, December, and January. Tournament time in March was not the time to work on conditioning, or to install an entirely new system.

Everyone remarked on how at ease I was throughout that week in Austin. I remember feeling a sense of certainty. I told the press, "Tennessee is going to win a national championship. I just hope I'm there to see it." I was still working like a dog—our entire staff stayed up all night long watching film before the title game against Louisiana Tech. But this time, I didn't take it out on the players. While we watched film, they went shopping or to the movies.

On the day of the game, we didn't practice at all.

We visualized.

The entire squad lay in a circle on the floor and closed their eyes. Mickie and I talked them through a series of situations and asked them to see in their minds what they wanted to do.

Final score, Tennessee 67, Louisiana Tech 44. Bridgette cried and cried afterward.

Our success that day was in part a result of the fact that I was a more mature, more self-confident coach. Previously, I had felt like I was bluffing. I worked everybody so hard because I thought it would make up for my youth and deficiencies.

I was less frantic in '87. I still worked hard, but I didn't work desperately. I was secure in my abilities, and I was secure in our players. I had developed relationships with them, so I sensed what they needed, I knew when to back off, and I understood when they needed a rest.

Making that breakthrough was a bonding experience. I became especially close to Bridgette. She practically became part of my family. Bridgette's mother, Marjorie, had asked me to watch out for her when I recruited her. Bridgette was from a family of eight children and the only one to go off to college, and Marjorie was nervous about letting her go. She asked me straight out, "Please take care of Bridgette. She's so young, and she's never been anywhere." So I did my best to take care of her. Some people even teased her and called her "Pat's little girl."

Once we understood how to win, it seemed like we couldn't get enough of it. Bridgette, as much as any player we've ever had at Tennessee, knew how to repeat success. In 1989, she led Tennessee to its second title in three years by beating Auburn in Tacoma, Washington. It was that same game in which Bridgette almost lost her teeth.

Afterward, she made me dance on a tabletop. Bridgette and I had a friendly wager on the game. She wanted to bet that if we won, she got to go shopping in my closet. But that was against NCAA rules. Instead, one afternoon the kids were all over at my house, dancing. They tried to get me to dance, and I said, "I don't dance." So of course, Bridgette made me agree that I'd dance if we won.

As soon as the game was over, Bridgette did a courtside interview with CBS. "What you really need to tune into is Pat dancing on a tabletop," she said to a national television audience.

I was forced to keep my word. At our victory party I caught a rhythm on top of a glass table, with Daedra Charles on one side of me and Carla McGhee on the other. I looked like a big country girl, while the rest of the team wailed and fell about with laughter.

Our players will ride with me now.

● ● ●

Success in my business is about putting the right people in the right place at the right time.

When you have the right tools on hand to do something properly, it makes a job infinitely easier. You don't try to change a car tire without a jack. Take it from me, someone who drove a tractor long before she ever drove a car.

Now, as a coach, my tools are people. You can't expect to have a successful working organization if you have the wrong people in the wrong jobs, no matter how many hours they may work. You don't put a shy person in sales, or a math wonk in service and parts. What you try to do is put people in positions that suit their natural abilities and inclinations.

Sounds simple, right?

But it's not nearly as easy as it sounds. Human beings are not socket wrenches. They are extremely complicated, enormously inconsistent, and they change emotional shape on you all the time. What you see is rarely what you get. I'm here to tell you that young women are especially complex. They can be alternately innocent and calculating, stubborn and malleable, selfish and affectionate. It isn't always apparent what their strengths and weaknesses are. They are riddled with insecurities and frailties, some of them pretty carefully hidden.

I've spent my life trying to understand our players. They still fool me all the time.

I'll give you my favorite example. It's a very common mistake to suppose that the most talented person in an organization is also the natural leader. Wrong. I am here to tell you that's not so.

In Eugene, Oregon, in 1981, Tennessee played a very close Final Four game against Old Dominion. It came down to the last eleven seconds. We were up by a couple of points, with the ball. I called a time-out.

I wanted to set up an out-of-bounds play to get the ball to Pat Hatmaker, our point guard and one of our best athletes. Pat was a local product from Knoxville, a sleek, muscled guard with fast hands. She was our quickest player, she was one of our best free throw shooters, and she was certainly one of our best ball handlers. The idea was to in-bounds the ball to Pat, so we could go down the stretch confidently. If Pat had the ball, I would feel comfortable with the offensive execution.

I wanted the ball in the right person's hand.

But when our team ran out on to the floor after the time-out, I saw them stop and gather for a second huddle.

Now that's not a good sign. When you have a meeting, and then your colleagues hold a second one without you, something's wrong.

They broke that second huddle, and took their positions. Mary Ostrowski, an All American, was to run the in-bounds play, which called for Pat Hatmaker to come back toward the ball. Mary slapped the ball to signal the start of the play. Well, Pat took off. Only she ran *away* from the ball and *never looked back.*

Susan Clower came up, received the basketball, and got fouled. Now, Susan was a great player, but she was not what I would have called our pressure player. She was far from our best free throw shooter.

So now Susan was in a pressure situation that she was not ready for, thanks to Hatmaker. Instead our most reliable player at the free throw line, Susan had to go to the line. Inside, I was livid. But outside, talk about communication. My body language, my eyes, everything had to be very positive and very poised. Because, immediately, Susan looked over at me.

How do you look back at a player in that situation? Here's how: I gave her the thumbs up sign and told her she was ready.

She hit the first shot—and looked right back over at me.

I gave her the high sign again, and she made the next one. It was key. Old Dominion took the ball out of bounds and threw it up and scored a long-range shot, but we won the game, 68–65.

For Susan, that was a great moment. For our team, it was a great moment. But as for me, I was still livid. I could not think about the great victory, because I was so concerned about what Hatmaker had done and the implications for us in the championship game.

I shook hands with Old Dominion's coach, Marianne Stanley, and headed down to the locker room. While I was en route, Mary Ostrowski caught up with me and said, "Coach, I've got to tell you something."

I stopped and looked at Mary.

She said, "After our huddle, we had another huddle."

"Yeah," I said grimly. "I saw it."

Mary said, "Hatmaker told us she did not want the ball."

I couldn't believe it. Our go-to player didn't want the ball.

When I came into the locker room for our post-game meeting, Pat Hatmaker, to her everlasting credit, sat in the front row. She looked right at me, prepared to accept whatever I had to say to her. I just went off on her. "Pat Hatmaker, I can't believe you wouldn't want the ball," I said. "I can't believe we put you in this situation, and you let the whole team down."

But then I realized that we had to play for a championship. It occurred to me that we would need Pat Hatmaker's help in the title game. I thought to myself, *Don't get so caught up in how upset you are with Pat and what happened today that you fail to prepare for tomorrow.* So, immediately, I cut myself off. I started to pump her back up. "We'll be okay; you're going to learn from this; now, let's move on," I said.

But we did not win the championship. Pat Hatmaker came back mentally ready and strong, but Tennessee got soundly beaten by Louisiana Tech, 79–59. And the person who learned the most that day was not Pat Hatmaker. It was the other Pat. Me.

I benefited more than anyone else that day, because I realized that I'd not done a good job of understanding the personnel I was working with. And I really had not understood our individuals specific to pressure situations. All of us handle pressure in different ways. That's when people will hide or bend under the fear of failure. Prior to ever getting on the court, you must have a working knowledge of how people will respond to pressure.

What I learned was: I was the person at fault. I don't think any coach, leader, or manager should be that ignorant of their personnel. We were playing in the semifinal game of the Final Four, and my whole offensive call was designed to get the ball to Pat Hatmaker, and Pat didn't want the ball. Not once had I sat down with her and asked, "Pat, how would you feel if we're in this situation?" Seven years into my coaching career, I should've known that.

Now, I know who wants the ball.

It's your chief responsibility as a leader, or manager, or CEO to know who you can delegate to and when. Most important, you'd better have the round peg in the round hole. When I do hand the ball to a player in the stretch, I need to know she's capable of handling it—and handling it on a sustained basis, not just a onetime basis.

The obvious question is, how can you know these things? By talking with people, first and foremost. But there are also some tools that can help you. One of them is the Predictive Index©, which I have used for the better part of the last ten years in an attempt to understand our players better. It is a survey that categorizes personality traits. Some people are authoritative, some are craftsmanlike, some are methodical, and so on.

I first began to experiment with the Predictive Index© in 1987, the year we won that first national title, at the suggestion of Bill Rodgers, a businessman and owner of a Knoxville car dealership. I don't depend on it or take it as gospel. The survey is by no means infallible, for the simple reason that no two people are alike. But there are some general tendencies in personality types, and examining them can be helpful. I ask all of our prospective recruits and incoming freshmen to take the test, because it can indicate their strengths, weaknesses, and needs.

Personally, I'm a Type A. What that means is, I'm authoritative. I'm one of those people who feels like I have an invisible hand in the small of my back, pushing me. I have a sense of urgency about everything, even doing laundry. No matter how much you beat me down I'm going to bounce back, like a pop-up toy. Also, I have to win at everything. I don't even let people *walk* in front of me.

Each year, with the results of the survey, we form personality profiles of our players. We bring in a sports psychologist to help us analyze them. But I always make our players part of the discussion. I share the results with them before anyone, and we talk about how *they* see themselves, and whether they agree or disagree with the analysis.

What's more, I give them my profile to read.

They need to see it.

They need to know what they're getting into.

Bringing together disparate personalities to form a team is like a jigsaw puzzle. You have to ask yourself: What is the whole picture here? We want to make sure our players all fit together properly and complement each other, so that we don't have a big piece, a little piece, an oblong piece, and a round piece. If personalities work against each other, as a team you'll find yourselves spinning your wheels.

A lot of coaches or managers try to force personnel into a system or framework that doesn't suit them. They have a certain way they think things should be done. What they don't understand, out of stubbornness or ego, is that it may not be the most intelligent use of talent. How many times have you seen a player languish in a lineup, not fulfilling her potential, but as soon as she is traded to another team, she bursts out of her slump? I see that a lot. When you force somebody into a slot, you're inviting disaster.

The Predictive Index© can tell you *how* to work with people. The better I understand our players' personalities, the more able I am to draw out their abilities. And the more aware I am of what situations they are less likely to be successful in. When you do something that's contrary to your personality, it uses up mental energy. Each of us only has so much mental energy. If you've got a person who is not a comfortable, natural leader and you ask him in every practice and every game to be the leader, at some point in time, you will drain him. And when one gets mentally tired, one makes physical mistakes.

When I look at the personality profile of a player, it doesn't matter what his or her physical body type is. I'm more concerned with the mind attached to it. If I understand the inner workings of someone, I know better how to motivate him or her.

Not that it always works.

Abby Conklin took the Predictive Index© three times. Each time, the results were totally different. So you can see what I was dealing with. I didn't do a lot of fancy psychoanalyzing with Abby. In one game during the '96 season, I was reduced to yelling at her, "Just shoot the damn ball, Conklin!"

It's not like I make our players lie down on a psychiatrist's couch. I don't want to pry into their psyches too much. But I do believe that there is a basic blueprint for coaxing performances out of athletes or any other talented people. The blueprint is this: knowledge, confidence, relaxation, results. Knowledge builds confidence, which causes you to be relaxed, which gives you good results.

The opposite of that, of course, is a lack of knowledge, which causes self-doubt, or a lack of confidence, which causes anxiety; both give you poor results.

The more I know our players, the better we will be able to duplicate the circumstances that are conducive to their best performances. I'll give you an example. The Predictive Index© describes Type D people as perfectionists. They walk around in a flinch mode, waiting for something bad to happen. They think about what will happen not if but when they make a mistake. So when I pull a player like that from a game, I don't yell at her. I ask her, "What did you do wrong?" She tends to already know the answer. My response is, "That's right. Now, I want you to have a rest, because I'm going to put you back in the game in a few minutes." If I don't reassure that person, she'll sit on the bench and play the game over again mentally. When she goes back in, she'll still be thinking about the mistake she made before. I don't want her thinking about the mistake she made before, I want her to play the game frontward, not backward.

Tiffany Woosley, a gifted guard for us from Shelbyville, Tennessee, had a profile that's called A/D Conflict. What that means is, she saw equal reward and equal punishment in certain situations. In that state of conflict, you can be indecisive under pressure. You want that reward, but you fear the consequences unduly if you make a mistake. Under extreme pressure, you suffer anxiety.

In Tiffany's case, she was missing free throws under pressure. She was far and away the best free throw shooter on the team, and an instrumental player for us from 1991–95. But in 1991 she tended to think too much about her shot. As her percentage dropped, teams began to pick on her.

When it got to be late in the game, they would foul her, hoping she'd miss. Which only put more pressure on her.

Shooting more free throws wasn't going to cure the problem. Tiffany didn't need to work on her shot. She had shot enough free throws to last a lifetime. This was a matter of finding a smart solution. I called Bill Rodgers, who's pretty good at analyzing the results of the Predictive Index, and we discussed ways to help Tiffany. Our coaching staff began trying to convince her that free throw shooting under pressure was a win-win situation. We wanted to take the idea of punishment out of her mind and build up the idea of reward, so she wouldn't dwell so much on the external pressures. The idea we wanted to plant was, "If you make it, who are they going to write about? Whose picture's going to be in the papers? Who's going to be the hero when you step to the line and drill two, and we win the game?"

Also, Tiffany was worrying too much about all the mechanics of the shot as she was standing at the free throw line. Wrong time to think. I want our athletes to go through their mental exercises *prior* to stepping to the line. As you walk from one end of the floor to the other, that's when you go through your thought process. But once you step up to that free throw line, there's only one thought in your mind: "The ball is going in the hole." That's all they should think under pressure. "It's in."

We worked with Tiffany, until, one night against Louisiana Tech at their Thomas Assembly Center, it finally paid off. It was a regular season game in front of a big crowd. They were ranked, and we were ranked. It was a back-and-forth game right to the end. With about two-and-a-half minutes to go, you could see Tiffany's wheels turning in her brain. Then they started fouling her.

When she stepped to the line, you could see this thought cross her mind: *This baby is in.* After all, she had shot thousands and thousands of free throws. She didn't need to go over her mechanics: I've got to bend my knees. That should have been instinctive at this point. All she wanted was a visualization of the shot going in the hole, period. When you've practiced that many free throws, step one's already been achieved: knowledge.

Step two is, you go to the line with confidence and say, "I'm draining this one." That causes relaxation. What do you get? Results.

We won by seven going away. Who'd they foul? Her.

Four different times that year, Tiffany helped win games for us in the stretch at the free throw line. They all, of course, had made the mistake of scouting her in the past, and had said: Foul Woosley. Then she got up there and drained them. She went on to set the women's free throw record at Tennessee. Then she came back the next year and broke her own record, hitting forty-five straight. All she needed to do to break the slump was to understand what was going on in her mind.

The personality profile gives me a tool when I need a way to reach a player. If all her life she's thrived on approval, then I use that to motivate her. I hunt for ways to draw her best out. To be honest, I push her buttons. For instance, I knew Michelle Marciniak thrived on attention. I was not above saying to her, before we played Connecticut in 1996, "Who's the bigger star, and who are they going to be interviewing on TV over there in the corner of the arena after the game? Jennifer Rizotti? Is it going to be her? Or is it going to be *you?* Which one of you is going to be there?"

I have even used a personality profile on occasion in recruiting. It suggested a way that I could communicate effectively with a prospect like Chamique Holdsclaw. Chamique was a highly sought-after player from Astoria, Queens, New York. She is, to my mind, the single greatest player in the women's collegiate game today. She has a deceptive, Gumby-like body that seems to almost change shape in midair. But if you met her you'd think she was just a quiet girl with braces on her teeth. Deep down she's full of attitude, but on the surface she's hard to read.

We weren't certain of Chamique. She kept saying, "I'm your home girl, I'm coming to Tennessee." But she had two more visits planned to other schools. She wasn't 100 percent committed, or she wouldn't have planned those other visits. She called Mickie practically every day. But we wanted to see if we were really right for each other, and if so, we wanted to know how to motivate her to come to Tennessee. So we took a look at her personality profile. It suggested that what she responds to best is a challenge. So we decided to form a couple of questions for her.

The first question we asked her was, "If you come to Tennessee, one of the top programs in America, how soon, as a freshman, do you feel you should be able to contribute?"

Her response was, "As soon as I lace them up."

That right there verified that we had a high A on our hands.

The next question was, "When the game's on the line, and we're down to the wire, what do you think we as coaches should do?"

Chamique said, "Give me the ball."

After that, I knew exactly how to talk to Chamique. And I knew what *not* to say to her, either. Chamique was not a benchsitter. She never had been second in her life—she had won four state championships at Christ the King. And she was not about to sit on the bench at the University of Tennessee, no matter how good the program was. With Chamique, what makes her tick is a provocation. You put the challenge in front of her, and if it's in her body, she's going to do it.

Last year, Chamique came into my office just before we entered the post season. It had been such a long, grueling year, and she said she wanted to talk. I wasn't sure what she was after at first.

She sat in a chair across from me and said, "Who do you think will win the national championship?"

I looked back at her, and I said carefully, "Who do *you* think will win?"

She said, eyeing me, "I think Connecticut will win."

I said, "I'm not ready to concede that."

Then Chamique said, still gazing at me, "I think Nykesha Sales is the best player in the country."

It suddenly dawned on me why she was in my office. Chamique was looking for a reason to keep our season alive. She wanted someone to throw down the gauntlet. So that's exactly what I did.

"I think you're better," I said.

I knew just what Chamique needed to hear. The way to motivate an A is, you lay it on the line. You say, "You've got godgiven ability, and abilities that you've honed over the years, and if you don't play to your potential, you're letting down all the people that mean so much to you." That's pretty strong motivation. It's like yanking the rug out from under her, mentally.

It sounds tough, I know. You're probably worried about our players' feelings. You might ask, "Won't that hurt their self-esteem if they don't perform?" What you have to understand is, this is what *does* make a player like Chamique perform. And I'm not afraid to use it. I'd be cheating our players if I didn't try to get the most out of their gifts.

Pressure is not bad, applied correctly. It can tell you a lot about people. Self-concept can grow or diminish, based on the pressures that people respond to. People can either flower or wither, depending on how you handle them. What we do with the Predictive Index is explore those responses, so we can figure out how to interact and work together in the best way.

I'll show you what I mean by telling you a bit more about some of our current players. On the 1998 team, we have two upperclassmen, Chamique Holdsclaw and Kellie Jolly. Chamique is not the most exacting player or vocal leader, but when she steps on the floor she inspires. She is worth twenty more points to the team—not in what she herself scores, but in what she brings out in *other* people. That's twenty points I wouldn't be able to get out of our team, no matter how long and hard I made them practice.

Kellie Jolly is a young woman from Sparta, Tennessee, and another high A, but with an emphasis on technical execution. She does things by the book, and precisely. But her precision cloaks an abiding competitiveness. Kellie is certainly not one of the quickest players on the team, but if you throw a loose ball on the floor, she's the one who will get to it. Her first instinct, if you steal the ball from her, is to *steal it back*. If she doesn't respect you or doesn't trust you, you've got a problem, because she'll look at you with her head cocked, as if to say, "What's your angle?"

Kyra Elzy is a sociable sophomore from LaGrange, Kentucky, and an elegant guard-forward despite her skinny flying elbows. LaShonda Stephens is a strong, quiet sophomore center from Woodstock, Georgia. Niya Butts is a small streaky sophomore forward from Americus, Georgia. Brynae Laxton is a serene junior forward from Oneida, Tennessee, who carries a 4.0 grade point average. Misty Greene is a three-point-shooter with NBA range from Decatur, Tennessee. Laurie Milligan is a senior with eligibility but was inactive due to injury.

Then there are our four incoming, highly regarded freshmen. Tamika Catchings of Duncanville, Texas, is the Naismith high school player of the year and a fluid athlete with great versatility. Kristen "Ace" Clement of Broomall, Pennsylvania, has work ethic, composure, plus an almost illusory passing ability. Semeka Randall of Cleveland, Ohio, was the USA Today high school player of the year and jumps like she wears a jetpack; she is almost too hard-working; I'm afraid she may hurt herself. Teresa Geter, of Columbia, South Carolina, is a fearless post player whose nickname is "Smooth" for her ability to glide around the basket.

Using the personality profiles, we look for potential conflicts. We carefully consider how to mold the personalities together. All of them absolutely hate to lose. Anytime you get five or more people who absolutely hate to lose, you worry about how they will mix. Kellie might be more concerned about exactness than the end result. Meanwhile Chamique says to herself, "I don't have to go to exactly that spot or cut exactly, as long as I score." While they might all be working hard in their own way, what happens is a bad pass or a miscommunication.

When our team begins to understand each other, they start altering their behavior to work more cohesively. Maybe Chamique cuts a little more precisely, and Kellie gives her some slack. The end result is cooperation and an intelligent, concerted effort. They say to themselves, "We're all going to look good if the ball goes in the basket and we win."

● ● ●

The greatest strength any human being can have is to recognize his or her own weaknesses. When you identify your weaknesses, you can begin to remedy them—or at least figure out how to work around them.

I hire people who have qualities I'm deficient in. By evaluating my own strengths and weaknesses, I can put people in position to complement me. It means setting aside your ego. But it's a far more sensible way of doing business than to insist on being right all the time. I'll give you an example. For a long time one of my weaknesses was an inability to see the whole court. The two teams would run out on the floor, and all I saw was Tennessee orange.

Finally, I decided to break down responsibilities among our coaches on the bench, so I didn't have to worry about what I was missing. Al Brown pays attention to time and possessions. Holly Warlick watches the offenses. And Mickie DeMoss watches the defenses. Holly is in charge of substituting for the perimeter players, Mickie for the post players. My job is to make executive decisions. I take input from all of our coaches, and then do what I do best, which is to pull the trigger and deal with the consequences.

With organized delegation of responsibilities, we can work calmly and rationally on the sidelines in crunch time, no matter how crazy things are in the stands or out on the court.

We each have vulnerabilities. We're human. Probably the most common mistake we all make is letting our emotions get in the way of rational decision making under pressure. When you have worked hard and invested in a project and things don't go your way, passion can take over. Instead of continuing to think and work in an organized way, you get panicky and try to do everything all at once or try to force the situation. Sound familiar?

There is no emotion more wasteful or detrimental than panic. And none more human. A classic example of allowing panic to compound a mistake is when you turn the ball over and then commit a foul on the defensive end by overplaying.

But you can control panic. I am talking from experience here. Self-control is the one quality a coach must have on the bench if she expects her team to hold together under duress. I have to handle the mistakes we make so our players will handle them.

In adverse situations, you don't get results by crying, or yelling at other people just to make yourself feel better. When you're twenty points down with five minutes to go, throwing a tantrum is not the smart way to work. The smart way to work is to take care of the first possession. And then the one after that. And the one after that. With each small thing you do right, you regain some confidence.

Let's say you are taking a multiple-choice exam. You open the test and realize you don't know the answer to the first question. So you move on to the second. You don't know the answer to that one either. Now you are so panicked you can't even read the third question.

Take a moment. Go through the test until you find a question you know the answer to. Then find another. After you have answered all the questions you are sure of, go back to the ones you aren't sure of.

I wasn't born with composure. I am extremely emotional. Believe me, poise did not come naturally to me. As a child, I was pretty wild. I remember breaking an old wooden flagpole at school by swinging on it. But out of fear of my father, I had to mask my emotions. There weren't many outward displays, good or bad, permitted in our house.

The feelings were there, but they roiled under the surface. I remember when my oldest brother, Tommy, went off to college. My parents drove him to campus and dropped him off. After they got back home that afternoon, I heard a strange sound coming from the front porch.

I looked out the window.

My father was sobbing. He was sitting in a chair on the porch, heaving, with tears running down his face. It's the only time I've ever seen him cry like that.

I remember, too, when my brother Charles went off to Vietnam. We all felt a lot then. Mostly concern. One night when I was about fifteen, a bunch of us kids were going to a movie in Clarksville. We were all standing around on the street, when some boy in the group made a crack about Charles. Fury came over me like a blackout. The next thing I knew, that boy was doubled over and sucking in air. I had belted him as hard as I could in the stomach.

That's one way of dealing with your anger. Generally, however, I don't recommend it.

I tamed my emotions. I learned to get the better of my quick temper. How? An analogy would be driving in snow. You don't slam on the brakes when you see an accident coming, or feel yourself slipping. You drive slow and steady. But it takes a lot of practice at driving in snow before you get a feel for it. The same is true in life. The only way to learn how to cope with panic and frustration is to put yourself in challenging situations, over and over again, until you have mastered your responses.

This may sound funny, but I believe that, with practice, you can literally control your heart and pulse. A few years ago I participated in a test for an academic study conducted by a couple of research specialists from Vanderbilt University. They took four head coaches of Division I-A programs, both men and women, and monitored our heart rates in big games. I had the highest sustained heart rate of any of the four. I'm told my heartbeat was at a steady, unwavering gallop. So obviously, I'm not the calmest person you've ever met.

But a peculiar thing happened during a time-out. My heart rate plunged. Late in the game, in pressure situations, I had the *lowest* sustained heart rate. It slowed precipitously. At some point I taught myself to calm down under pressure and to suppress my feelings, in the interest of winning.

When you give in to excessive emotion, you betray your weakness and vulnerability to others, and you cloud your thinking. It's like I tell our players, when they get tearful on me. "Hey, I'd like to cry sometimes, too. You think I don't? But what would you do if you looked over at me on the bench, and I was in tears?"

More important, what would our opponents think? They'd think I'd gone to pieces, and they'd take advantage of it.

Whether in basketball or business, you have to cultivate a certain detachment if you want to succeed. You work smart by understanding what you need and looking at the best way to get it. Not by threatening to quit or sue. Or by crying.

None of those responses would have gotten me very far at an old southern university like Tennessee. I've always wanted to promote the game of women's basketball. But I knew that at a deeply traditional Southeastern Conference football school, it was going to take some prudence. No amount of argument was going to get us a bigger budget or a better locker room.

To be perfectly frank, my sorority training came in handy. When I needed to ask for something from our administration, the Chi Omega came out in me. She'd request those resources we needed to succeed. Pat Summitt might barge around the sidelines of the basketball court screaming, but Miss Chi Omega, thank goodness, knew how to talk to people courteously.

In 1972 Richard Nixon signed a law called Title IX, stating that girls and women were entitled to equal opportunity in education on the playing fields. I was in the right place at the right time: Tennessee was among the first Division I football schools to make a commitment to uphold the law and to prove that women could lead. Long before it was the popular thing to do, Tennessee said yes to women's athletics, and specifically to basketball, thanks to then-president Dr. Ed Boling. That's why they hired me in the first place. So how smart would it have been to tell them they weren't doing enough?

Even so, the bad old days were pretty grim. The year before I arrived, the team sold doughnuts to buy uniforms. On road trips our team used to sleep four to a room, because there was so little money for hotels. We would cram into two vans and drive eight to ten hours to games. The yearly budget for the women's athletic department was $5,000—for six sports.

When I arrived at Tennessee in 1974 as a graduate assistant, I took home $250 a month. The following year I became a full-time teacher and coach with a starting salary of $8,900 a year. When we won our first national championship in 1987, I was making $42,465. But I didn't get into this business for the money, or I would have gotten out a long time ago.

I could have gotten angry about it. But getting angry wasn't going to help. I had to work smart. Maybe I should have shouted and waved around a copy of Title IX, on principle. But I genuinely felt that that would have set our cause back. Part of working smart is having the discretion to know when you need to impress, intimidate, or befriend.

There are two ways to break through a glass ceiling. You can scream and kick at it and try to shatter it with your high heels. Or you can learn to cut glass. I chose to be a glass cutter.

Glass cutting requires patience and positive thinking. If I had resented my employers or complained about my paycheck, there is no way I could have survived at Tennessee. Instead, I trusted in their good intentions and focused on the job at hand, which was to run an honest program, win games, graduate players, and maintain discipline. I made sure we did those things thoroughly and well. And I never asked for more than I needed. If the men's basketball team got twenty new pairs of game shoes, I didn't go to the administration and slam my fist on the desk and demand twenty game shoes for the women. I asked for three pairs. Because that's all we needed.

Did I have a legal right to demand twenty pairs? Yes. Would they have gotten me anywhere? No. I never looked at the men's program and complained about what they had and we didn't. First of all, nobody likes a complainer. Second of all, the men's program was irrelevant to me. We were in a unique situation. Tennessee is one of five schools in the country that has a separate athletic department for women. We had the ability to raise our own money and prove our independent worth. The men's football program was very generous to us, in terms of helping to fund women's sports. But we also did our best to pay our way. We proved that we were willing to help ourselves and not just ask for handouts. And in the long run, the administration appreciated it.

If you ask for what you need, and no more, people will be inclined to give you what you want. And they'll be more inclined to listen to you on those occasions when you do take a stand. In 1979, I went to bat against the state of Tennessee over the kind of basketball being played in our high school system. High school coaches were still teaching the six-player game, out of the mistaken notion that young women were too weak to run full court. Three girls would play on the defensive half of the floor, and three on the offensive. Tennessee was one of the last three states in the union still playing such an antiquated version of the game, along with Oklahoma and Iowa. I came out publicly in favor of modernizing the game, scandalizing half the state and enraging a lot of parents. Fortunately, the game changed.

Sometimes, being accommodating is part of working smart. For years Tennessee started school in late September. We were on the quarter system. Why? Well, because people were bringing in their crops, and they needed their kids at home to help. Southern universities have always been very accommodating.

Working smart requires patience and, frankly, a certain amount of calculation. You can't accomplish everything in one swoop; you have to pick your spots and know when to compromise. We spent a lot of years etching away at that glass, and it was slow, painstaking work. And sometimes it bred a frustration that was hard to disguise. But today the women's athletic department has a budget of over $8 million. Last year the university president, Dr. Joe Johnson, made me the highest paid female coach in the business, putting me on a par with most male coaches. It was back pay.

But strangely enough, I'm not what you would call a feminist. I don't really care for that word. What I am is a fairly conventional southern woman. I cook dinner for my family just about every night. The last thing I do before I go to sleep, and the first thing I do when I wake up, is a load of laundry. There is no question that my traditional southern credentials advanced the cause of Tennessee basketball. I was the sort of woman that the powers-that-be were familiar with, and I appealed to them. On the other hand, ironically, everything I've achieved and fought for as a coach, like equal opportunity and equal pay for equal work, is pretty deeply feminist. So I don't really know what you would call me. Subversive?

All I know is what experience has taught me.

Working smart is about being realistic and economical. It's about not wasting your energy on emotions that are detrimental to yourself and those around you, like panic or resentment. It's a pretty magical ability to have, once you acquire it. Everything becomes easier. Basketball, politics, driving, relationships. In the space of just a year at Tennessee, from 1986 to 1987, we went from feeling like we might never win a national championship to feeling like we could never be counted out again. All because we learned how to work smart, instead of just hard.

Working smart is about understanding what you are best at, and what you are worst at, and what you will settle for in the interest of progress. It's about arriving at a balance.

Even if you're balancing on two wheels.

Q & A *Carla McGhee*

Forward, 1987, 1989, national championship teams; Olympic gold medalist, 1996; Columbus Quest, ABL

Q: *How does Pat get people to play for her and put up with her?*
CARLA McGHEE: *She's very honest. She's up front. You have to be that way, too, to stay with her. Once you learn to be honest with her, you have a friend and an ally for life. But you need to trust her. She breaks you down and rebuilds you. She doesn't tell you she's going to lead you to the Promised Land.*

Q: *Did you always trust her?*
CARLA McGHEE: *No. I was from the north, where you don't trust anybody, much less a coach. When I first got there, I was like, "Oh, man, me and this lady are going to have a* problem."

Q: *Did you?*
CARLA McGHEE: *Yeah. My freshman year we had a very heated argument. You don't want to catch the wrath of that lady. I was so rebellious, and I was cocky. I kept saying to Mickie and Holly, "Why is she picking on me? Why is she always on me? I'm tired of it. I could have gone to the Army or Navy and gotten off easier." She spent hours dogging me out. Then one afternoon, she wanted to talk. I said, "Pat, you need to go on, before I say something we'll both regret." I started to walk away from her. She said, "You get back here. You say it." I told her I wanted to transfer. I said, "I think I need to play for a black coach. I want to go play for Vivian Stringer." She was calm. She told me to think about it, and if I was serious, she would help me transfer. But I knew what she was really going to do. She called my mother. My mother wasn't even on my side. My mother was on Pat's side. I wasn't going anywhere. But after*

that we talked, and it brought us closer. From that point on, I knew I could tell her anything.

Q: *Do you still talk?*
CARLA MCGHEE: *Last year I wasn't playing well. I was tired of basketball after the Olympics, and I hit a wall. I've been out of school for seven years. But she calls me up. She says, "Carla, what's going on with you? You suck it up and you play. You committed to that team, now you go out and play." No one else could have talked to me that way.*

VIII

Put the Team Before Yourself

Teamwork does not come naturally. Let's face it. We are born with certain inclinations, but sharing isn't one of them. If that sounds cynical to you, just watch a group of children playing. I enjoy studying children, because they are so unself-conscious. When two or more children get together in one room, what do they fight about? Sharing, that's what. They *hate* to share. Tears roll down their faces over the cheapest plastic toy, simply because another child wants to play with it. Not long ago, I went to a Halloween carnival with my son, and all of the little costumed clowns and princesses were having nervous breakdowns at the idea of sharing. Pirates wailed, monsters wept. Spiderman went to pieces right in front of me.

I've seen whole teams act that way.

Guess what? In the end, those teams lost.

My point is, teamwork is taught. You don't just lump a group of people together in a room and call them a team and expect them to behave like one. No organization will succeed without teamwork, no matter how many all-stars you have. Everyone knows that. I'm merely stating the obvious. What's not so obvious or easily stated is, *how* do you create a successful team? How do you convince a group of highly talented individual performers to set aside their personal feelings, ambitions, and agendas in favor of a unified effort? It's no easy matter. As a coach, I have to be at my most inventive and articulate when I talk about teamwork. But basketball happens to be a wonderful tool with which to teach it.

Every year, a whole new cast of diverse characters arrives at Tennessee. I can't physically force those players into a harness. I can't automatically *make* them play together. I have to use the full range of my teaching and training techniques, and I have to redefine a lot of their ideas about themselves.

I request, I plead, I threaten. I say, "Anyone who doesn't like it, I've got a seat on the bench right over here next to me." I talk about teamwork until I have no voice left. But when I'm done with my speech, some of them still look at me skeptically, as if to say, "Yeah, but what's in it for me?"

Without an incentive, people simply won't work together consistently. But if you can grasp the real incentive behind teamwork, instilling it suddenly becomes a whole lot easier: Teamwork is not a matter of persuading yourself and your colleagues to set aside personal ambitions for the greater good. It's a matter of recognizing that your personal ambitions and the ambitions of the team are *one and the same*. That's the incentive.

Teamwork is really a form of trust. It's what happens when you surrender the mistaken idea that you can go it alone, and realize that you won't achieve your individual goals without the support of your colleagues. Once you buy into it, you will feel a sense of relief. It's like relaxing into a chair after a long day on your feet.

Even so, teamwork is a highly tenuous state. It has to be tended to and cultivated every day, because it doesn't take much to disrupt it. A single unhappy troublemaker, a murmured complaint at the end of the bench, can undo it. So can personal jealousies. Whispering campaigns. Meddlesome parents. When you're dealing with highly charged, competitive individuals, egos invariably clash. The most well-intentioned of us will unconsciously cling to self over team.

Take me, for instance.

Tyler is starting to participate in sports, which has put me in an interesting position. I'm his mother. But when I watch him play, all my coaching instincts come to the forefront—and so does my ego. Now, I don't ever want Tyler to be confused as to who I am, his mother or his coach. Also, I don't ever want him to feel pressured to perform athletically simply because he's my son. I want him to be athletic for the sole reason that it's healthy for him. I've purposely refused to push basketball on him. Whenever we talk about what he wants to be when he grows up, R.B. and I tell him, "Just don't be a coach or a banker."

Tyler plays a little baseball, and he plays soccer. That's right. I'm a Soccer Mom.

Now, there are few things more potentially disharmonious than a parent who doesn't understand his or her proper role in the team concept. Parents think their daughter should be playing more or that they know more about how to coach her than I do. I ask them to trust me and let me do the coaching. I ask for their support in making a cohesive unit out of our players. When I discipline or bench a player, our parents must understand that I have to do what I think is best for all. Their proper role on our team is to support their daughter and our team.

But when Tyler came along, Mickie and Holly got these knowing looks on their faces. They said, "Just wait 'til Tyler starts playing sports, and we'll see how *you* act."

I said, "I'm not going to act like some Little League parent. I'm not going to do it."

But that was before I went to his first soccer match.

As Tyler ran on to the field that day, I was so proud of him. He looked adorable in his shorts and his knee socks and his cleats. Then the game got underway. Now, I don't know a lot about soccer. But as the game progressed I couldn't help being a little disappointed, because Tyler was hanging back.

He wasn't aggressive. It seemed like a lot of those kids were playing harder than he was. Some of them were really out front, running toward the goal and kicking up a storm. From where I stood, Tyler was being awfully passive. As the game went on, I started worrying about it.

Finally, there was a time-out, and Tyler's coach substituted for him. Tyler came jogging over to the sideline, and the first thing he did, naturally, was look me right in the eye, expectantly. He said, "Mom, how'd I do?"

He wanted my approval. I knew that how I reacted was so important. I could influence his self-esteem for life, right then and there. So I said, "Son, you did great. You did just great."

He stood next to me, watching the game. Boy, I was really struggling not to say anything more to him. After a minute, finally, I couldn't stand it. I put my hand on his shoulder, and I leaned down, and I said, "But you could be more aggressive! You didn't kick the ball. Get in there! Be competitive! Be aggressive!"

Tyler looked back at me with his big, somber blue eyes, and said, "Okay."

When he went back into the game, I was one proud mother. He kicked the ball. He ran so hard, he knocked people down. He was *aggressive*. Boy, did I puff up. I was pretty full of myself, thinking, *That's my boy*.

Well, at halftime the coach went over and talked to Tyler. Afterward Tyler walked back toward me. I could tell from his body language that something was wrong. He scuffed along, his head hanging down.

I said, "What's the matter?"

Tyler said, "Mom, I'm so confused."

"Why?" I said.

He said, "Well, you told me to get in there and kick the ball and be aggressive. But my coach told me I was supposed to be back on defense and protect the goal."

I went pale.

"What do I do?" he asked me.

"Son," I said, "you do *exactly* what your coach tells you to do."

● ● ●

Teamwork is what makes common people capable of uncommon re-sults.

Let's say I hand out pencils to our twelve players. I tell them, "Now, I want each of you to break your pencils in half." They will do it, no problem. You'll hear the snapping of individual pencils all over the gym.

But what if I take twelve pencils, and I bind them together with a rubber band? Now try to break them.

You can't.

That is the basic principle of teamwork.

Analogies are useful in teaching the team concept. People will buy into it a lot more readily if you can show them what you mean and not just talk about it. Another analogy I like to use is a potluck dinner. Only I don't just talk about it. I throw one. From time to time, I host a potluck dinner for our team.

"Everyone brings a dish," I announce.

Every player is responsible for contributing just one thing. Maybe Chamique brings the beans. Kellie makes the corn. That's all they have to worry about, no more and no less. They gather over at my house, and we sit around and eat and talk. The lesson is obvious. If they perform their assigned role, if they each fulfill their small share of responsibility and bring that specific dish—whether they like that dish or not—then we all get a big dinner.

Not everyone is a born leader. Role players are every bit as essential to the success of a group as the leader. The last thing you want is a team full of A personalities who think they can do it all. It wouldn't work. They'd kill each other. Our team would resemble an old B monster movie. Mothra meets Godzilla. What you do want is a good mix of personalities. Some are leaders, some are role players, some are contributors. Everyone has different abilities. Everyone brings a different dish.

Role playing is uncomfortable, especially for people who are competi-tive and diverse. You may fight the team concept because it means yield-ing, something you are instinctively opposed to doing. But you can train yourself to become a team player—by keeping a disciplined eye on the larger goal and realizing that when you help each other, you help yourselves. The military creates unit cohesion by using severe physical training and emotional bonding to convince soldiers of their interdependency. Sports teams tend to operate the same way. In a more benign office setting, team play can be taught with some tried-and-true seminar tools. We're always experimenting with them at Tennessee. We've tied ourselves together with skeins of yarn. We've blindfolded team members and led each other around the room. Sometimes it may seem like silly stuff. The bottom line is to learn that when you aid in the success of a team member, you'll be successful yourself.

But there is a deeper meaning, and an ethic, to team building that can't be taught with a tricky mental exercise or a cute analogy. If teamwork is about trust, then honesty is vital. Before you can work together, you have to be honest with each other.

You don't trick someone into doing something they don't want to do. There is no easy way to slide through the conversation when you ask someone to step aside and sit on the bench. When you talk about unselfishness, you have to be candid, or you'll invite discord.

If you deceive someone, if you insinuate that he will receive more personal gain or satisfaction than he can realistically gain, he will be susceptible to feeling that the team aim was counter to his individual success. He will think, "I set aside my own interests in favor of the team's, and I didn't get what I was promised. I got cheated."

It's important and only fair that people know up front what your philosophy is. You have to be clear about what their expectations should be. If I'm recruiting a role player, for example, I don't say, "I think you're going to get thirty minutes a game, and I think you ought to be able to average twenty points." Unless I really believe that, why would I ever try to influence someone to come into our organization under such obviously false pretenses? I'd be asking for trouble. And you would be right to distrust me.

People will perform so much better if they understand their specific role and what is expected of them. It's like the potluck dinner: It doesn't work if it's disorganized and unclear. If people don't know what they're supposed to bring, you don't get a good dinner. Some people bring too much, others bring nothing at all.

Too often, managers hesitate to tell it like it is. They tell people what they want to hear versus what they need to hear. We are very clear on what we do at Tennessee. We tear down individual self-concepts and rebuild them within the team.

We had a situation in 1996 that could have been awkward. We had almost too many high-profile players on that team. Michelle Marciniak and Latina Davis were seniors who had gotten a lot of attention—until Chamique Holdsclaw arrived. When Chamique came in, everything changed. Chamique had a spectacular rookie season, averaging 16.2 points and 9.1 rebounds to lead us in both categories, and toward the end it was clear that she was probably going to win All-American honors. I knew that that might not go over too well with our upperclassmen. Chamique was a freshman, while they had been working for four years.

I called Michelle and Latina in, and I told them straight out that Chamique would probably make it and that they probably would not.

I said, "She has the best credentials and she has the best chance of being All American. Now, both of you want to win a national championship. Which would you rather have? Would you rather be an All American, or would you rather win the championship?"

Latina and Michelle both said, "We want the championship."

I assured them that if they would continue to help Chamique, we would all have enough individual honors to go around. She could be the All American, and we could win the championship, and they would get their share of recognition. Winning a title far exceeds any plaque, I tried to explain. Once you have experienced it, you know that. But if you haven't, you don't. You might just get jealous.

Michelle and Latina swallowed whatever feelings they had. What happened next with that team is a credit to both of them.

Latina became the Most Valuable Player in NCAA East Regional.

Michelle was the MVP in the Final Four.

Chamique was named Kodak All American. And Tennessee was national champion.

Team building starts by recruiting good people and turning them into willing role players early on. You have to stress from the outset that no one individual is more important than the other, whether you are the go-to player, or you are the twelfth player. It's the only way to preempt jealousy.

If you have a player or colleague who thinks she is somehow more valuable, then you've got trouble. Athletes are especially inclined toward this kind of thinking. They have a natural tendency toward elitism.

Perhaps the best role-playing team we've ever had at Tennessee was our 1987 squad. I cite it all the time. We broke through and won the national championship with an assembly of unsung players. People forget that there was not a single All American on that team. Although players like Bridgette Gordon, Tonya Edwards, and Carla McGhee would go on to great things, at the time they played supporting roles to unheralded veterans like Dawn Marsh, Shelley Sexton, Sheila Frost, Lisa Webb, Melissa McCray, Karla Horton, Cheryl Littlejohn, Kathy Spinks, Jennifer Tuggle, and our two walk-ons, Gay Townson and Sabrina Mott.

We were only ranked No. 7 in the country. We had the worst record in the Final Four, at 26–6. We had to go up against Long Beach State, and their All American Cindy Brown, which was the highest scoring team in the nation, and then Louisiana Tech, with Teresa Weatherspoon. Nobody had any respect for us. They thought we were wide-body country girls. Cindy Brown called us "those corn-fed chicks from Tennessee."

But there was something bonding in that lack of respect. We decided to believe in each other, since nobody else would. Going into the national championship game, Louisiana Tech was 11–1 against us, including a twelve-point loss earlier in the season. But rarely have I seen all five members of a team each perform their assignments so exactly. We knew what Tech was going to do before they did it. Even though we didn't have a star or All American, three different players scored thirteen points each, and a freshman, Tonya Edwards, was MVP. We dominated from the outset on the way to our 67–44 victory.

That's what teamwork will do.

But one selfish player can undo it all. I've started to recruit some players and actually made a decision along the way not to offer them scholarships because I suddenly felt that it wasn't a good fit. It doesn't take you long to realize when you have a self-centered person in your midst. The amazing thing is that we have so many young women who are committed to the team concept. When one isn't, the negative attitude really stands out. It shows up like an X ray.

Sometimes, we have to break down our players emotionally in order to teach them teamwork. We build them right back up, again, of course, within the system. But it's a painful process. It's especially hard on our freshmen, who don't yet understand our methods. They think I pick on them, or that I don't like them. There can be a lot of tears those first few months.

The first couple of semesters at college can be a confidence shaker for anyone, much less an athlete. They come to Tennessee full of confidence and swagger. They were all-everything in high school. They were recruited by the best schools. There were maybe one or two other players in their entire career who came even close to them in ability. Well, you can have a false sense of confidence and security when you're a notch, physically, above everybody else. But all of a sudden, you step into the Tennessee arena, and you're playing the toughest schedule in basketball. You realize, "These people are as good as me."

Then I get a hold of them. In some cases I'm the first person to really criticize them or tell them that they are doing something wrong. The floor drops out from under them. I can see it in their faces.

I almost ran off Kyra Elzy just last year. The only reason Kyra didn't quit school as a freshman at Tennessee in 1997, was because I had prepared her mom, Sheryl, for what to expect. Sheryl is a corrections officer in LaGrange, Kentucky, and I'm very fond of her. One reason Sheryl hoped Kyra would go to Tennessee was because she felt that I coached with the kind of discipline she had tried to raise Kyra with. I was completely frank with her about how difficult Kyra's freshman year would be.

"Now, Sheryl, Kyra's going to call you and want to come home," I said. "She's going to cry and tell you she's unhappy. I'm asking you, right now, to tell her no. Don't let her come home."

Kyra will tell you straight out that you couldn't pay her to go through her freshman year again. She makes it sound like boot camp. It wasn't quite that bad, but I did stay on her back. The reason was, I saw so much potential in her. We needed Kyra to play a significant role as a freshman, and I knew she was capable of it. I didn't think we could win a national championship without a defensive stopper on the perimeter. Kyra, at the two-guard spot, had the best chance of doing that for us. But to be a defensive stopper, Kyra had to develop mental toughness. So I had to grow her up—fast.

"Kyra Elzy, are you too *good* to take a charge?"

"Hold up. Everybody on the line. We're going to run a Big Three for Kyra."

For the first few months, Kyra was miserable. I really went to work on her. She was eaten alive by opposing teams. Old Dominion and especially their senior point guard, Ticha Penicheiro, had a field day. Penicheiro put up twenty-five points as Old Dominion beat us, 83–72. Afterward, when Kyra came to practice, I told her, "You'll get another chance at Penicheiro. And when you do, you'll be ready." But I also stayed on her.

Kyra had, and has, so much untapped ability. And I was, and am, determined to get it out of her. She didn't understand that at first. It took Mickie to explain it to her. Like I say, sometimes Mickie's role is to sweep up the broken glass I leave behind me.

"Stay positive," Mickie told Kyra. "When Pat starts calling your name out, just think to yourself, 'I must be special for her to say my name so often.' "

I challenged Kyra every way I knew how. I barked at her, I teased her. I told her she was way too nice. "I'd take you to lunch," I said. "But I wouldn't take you to war." I told her everybody was saying we couldn't win a title because we were so weak at her guard position.

"We're a two-guard away from a national championship," I taunted her.

After I said it, I held my breath. I looked at her and thought to myself, *You'd better respond, young lady. Don't you fold on me.*

One afternoon, my phone rang. It was Sheryl, calling from LaGrange. Sheryl said, "Well, Pat, I got that call you told me about."

Kyra had called her mom, crying. She had asked to come home. She told Sheryl college just wasn't for her. She said it was the worst December of her entire life.

The whole team felt the same way. I would make them practice for three hours, raging at them the whole time. Afterward, the team would straggle into the locker room and put on a Counting Crows song, called "Long December." They played it over and over. Day and night, you could hear singer Adam Duritz's lament, his voice floating out of our locker room.

Sheryl said, "Kyra wants to come home."

I said to Sheryl, "Well. What did you tell her?"

Sheryl said, "Pat, it was one of the hardest things I've ever had to do. But I told her she couldn't come."

Sheryl, bless her heart, talked to Kyra for half the night. In doing so, she played her own role in our '97 championship. She explained to Kyra that four hard years was nothing compared to the thirty-five or fifty years of hard labor she'd be looking at if she quit school. She comforted her and encouraged her. But she didn't give in.

When I say that without Kyra we wouldn't have won our fifth national championship, I'm not exaggerating. I told her, after that first Old Dominion game, "You'll get another shot at them. And you'll be ready." Kyra just looked at me, like, "This lady is crazy." Nobody thought I was serious. My dad would say, "Why are you playing Kyra Elzy?" And I'd say, "Dad, she's going to be a defender for us in March."

That she was. The night of the national championship game in Cincinnati, before we went out on the floor against Old Dominion, I reminded Kyra that this was her shot at revenge. "Make Penicheiro have nightmares about you," I said. Kyra did precisely that. She was Penicheiro's own personal bad dream. Old Dominion had twenty-six turnovers—eleven of them by Penicheiro. It was the most she had given up all year. Afterward, Penicheiro was *still* thinking about Kyra. "She had those long, slender arms that seem to go on forever," Penicheiro said.

When the buzzer finally went off at the end of the game, Kyra came straight over to me.

"So," Kyra said. "Are we still a two-guard away from a national championship?"

"No," I said. "We've got a two-guard." Then I wrapped my arms around her and hugged her.

The 1997 team was full of role players. Looking back on it, it seems like in every game of the post season, we asked a different player to step forward and do something out of the ordinary to help us win. On each occasion, they came through for us. But it took the better part of the season to train them into it.

Another player who performed a crucial role for us in the post season was Kellie Jolly. Kellie was known for her ball handling, but not for her offense. Generally she didn't attack the basket. But against Connecticut in the regionals, we asked her to score. We figured the Huskies wouldn't expect her to look for her shot. We thought if she could start out aggressive and set a tone, she might give UConn something unanticipated to worry about. It was our way of saying, "We're going to come at you."

Remember, Connecticut had manhandled us, 72–57 earlier in the season. They were unbeaten at 33–0, and the huge favorite. We needed some kind of jump start against them, and Kellie was our point guard and mood setter. If she could get off to a big start, we knew it would filter throughout the team. She could take all kinds of pressure off the players who had been our scorers all year—specifically Chamique. Also, by breaking down UConn's point guards, she could breach their first line of defense. If you can loosen up a zone with your point guard, they've got to step out another foot, and then your passing is easier and your penetration is better.

On just our second offensive possession of the game, Kellie took the ball, drove the lane, and shot a layup.

We went crazy on the bench. She was coming off her anterior cruciate ligament injury, from which she had recovered in just over two months, and she was gutsy enough to take the ball to the hole on the second play of that game. She never looked back. And neither did we.

Kellie had nineteen points that night. It was a career high.

In the title game against Old Dominion, another freshman stepped forward to share the glory with Kyra. We had to find still another way to take some pressure off our proven scorers and put some pressure on the Lady Monarchs. We turned to Niya Butts. All year, we took flak for playing our freshmen so much. My own father and brothers wanted to know what I was thinking. But there is no reason a freshman can't be an impact player, as long as they know what dish to bring. In Niya's case, we gave her one very specific job. We limited her shot selection to a single option.

Niya was only allowed to shoot layups in post season. People said after the championship game: "Gosh, Niya Butts has never taken the ball to the hole like that before." Well, she only had one thing she was allowed to do. I said to our point guards, "Don't put Niya in a position where she needs to take outside shots. She's not ready for that."

Niya had a great game, shooting layups. She scored eight points in eight minutes.

These days, Kyra and Niya aren't the stars they were in high school. They aren't the most recognized members of our team. But they are confident, selfless role players. Whatever happens in the remainder of their careers, they know they had a part, a significant part, in a national championship.

● ● ●

To me, teamwork is a lot like being part of a family. It comes with obligations, entanglements, headaches, and quarrels. But the rewards are worth the cost.

I have a heart for those players who sit on the bench. I know how hard it is and what it can cost in self-esteem. It's like being the most thankless member of a large family. So it's all the more gratifying when I see one of those young women step forward and contribute uncomplainingly.

I believe that sitting on the bench for a summer absolutely made me a coach. My experience with the U.S. gold medal team at the Pan Am games in '75 changed my whole outlook. I am very aware and sensitive to the women who play that role for us. Of course, I thought I should be playing. What I gained from the experience was the conviction that benchsitting is one of the most important and difficult positions on our team. In my eyes it is almost as important as having a go-to player.

I particularly remembered that experience when I became head coach of the Olympic team that won the gold medal in Los Angeles in 1984. That job aged me years. I've never had anything stress me like that. For two-and-a-half years, not a day went by that I didn't think about the Olympics. The task of convincing players like Cheryl Miller, Lynette Woodard, Anne Donovan, and Denise Curry to blend together was daunting. We couldn't have asked for better talent. It was an all-star collection. My main job was not to over-coach and to get those young women to play together.

How do you establish roles with such an array of talent? It was one of the trickier jobs I have ever taken on. It was easy enough to convince them that when you win by a thirty-two-point margin, everyone has fun, and they would all get to play in Los Angeles. But there was no way everyone could start. How was I going to ask them to share playing time without putting them at each other's throats—or mine?

I decided to address it right up front. At our first meeting, I stood up.

"Seven of you will be sitting on the bench when the game starts," I announced. "And seven of you will be on the bench when the game ends. Seven of you who are superstars within your own programs are going to have to play roles. Can you handle it? Can you be a cheerleader and supportive of the person playing in front of you?"

The next thing I did was, I allowed them to make a crucial decision in shaping the team during the Olympic Trials. We were down to eighteen players, and we had to make the final cut to a roster of twelve.

I told *them* to do it.

I passed out confidential ballots, and I asked them to vote on the twelve players they thought should go to Los Angeles. When the coaching staff totaled up the player votes, the twelve who won matched the list that we, as coaches, had made. Our first choices were the same as those of the players. What that meant was that some of these women had quietly voted for others instead of themselves in the interest of sending the best team to L.A.

It also meant that the squad went to the Olympics believing that it was *their* team. Not mine. They felt that all-important sense of ownership and were willing to play their assigned roles without complaint. I took the twelve players they wanted. It preempted potential problems. If you want to have a team, you have to involve the team members in the decision-making process.

When I talk about team building, I don't mean that everyone has to agree, or play exactly alike, or *be* alike. The aim is to build a team, not clone yourself. You have to value people for their different qualities and abilities. The ultimate argument for diversity is not that it is politically correct, but that it is healthier, more interesting, and more conducive to success. That's why I have a male assistant, Al Brown. It's why I have two other assistants, Mickie DeMoss and Holly Warlick, who disagree with me so often. When you put differing perspectives and backgrounds in the same room, you get a bigger, more complete picture. Why would you want to know less, instead of more? Some people want to be surrounded by replicas of themselves. They want to work with people who look and sound familiar. They might as well go to work in a wax museum.

Teamwork is not created by like-mindedness. It's an emotional cohesion that develops from mutual respect and reciprocity and from coping with good times and adversity. As in a family, you have to be generous enough to take pleasure in someone *else's* success, not just your own. And have the smarts to realize that no one succeeds alone. As Alex Haley once said, "If you see a turtle sitting on a fence post you know he didn't get there by himself."

Like I say, at Tennessee, the family analogy is a pretty literal one. Tyler believes he has an important role on our team. He thinks he's our good luck charm. We have had three championships since he came into this world, so there might be a correlation.

But he also plays the role of comforter for all of us. And sometimes, little boyfriend. For a while he was going steady with Kellie Jolly, but I'm told he recently threw her over for Brynae Laxton. Anyway, whenever we are in need of a laugh or some perspective, Tyler seems to provide it. One afternoon last year, Kyra Elzy really needed a laugh.

On road trips, Tyler likes to sit in the back of the bus with the players. Often, he squeezes into the last row, sandwiched between Chamique and Kyra. He and Chamique have a private club, with a special handshake and initiation. No one else is in it, just them. They sit in the back of the bus and trade secrets. He's pretty good buddies with Kyra, too. He calls her "Cousin" Kyra.

Like I said, during the '97 season Kyra was usually in trouble with me for one thing or another. Tyler was sitting with her and Chamique in the back of the bus after a particularly woeful game. As we drove, I wasn't speaking to anyone. Our players' eyes were puffy. Everyone was silent, no one more so than Kyra. Tyler felt for her and decided to comfort her.

"Don't worry, Cousin Kyra," Tyler told her. "My mom will only be mad at you for a couple of days. She won't fire you."

To me, the greatest reward for being a team player, far outweighing any personal gain, is that it means you will never be alone. Think about that. Life has enough lonely times in store for all of us. The wonderful thing about partnership is that it halves your sorrows and compounds your joys. When you are pressured, teammates will lessen the burden. When you are exultant, teammates will only multiply it. The amount of success you are capable of enjoying, and the pleasure you are capable of feeling, is equal to the number of people you are willing to share it with.

Go ahead, try it. Share a little.

Q & A   *Mickie DeMoss*

Assistant Coach, 1985–present

Q: What really bothers Pat?
MICKIE DEMOSS: *People who are laid back. It drives her crazy. If you look at the players she has been hardest on, they had a laid-back attitude. That's just a thorn in Pat's side. Don't be laid back. You can be a lot of things as a player, but don't be laid back.*

Q: How does she motivate them?
MICKIE DEMOSS: *A kid will get glazed for whatever reason, and she'll say something to just blow her mind. To get her out of it. She'll surprise me with how in tune she is with people's moods, insecurities, fears. There are some days she'll purposely not say anything to a player. She'll say, "I don't even want to see her. I don't want to talk, we'll talk tomorrow." She can be strategic that way, when she wants kids to think on something, or sleep on it. Or she'll say something that makes them want to stick it to her. That's her whole intention and strategy: She wants them to come back and stick it in her face. "I'll show her." That's what she wants.*

Q: Is that why Tennessee is so tough in the big games?
MICKIE DEMOSS: *I have to believe some of it is Pat's ability to instill so much confidence. The kids have confidence in themselves, and they have confidence in her. I don't know what comes first. Maybe it's one and the same. She's so good at hiding her emotions. If she's nervous they'd never know it. If she was doubtful, they'd never, ever know it. She genuinely thinks we're going to win every ball game. She projects it. She could say, "Here's the plan. We're going to run backward down the court, and take our bras off, and swing them around our heads." And they'd nod their heads and say, "Sounds like a winner, Coach. When do you want us to start running?"*

IX

Make Winning an Attitude

I'm a believer, by nature. I believe in God. But I'm also careful to observe superstition. I give credence to the existence of ghosts, I don't contradict the advice of witch doctors, and I *know* crickets are good luck. There are a lot of skeptics in this world, but I'm not one of them. I'm reverent to the bone, probably because I spent so much time as a child spooking myself in country graveyards, or sitting in our old wooden pew at Mount Carmel United Methodist Church in Montgomery County. We went to Mount Carmel every Sunday morning and on a lot of weekday evenings, too. I was married there. So it's pretty hard to shake my faith in the church. My brother Tommy managed to interrupt my devotions once, by dropping a grass snake in my lap in the middle of Sunday service. That caused a temporary break in my prayers, I can tell you. But I just ran outside and screamed for a minute. Then I came back in.

Belief is actually a fairly practical matter. Most people think of it as something mystical, or, at least, highly conceptual. I don't. To me, the strongest kind of belief is grounded in reality. Like anything else, it's largely a result of focus, hard work, and other verifiable things. I heard once that magicians believe that if they practice a trick over and over, eventually it becomes genuine magic. To me, that's how belief in anything works.

Let me verify something for you. After twenty-four years as a head coach, after watching countless teams ebb and flow, observing them blow leads and rally to great heights, this much I know for sure: With a combination of practice and belief, the most ordinary team is capable of extraordinary things.

That's why belief is at the core of everything I teach our players. I ask them to believe in each other and to believe in our principles. Of course, it is much easier for me to preach belief with five national championship banners hanging above their heads in practice. Our success is certainly verifiable. But it wasn't always that way. Remember, Tennessee only started winning titles ten years ago. Somewhere along the line, like anybody else, we had to learn to believe in ourselves. Once we finally did, we discovered that it wasn't a very mysterious process at all. It was a simple matter of attitude.

Attitude lies somewhere between emotion and logic. It's that curious mix of optimism and determination that enables you to maintain a positive outlook and to continue plodding in the face of the most adverse circumstances. But while attitude is a state of mind, it is also based on a few hard certainties. There is nothing mysterious or illogical in the certainty that you are willing to work harder and longer than your opponent, even when you are behind in the game. That small piece of self-knowledge gives you something to hang on to. It's how comebacks are born.

Our attitude with our players in a tight, important game is, "You couldn't be better prepared. You know exactly what to do. So go do it."

There was a thought we posted on our locker room wall in midseason in 1997, while we were losing ten games on our way to our fifth title. Every locker room has its slogans. They are clichés, sometimes to the point of being ineffectual, like elevator music. But our walls were a testament to what that team went through. Every day we would give out a thought for the day. One of them said, "Fate saves a warrior when his courage endures." What it means is, if you keep fighting, blindly, in a positive and courageous way, sometimes chance will rescue you.

When I say winning is an attitude, that's what I mean. No one ever got anywhere, accomplished anything, or survived any amount of ill luck, by being negative. As a boss, it's one of the first things I look for in someone I'm hiring. I don't care if the person in question is a student manager or an assistant coach. His or her attitude is paramount.

With attitude, you can determine your own performance. But more than that, you can help determine the performance of others. A single individual with a strong positive attitude can lift those around her. She can change the course of events. Sometimes a positive person can walk into a room, and immediately the air feels different. It's as though her presence literally converts ions from negative to positive.

Attitude is a choice. What you *think* you can do, whether positive or negative, confident or scared, will most likely happen. When you doubt, you create a negative. It will affect your performance, and probably drag others down, too. How many times have you watched someone fail, because they were full of self-doubt? Afterward, what do they say? "I knew it."

I love to have dreams about winning. I dream all the time about playing and winning. We don't often lose in my dreams.

But when we do, it's never a good sign.

If I dream about a loss, it usually means I doubt myself. In 1993, we had to play Iowa on their home court in the Mideast Regional Finals of the NCAA tournament. Iowa was a tough team, coached by Vivian Stringer, someone I have a lot of respect for. The night I learned that we had to go to Iowa City, I dreamed we weren't ready for them. We played awful in my dream. We turned the ball over, we loafed on defense, our shots bounced off the rim.

A few days later we played Iowa, for real. We lost, 72–56.

This next part of the story will convince you once and for all that I'm crazy. That whole season, I was bothered by the number thirteen. It seemed like it followed me everywhere. It dogged me, it haunted me. I saw it every time I turned around.

If I looked at the clock, it would always be thirteen minutes past the hour. Let's say I woke up in the middle of the night and glanced at my digital bedside clock. It would say 1:13 A.M.

Or maybe I'd be in the kitchen cooking dinner. My gaze would wander to the clock on the stove. It would say 7:13 P.M.

This went on all year.

After we lost to Iowa, I said to myself, "You've got to make thirteen a positive number. There's nothing wrong with thirteen. Just keep telling yourself that."

But the next year, same thing. I saw the number thirteen everywhere. I saw it on license plates. I saw it in clothing catalogues. If I checked my watch to see if it was lunch time, my watch said 12:13.

Well, at the end of that year we lost to Louisiana Tech in the first round of the NCAA regional tournament.

In 1996, I was determined to do something about that stinking number. I wasn't going to let a couple of digits, two puny little numerals, get the best of me. Out of pure contrariness, I installed a match-up zone defense, a one-one-three set. I called it "Thirteen."

I said grimly, "Thirteen is going to be good for us."

I forced myself to think of the number in positive ways. If I had to choose a number I'd choose thirteen. If I played a lottery, I played thirteen. One way or another, I was going to make it work *for* me.

That March, we played Virginia in the NCAA regional finals. Now, we hadn't used the Thirteen defense much all year, and I had almost forgotten about my obsession with that stupid number.

As I got ready to go to the game, I glanced down at the digital clock next to my bed. You can guess what time it was.

The clock said 4:13.

But I told myself, gritting my teeth, "It's our lucky number."

We went out and trailed Virginia by seventeen points with fourteen minutes to go.

But I think that game is when we finally broke the spell. Would you believe it if I told you we went on to win?

I've never seen a team maintain its composure and positive attitude so well in the face of such overwhelming odds. There wasn't a negative thought on our bench. Afterward, Billie Moore, who coached me as an Olympian and who has been a lifelong mentor, told me that it was the calmest and most self-assured she had ever seen me on the sideline.

But someone else, not me, really set the mood that day. It was thanks to Al Brown, as much as anyone, that Tennessee didn't fold. Mickie DeMoss and Holly Warlick are my right and left arms. But Al was my pulse on that occasion. It was a great example of one person's winning attitude suffusing the entire team. And bench.

In the time that Al has worked with us, scouting opponents and breaking down film, I've never once heard him say, "I don't think we can beat that team." I've never seen him get upset or lose his temper, either.

Al and I had gone for a run together the day of the Virginia game. As we ran, I bit my lip, worrying about the Cavaliers. I asked Al what he thought about our chances. He said, "I think we're going to be fine. We ought to beat them. It'll be emotional at first. But at the end of forty minutes, we'll be fine."

When we were down by fourteen, I drifted down the sideline to where Al was sitting.

I said, "Well, what do you think?"

Al said, almost casually, "We're all right. They're going to play right back to us."

And that's exactly what happened. As Al predicted, Virginia's hot streak couldn't last forever. They cooled down a bit, and we regained our composure. Gradually we picked up a rhythm. We contested every possession, and whittled away at the score.

Michelle Marciniak was really struggling in that game. I had sat down with her and gone over personality profiles of the team, with the aim of getting her to understand how she could best deal with her fellow players in a pressure situation. I explained to Michelle that with a player like Pashen Thompson, you did not need to attack her; you needed to talk to her in a very gentle way, saying, "Pashen, we really need you now, we're counting on you." But when we got so down to Virginia, Michelle was pressing, and she started yelling at people, especially at Pashen. So I brought Michelle out of the game. But I didn't yell at Michelle, either. Al had transferred his calm assurance to me, too.

I sat her down and I said, "Look, Michelle, you're all right, but we need you to calm down. You need to speak to Pashen the way I'm speaking to you."

Then I remember looking her right in the eyes, and saying, "Do you understand? You need to talk to Pashen the way I'm talking to you right now. Same tone. Look her in the eye, let her know what you need from her."

Michelle went back in, and she and Pashen finished out strong for us. We came back and won, 52–46.

If we hadn't, I probably would have broken every clock in the house.

Still another year later, before the '97 championship game, I had my last encounter with the number thirteen. I always stay in the locker room, getting myself focused, until almost exactly two minutes before the tip-off. At about the two minute mark, I tell myself, "Let's get out there and get going." In Cincinnati, I walked out into the arena as our team was warming up to play Old Dominion for the title. I looked up at the game clock.

It said: 2:13.

I smiled. I said, "Yes. We're going to win."

●　　　●　　　●

I've said that success in my business is about putting the right people in the right place at the right time. But all too often it doesn't work out that way. Oftentimes, the wrong person is in the wrong place at the wrong time. What then?

You'd better have a winning attitude.

It may be all that's left you.

In any job, you have to deal with the unpredictable. You can't determine the weather, luck, or other people's opinions. But when things don't go as planned, there is one thing you can count on: your own outlook.

That's when attitude can provide that knife-edge of difference between winning and losing. At Tennessee, we have won games by the margin of a single good thought.

There are some concrete ways to create a winning attitude. But nothing beats practicing it. When you prepare to win, belief comes easily. Let's take sales as an example. When you have a big presentation to make, the best thing you can do for your confidence is to practice, over and over. When the day comes, you want to go in relaxed and calm, able to talk about what you have to offer. The presentation is such that it's informative, professional, personable, and delivered in a way that will gain the attention of the people you're talking to. You aren't wondering what the competition is doing. You are controlling what you can control, which is your own performance.

We simulate and prepare. We expect to win because we rehearse it. I believe you get what you deserve. That's why we force our players to make decisions in practice. We put a time and a score on the clock, and let them make mistakes. We work late-game situations, we put the ball in their hands and tell them to make the calls.

That sort of preparation manifested itself as winning conviction in the 1996 season, when we played Connecticut, as usual, in a heated Final Four game that came down to the wire. We went into overtime. Now, UConn had beaten us four times out of five. But on that night, as we huddled in a time-out before the start of the extra period, we were a confident team. Why? Because it was Tennessee's third overtime game of the year. I told our team, "We're okay. We've been in this position before. They haven't." Final score: Tennessee 88, UConn 83.

Many times you have to hand off an important job to someone who isn't necessarily your first choice. Maybe the person you wanted to take the shot is on the bench in foul trouble, or is denied the ball. In any business, you're going to have people in roles where they're not always 100 percent comfortable. An intermediate, or a substitute, has to step forward. It's not something this person is going to do on an everyday basis. But it's a fact of life—we all have to do jobs we didn't plan on.

How do you ask people to perform out of character, or above and beyond their capabilities? Maybe someone who is passive needs to be aggressive. A follower is suddenly forced to become leader. Now, he may not be able to do it on a sustained basis. But you would be amazed at how individuals can rise to an occasion—and more than once, too.

When we have to ask that of a player at Tennessee, we call it "dialing up." Dialing up is the state a player reaches when she plays a cut above her norm, or when she does something out of her comfort zone. You can recognize when someone has dialed up by her peaks and valleys. She might have a great game one night, scoring twenty-five points, but the next game, she's barely in double digits.

What we try to do with the Predictive Index is to figure out how best to dial people up mentally, on a consistent basis. We determine what really inspires our players individually, so that in a big game when they need to play a crucial role for us, they're brimming with the belief that they can do it. We want to know what to say to this player versus that player, to get her into that mentally charged-up state.

With the right attitude and mind-set, huge obstacles are suddenly surmountable. A good example was the role Pashen Thompson played in our run to the NCAA championship in '97, and especially in our pivotal tournament game against Connecticut. Going into the game, UConn was not only ranked No. 1 and unbeaten at 33–0. They also had Kara Wolters, considered the best big player in the country.

Now, Wolters was 6-foot-8. We didn't have anybody who was bigger than 6-foot-4. How were we going to defend against her?

With Pashen Thompson, that's how. Pashen was 6-foot-1, but she was going to have to go up against Wolters, and win. So we had to dial Pashen up. We had to convince her to be more of an outward leader and a physical player than she was accustomed to being. We thought long and hard about how to do that—what would give her the attitude she needed?

First of all, we wanted her to know she wouldn't be alone out there. I said to Pashen, as well as to Tiffani Johnson and our other post players, "We're going to guard her early. Put an orange uniform on Wolters before she ever gets to the paint. When she takes a shower tonight, and she gets ready to take off her uniform, it's going to be orange."

The next thing we did was show Pashen physically the way we thought she could beat Wolters. If you show Pashen how to execute, she will imitate it. She's got a great memory. So we gave her some techniques and knew she would retain them and use them in the game.

But we also needed to inspire Pashen; we wanted her to play at a level she hadn't really considered herself capable of before. Now, Pashen was a senior. She understood that the WNBA and the ABL pro leagues were looming as an opportunity. She also knew that the UConn game would be on national television. So I said, "If you want the type of pro contract you've been dreaming about, you'll have to take care of business in these next games. They're all on TV."

I also told Pashen the leagues would be calling me, after the season, asking about our seniors. I said, "They're going to be calling me about you, Pashen. What should I say?"

Articulating what's at stake is a good way to force people to believe in themselves. There is nothing wrong with stating the rewards and conse- quences of a situation when you're trying to dial up a performance. Now that there is a WNBA and an ABL, careers are at stake, and players must come to terms with their ambitions. There was an extra carrot out there for our players to be inspired by. I used it.

We also knew that Pashen's whole family, and everybody else in her hometown of Philadelphia, Mississippi, would be watching the UConn game. Pashen is interested in three things: her family, doing the right thing, and success. We used that, too. Al Brown sat down with her and said, "Pashen, this is your chance to be Miss Mississippi. This is a game that'll go down in everybody's memory. They'll remember it for the rest of your life. You don't want to disappoint your family, your teammates, your coaches, the University of Tennessee, the fans, or anybody else. This is your chance to go out and show people exactly who Pashen Thompson is and what she's made of."

Now normally, Pashen wouldn't say boo if the gym were on fire. She is really a straightforward, genuine young woman who wants to be a social worker when she is done with basketball. She is sweet, soft-spoken, and devoted to her church.

But she came out on to that floor in the Connecticut game like her uniform had burst into flames. In the first two minutes, she literally almost started a fight.

My head swiveled around, and I stared at her.

Next thing I know, Chamique Holdsclaw had to grab Pashen and pull her away from Wolters.

"Pashen?" I said.

Chamique had this surprised look on her face as she pulled Pashen away, like: "Who did that?"

I looked down the bench at Mickie and Holly. They were in shock, too.

"Pashen?" Mickie said.

It was just two minutes into that game, but I could see it then and there. We were a different team from the one that had been so soundly beaten by Connecticut earlier in the year. Her performance gave us confidence. Thank you, Pashen.

We held Wolters to just seventeen points.

Every accomplished person I know has the ability to adjust his or her attitude and dial up for the big occasion. Coaches or office managers, particularly, have the power to manipulate group attitudes, for better or worse.

If a player makes a mistake, and she runs down the floor still carrying the mistake, it only causes more mistakes. And, of course, that infuriates coaches. So what does the coach do? The coach overreacts, gets the big hook out, and yanks the player out of there. But when you use the big hook, what you are saying to that person is, "I don't believe in you; I don't trust you."

It's critical to understand that, when someone is sensitive to criticism, you can drive that person further into the tank by hooking them. You can ruin his attitude by making him feel like a loser.

Or you can inspire him. You can say, "What did you do wrong out there?" Let him tell you. If he doesn't happen to hit it on the head, then you can enlighten him. But most important, you refocus the person on winning, not losing. We have had players who were prone to feeling hangdog, and we used a simple technique with them.

Some of our players actually write "Sprint" and "Refocus" on their gear. We put it on their socks, or on their tape, or on their wristbands, to remind them not to have that letdown.

Another method I use to instill positive attitude is "targeting." I single out one person as the recipient of a patented Pat Summitt harangue, for the benefit of all. I intentionally lean on her. I hassle her, put pressure on her, and generally make her the uncomfortable focus of my harsher attentions. The reason I do it is not that I like to pick on people. The reason is, I know that if I can get a strong, positive, uncomplaining response out of that one player, the entire team will follow.

My targets tend to be our leaders. I only target those who can handle it. But that's the whole point of the exercise: *Handling it* is what we're after from the whole team. When our players see that Daedra Charles can absorb the worst I throw at her, and maintain a good attitude, they think, *If she can take it, I can, too.*

It's not fun to be my target. My target gets a lot of criticism and praise, sometimes in the very same breath. Our players know exactly what I'm doing when I target them. But it makes them crazy anyway. I even call their mothers, like I did with Daedra Charles. In the fall of Daedra's senior year, I phoned her mother back home in Detroit and said, "I just want you to know, I'm going to be on her case."

Sometimes I hurt a player's feelings when I target her. I realize that. "Get over it," I tell her. It's not that I don't care. I care so much, I've scarred the inside of my lower lip for life. But I want the player to channel it the right way. "Don't get your *feelings* hurt," I tell her. "Take it out on the basketball court."

In 1991 everything fell on Daedra's broad shoulders. Whatever happened, good or bad, I acted like it was Daedra's responsibility. I knew she could take it, which is exactly why I targeted her—even though Daedra herself didn't think she could. Daedra is the type of person who doesn't like to be yelled at, and she had a problem with it at first. She would call her mother, complaining, "She rides me all the time." Her mom would say, "She just wants you to be better, that's her way of motivating you."

The reason targeting works is because a player who can endure adversity literally empowers other people. She can uplift her teammates and instill rock-solid conviction. The message was, if Daedra Charles could survive what I dished out all year long, then we can win a title. Our players genuinely believed that nothing was harder than what Daedra Charles went through with me climbing up her back.

One of the more intense dialing up experiences I ever had was with Daedra in her last Final Four as a Tennessee player. We met Stanford in the NCAA semifinals in New Orleans in 1991. During the first half, nothing was falling for Daedra. She was nonexistent. You could practically see her shaking her head and thinking, *It's not my day.* Now, Daedra was the beating heart of our team. If she felt that it wasn't her night, the whole Lady Vol squad was bound to feel the same way. At halftime we went to the locker room trailing by eight points.

I had to find a way to snap Daedra out of it, or we were going down. I knew that, for sure. I also knew something Daedra didn't. I knew she had just won the Wade Trophy, the award given to the best player in women's collegiate basketball. It is the biggest individual honor a player can win. I had planned to wait until after the game to tell her. Unless I needed to use it before then.

After addressing the team at halftime, I cleared everyone out of the locker room, except for Daedra. I said, "Everybody out, except for you, Dae. You stay here."

Mickie and Holly and the rest of the team filed out into the hallway. I was alone with Daedra, whom we sometimes called "Night Train."

I said, "Train, what's going on with you?"

Daedra said, "Pat, I'm doing my best. I really am. I don't know what's wrong."

I said, "Let me tell you something. I wasn't going to tell you this. But you have just won the Wade Trophy. The highest honor in college basketball."

Daedra had no idea how to react. She couldn't even smile.

I said softly, with emphasis, "You have won the most prestigious award anyone can win."

I paused.

Then I said, my voice rising, "And you're playing like you never picked up a ball before in your life!"

Then I got on her hard. I got on her so hard, my neck turned red. You could hear me out in the hallway.

I said, "You're dogging it. The people who voted for you are sitting out there, thinking, 'What have we done?' Now you go out there and stop dogging it. You show them you deserve it!"

I went on and on. My tirade must have lasted five minutes.

At the end of it, Daedra just looked at me meekly and said, "Rebound."

Then she practically tore the locker room door off. Back on the court, she gathered that team together and said, "Get me the ball. Just put the ball in my hands."

Daedra hit the floor like she was shot out of a cannon. She was climbing over people's backs to get to the ball.

We beat Stanford, 68–60.

A day later we won the championship, defeating Virginia in overtime, 70–67. We had another halftime drama in that game. Daedra is almost as superstitious as me. Before every game that season, she kissed Tyler on the forehead. He was just an infant, six months old, so he was usually with me in the locker room before our games. But in all the pre-game intensity and excitement, she hadn't gotten a chance to kiss him. He was with R.B. up in the stands. Well, after halftime, Daedra insisted on kissing him. I agreed. If Daedra didn't kiss the baby, who knew what awful thing might happen. Tyler was asleep, so we had him passed down through the stands, from one Tennessee fan to another, just so Daedra could kiss him.

I'm always looking for new ways to instill belief, and I don't care whether I have to use a superstition, or a personality profile, or a locker room speech. It's a matter of whatever works. That's why we started experimenting with sports psychology in the mid-eighties. A graduate assistant named Tina Buckles brought us the idea of using imagery and visualization. We tinkered and worked with it all season long in 1987. Different things work for different people, and that team liked it, so we kept doing it.

Regardless, I was determined to do whatever I could to bolster our players' attitudes. Certainly no one thought we were capable of winning a title that year. The big change in our fortunes, from feeling that we couldn't win the big one, to feeling that we wouldn't be denied, was in large part due to a simple shift in attitude. Attitude is what carried us.

I worked especially hard with Bridgette Gordon on her attitude. In her case, she needed to improve her overall demeanor. When she first arrived at Tennessee in 1985, she was a head-hanger. She physically drooped, and she mumbled. She was always ducking her head and murmuring at me. "Get your head up," I said. By her senior year, Bridgette would be so outwardly confident that she was the player who spoke on our behalf at the White House. She even gave President Bush a special gift—a poster of herself.

But back in 1987, the morning of the championship game in Austin, Texas, I felt our team as a whole needed a little something extra. We needed to create a top-dog mentality instead of an underdog mentality.

That's why we decided to visualize, instead of having our regular game day shoot around. It was the most confident gesture we could have made. What it said to our players was, "We are so sure of you, and of ourselves, that we don't need to practice."

I don't believe we ever actually touched a basketball until the tip-off. We lay down in the jump circle, right there on the court. I remember that the lights were down low, and there was just one spotlight beaming down in the middle of the court. There was a hush in the arena. Everything was still. Even the television crews and technicians stopped moving, and became transfixed by the silence.

"Close your eyes and relax," I told the team.

I gestured to Mickie to take over, because she had done the scouting on Louisiana Tech. Mickie just raised her eyebrows at me. I punched her. She pointed to herself and went, "Me?" I nodded.

"Okay, ladies," Mickie said. "Visualize yourself on the person that you're guarding. They're in a one–two–two offensive set, and the right wing pops out and receives the pass. The weak side post back screens for the point guard. Now, how do we defend this? Denial. Ball pressure on the point guard. Play to the outside of the stack. Force them to the baseline. . . ."

Mickie talked for ten straight minutes. She led the team through every potential situation we might face, while she and I exchanged sign language the whole time. It was risky. But it worked. Our team came out and played like they had ESP. Our players beat their players to their spots.

You have to take risks. You can't steal second with your foot on first. I firmly believe that, and I believe in calculated gambles. A large part of dialing up is getting our players to take chances, whether to go for a steal, or take the ball into the teeth of the defense. It's important that they be willing to go beyond their limits, to go beyond anything they've done in the past. That's why we work on their mental game as much as their physical game. We force them to expand on their talent and on their view of what they're capable of. If we have a player who hasn't wanted the ball in a pressure situation, we get her to try it.

To persuade a player to take a risk, sometimes you have to throw a little emotion into the mix and gear her up. But there are other times when you need to slow down and provide some cool logic to paint the real, true picture of what needs to be done.

Ideally, a good leader knows how to do both. You've probably worked with people who are too emotional. He lets his emotions fly all over the room with no ability to reason. You probably avoid him because he's simply too much trouble. Another attitude that's difficult to work with is the flat-liner. He's Spock-like, to the point that you think, *Gee, I'm dealing with a robot here; does this person not have any feelings for me as a human?*

It is extremely important to make sure that your leaders have that crucial blend of emotion and logic, because their attitude will infuse your entire organization. That's why I expect our players to be mentally tough and businesslike and not to carry their emotions on their sleeves. I don't want them to be robots. But I don't want them flying all over the place either.

I targeted Lynnette Woodard, when she was the captain of the Olympic team in 1984. I warned her from the outset that a part of her job as team captain would be to handle my criticism, or anything else I might dish out to her, with equanimity. I said, "You may think I'm picking on you, but what I'm really doing is sending a message to the team."

I sent my message one afternoon when I used Lynette to set the tone defensively. I felt that if I could get Lynette to play top-notch defense, the rest of the team would follow suit. With all the talent on the Olympic team, offense wasn't going to be our problem. The difficulty would be getting them to defend.

That day in practice, I made Lynette take three straight charges. We were doing defensive drills and I made her set her feet while a teammate went barreling into her and knocked her flat on her back.

The first time she hit the floor, she just sat there for a second.

"Get up," I said, with no sympathy.

Lynette got up slowly, but uncomplainingly, and set herself back into position.

"Same thing," I told the offense. They prepared to run the same play. Here came the ball handler, again, right into Lynette. She hit the floor again.

"Get up," I said.

Lynette looked at me.

"Get *up*," I said impatiently.

Lynette rose. By now the other players were lifting their eyebrows. I thought Lynette might say something, or at least glare at me, but she didn't. "Same thing," I ordered. Lynette sort of wearily took her position again. No sooner did she get set again, then, whammo. Down she went, a third time.

Lynette slowly rearranged her limbs.

"Get . . . *up*," I said.

Did I run that drill just for the pleasure of seeing Lynette hit the floor? Of course not. I did it to develop an attitude. If Lynette could take three straight charges and suffer my lack of sympathy without complaint, so would the rest of them. Sometimes your best example is a tough one. Defense is especially vital in international play, because international play is traditionally very physical, and very offensive. Shooting over 60 percent isn't at all unusual. Everyone would bring a potent offense to L.A. But the winner of the gold medal would be the team that could bring an offense *and* a defense that wouldn't quit. And that's just what we brought, thanks to Lynette. The team rallied around her.

Targeting works because it gives our team a small piece of belief to hang on to. Often, belief is made up of the specific knowledge that you've endured a situation before, and you can do it again. A small piece of knowledge, like faith in your colleagues, or the understanding that a player will take a charge for the benefit of the team, can be invaluable. These things add up to certainty.

● ● ●

Belief in yourself is what happens when you know you've done the things that entitle you to success. Real confidence is not groundless. It is based on everything you've practiced all year long. It's based in your experience and how much homework you have done. The same is true of every profession, not just basketball.

Now, I'm not saying that with belief, you will never lose. I can't promise you that success will be yours automatically, simply because you keep your chin up and your eye on the target. But I am suggesting that attitude will give you a fighting chance, every time. And if you do lose, attitude cushions the disappointment. At least you have the knowledge that you gave yourself every chance to succeed. It allows you to still like and respect yourself when things don't go your way.

The night I tore knee ligaments in my senior year of college, in January 1973, I remember the doctor saying, "I don't know if you will play again. . . ." But before he ever finished that sentence, my father cut him off.

"Play?" my father said. "She's going to make the Olympic team."

I have used that confidence ever since. Over and over again in big games, a little bit of conviction has made the difference for us. In 1982 we were playing Southern California's powerhouse team in the NCAA regional finals. The winner would go on to the first NCAA-sponsored Women's Final Four. We had absolutely no business thinking we could upset them. The Trojans were so confident, they came from the West Coast to Knoxville with their suitcases and gear already packed to go on to the Final Four in Norfolk, Virginia. But we played them right down to the wire.

When we called our last time-out, the first thing I said to our team was, "We're going to win this game." We talked about what we wanted to do, and then we got ready to break. I looked at our players again and I repeated slowly, *"We're going to win this game."*

We went into overtime. Final score: Tennessee 91, USC 90.

I've even managed to translate my belief and attitude to Tyler. He thinks he can *will* us to win. Back in 1996, we lost to Stanford, badly, 90–

72. Late in the second half we were getting absolutely killed, by more than twenty points. Even though it was clear that there wasn't much hope, I stalked up and down the bench. Finally I wandered down to one end, where my son was sitting.

Tyler looked up at me. Then he held out his hands and shrugged. He said, "Mom, I'm doing everything I can."

There is no question that belief can work in strange ways. Whenever I forget this, I just go home to Henrietta and visit a man named Mister Johnny. Mister Johnny Bellars removes warts by rubbing on them. He has taken warts off Tyler and a lot of other people in Cheatham County. The power to take away warts was passed down to him years ago from a dying old man named Blue. If you met Mister Johnny, you'd understand why I don't bother with a dermatologist when it comes to warts. Mister Johnny wears thick glasses, but he can stare a hole right through you. He sits on his side porch, in an old folding chair. His hands are stained brown by tobacco. He sits in his chair chatting with you, while he stares at you and softly rubs on your wart with his thumb.

After about ten minutes he stands up and leads you to his gravel-covered driveway. He picks up a stone and hands it to you.

"Okay, spit on it and throw it over your right shoulder," he says. "Then don't look back."

Mister Johnny has removed many a wart that way. I had a great uncle with the same power. Only he used a slightly different method. After he rubbed on my wart, he made me bury a dishrag in the backyard.

That way works, too.

Q & A *R.B. Summitt*

Husband, 1980–present

Q: *What makes Pat so competitive?*
R.B. SUMMITT: *I think she had to survive an extremely tough, silent, demanding father, combined with three brothers who gave her no quarter, even when she was the baby. It caused her to never feel safe or satisfied unless "they," all the demons, had been soundly beaten. When you are talking to a deaf person, you keep raising your voice until you can be heard. In this case Pat had to really do something to get any comment, let alone praise, from her dad or her brothers. An individual either gets tougher in that environment, or succumbs to it.*

Q: *Is that competitiveness hard to live with?*
R.B. SUMMITT: *At times, but the positives far exceed the negatives, because that competitiveness builds strength into a relationship. And it helps if you're competitive too. What I've always understood is that competitiveness is first cousin to leadership. Look, breaking the trail is hard. You have to be competitive to do it. I used to laugh because they paid her so little, and she loved it so much. It's difficult for a lot of folks to understand the fulfillment. But you like to think you knew what you were doing when you picked your partner. A lot of people thought I was crazy, or I had no sense, or I was just blind in love. Now I think people are beginning to realize she's a whole lot of person.*

X

Be a
Competitor

I wear two or three gold rings on my right hand, and every
year, they are flattened by the end of the season. I like to kneel or crouch
on the floor during games, and at least once during the course of a forty-
minute contest, you will hear a loud whack from the sidelines. That's me.
I have just slammed my hand down on the hardwood floor of the basket-
ball court. I do it so hard and so often that by the end of March my rings
are pancaked. They're practically square. I have to send them to a jeweler
to be fixed.

You're talking to somebody who would fight a bear with a switch. I'm a
competitor. I'm liable to take you on in just about anything, whether
cooking, or jogging, or arm wrestling. A few years ago, I was driving to
Sneedville, Tennessee, when I understood that I wasn't exactly average in
this regard. I realized that day just how competitive I could be. I was on a

banquet swing from town to town. I would pull into a small town and give a fund-raising speech to the local Tennessee supporters, talking up our program. Afterward I would eat practically the same meal at every stop.

On this trip one of our former athletic directors, Gloria Ray, was with me. Sneedville is a small town near the Kentucky border. But they promised to put on a big spread for us. So we had that to look forward to.

We were punchy and bored from driving for two hours straight, when, out of pure idleness, I wondered aloud what was for supper in Sneedville.

"What do you suppose they'll feed us?" I asked Gloria.

"Probably roast beef," she said wearily.

I considered that for a moment. Then I said, "No. Ham."

"It's bound to be roast beef," Gloria repeated.

"Want to bet?" I said, bridling.

"Okay," she said.

"Let's bet on the side dishes, too," I said.

Gloria thought about that.

"Peas," she said.

"Green beans," I shot back.

"Twice-baked potatoes," she said.

"Mashed," I retorted.

We bet on every single dish, down to dessert.

"Pie," she said.

"Cobbler," I answered.

An hour or so later, we pulled into Sneedville. There must have been twenty-five people standing around, waiting for us to arrive. I put the car in park, and Gloria and I jumped out.

But before anyone could greet us, we both yelled out, "What's for dinner?!"

Competitiveness is not always compatible with good manners, as I have just illustrated. It's not the most sociable quality you can possess. People won't always like you for it; it won't win you a lot of friends and dates. If being well-liked is your aim, I can't help you.

But competitiveness is what separates achievers from the average.

Only by learning to compete can you discover just how much you are capable of achieving. Trust me, you have more within you than you realize. Competition is one of the great tools for exploring yourself, and surprising yourself. Too many people elect to be average, out of timidity. As I look around, I see scores of underachievers. The world is full of them. The reason so many people underachieve, instead of overachieve, is simply because they are afraid to make a mistake, or to fail, or to be wrong. They're afraid to find out what's inside of them.

Competitiveness is the opposite of complacency. It's disquieting and uncomfortable. It requires commitment, and risk, and soul-searching. When you choose to compete, you take a huge gamble. You might just lose. You might just have to admit, "That's the best I can do."

I've known a lot of young women who were reluctant to compete. They either wanted to be liked, or, worse, they felt it was unladylike. I've spent the better part of my career trying to convince them otherwise. For instance, it seemed like I spent half of the 1987 season teaching our team to throw away their good manners on the court.

They were so nice, they drove me crazy. They would bump into each other, and say, "Excuse me."

I told them, "Ya'll are too nice. You're way too nice to each other. When you score it should be, 'in your face.' "

I got so sick of seeing our players be polite on the court that I decided to do something about it. We got some big padded cushions, similar to tackling dummies. Mickie and Holly held them up and used them to push our players around. They would bump and shove our post people in the middle, to accustom them to uninhibited contact.

When they complained, I called them "sissies."

"Bunch of babies," I said, sneering. "Sissies. *Nice* girls."

One player who was especially well-mannered was Shelley Sexton. "You know what happens to nice girls?" I said. "They finish last."

Three months later Shelley came off the court in the closing seconds of the NCAA championship game, our 67–44 victory over Louisiana Tech.

"See, nice girls don't always finish last," she told me.

I kind of liked it when she said that. It showed a competitive spirit.

It's not only important to compete, it's also important to compete against the best. You have to set high goals in order to achieve. That's why we routinely require *over*achievement at Tennessee. We don't always get it. But my experience is that when you ask for a lot, you just might get some of it.

At Tennessee, we expect to go to the Final Four. Every player who has stayed here for four years has been to the Final Four at least once in her career. The reason we get there so often is because we demand it, and we say it out loud.

We don't get there by saying, "We'd just like to win fifteen games."

It's my experience that people rise to the level of their own expectations and of the competition they seek out. For that reason our teams practice against male players almost every day. Day in and day out, they go up against men who outweigh them and who can outjump them. I tell our players, "The hardest thing that you're going to face is practice." When I was a graduate teaching assistant, I would recruit men from the physical education classes I taught to come and work out with us. Why? I wanted to simulate tougher, bigger teams in scrimmages. If you can get by a guy who's 6-foot-6 and 250 pounds, then you aren't likely to have a problem with a woman who's 6-foot-2 and 150 pounds.

I got the idea of practicing against men from Billie Moore, the Olympic coach in 1976. Billie was the first woman to ever speak to me harshly, or to drive me. I have never in my life had to condition and train at such a level of intensity or under such demands. I have never faced anything like her, before or since. You could not please her. In this day and age, people think that negative reinforcement is not politically correct. But Billie taught me how to get the most out of myself. I got my aggressive verbal and physical style from Billie.

Billie tells a story about me, when I was training with the U.S. team. She was the first women's coach I knew who used to make us scrimmage against guys, because she felt it would better prepare us for international play. We were aware that in the Olympics, we would have to guard a 7-foot-2 inch Russian center named Uliana Seminova. Now, I am no midget; I am 5-foot-11. But I had little chance of succeeding against Seminova. We never did solve the problem; we got the silver and the Russians got the gold. But it made me a competitor.

One afternoon Billie saw me getting pushed around by my male scrimmage partner. She started yelling in my face, "Put a body on that guy."

She claims that the next trip down the floor, I put him in the sixth row.

First they tell me to lose 15 pounds and I lose 27. Then I put a guy in the bleachers. Are you starting to see a pattern of excess here?

I ask our players to give more of themselves than they think is possible. I know they have more inside of them. I *know* it. That's why I set such high standards for them physically. I want them to learn how to dig deeper.

By doing things when you are too tired, by pushing yourself farther than you thought you could—like running the track after a two-hour practice—you become a competitor. Each time you go beyond your perceived limit, you become mentally stronger.

You think, *I'm a little tougher than I thought.*

The next time you have stretched yourself, try this: Think, *Well, maybe I can go even further.*

And after that, if you have continued working, think, *I wonder if I have a little more in me?*

Pretty soon, you are exploring your real depths.

My demands on Abby Conklin were extreme. I admit it. But nobody had ever asked anything of her before. No one had really tested her. So I tested her. And before she left Tennessee, she knew how much she had in her.

Abby's father didn't believe she would make it at Tennessee. As a high school senior in 1992, Abby had a choice between Tennessee and Purdue. Her dad, Harlo, kept subtly pushing her toward Purdue.

Harlo owns his own nursery in Charlestown, Indiana. At the end of every day, he sits up on his wooden porch and relaxes. One evening, Abby got so tired of hearing him talk up Purdue and run down Tennessee, that she decided to confront him about it. She sat herself down next to him.

She said, "Dad, why are you pushing me so hard not to go to Tennessee?"

He said, "Babe, to be honest, I don't think you're good enough to play for them."

Abby just got up and walked away from him without saying a word. But she was upset. She called me and told me about the conversation. So I got on a plane and flew to Indiana.

I sat with Harlo on his porch.

"Harlo, what's your concern?" I said. "Why don't you want Abby to go to Tennessee?"

"To tell you the truth, Pat," he said, "I think she's a step too slow for you."

"Harlo," I said. "Would I come up here and tell you how to grow flowers?"

He shook his head.

"All right then," I said. "What makes you think I need you to tell me how to recruit?"

Harlo just stared at me.

"Why don't you let me make the decision about Abby?" I said. "I wouldn't dare come in here and tell you how to run your greenhouse. I wouldn't tell you what to plant or what to sell. And I wouldn't come all the way to Charlestown, Indiana, to recruit someone to sit on my bench."

So Abby decided to come to Tennessee. Her freshman year, she almost transferred, I got on her so bad. "I know what you're thinking," I said. "You're thinking about transferring." Abby just looked at me, like, *How does she know?*

Abby struggled with self-doubt a lot. I always felt that I had to pull something out of her. I'm not sure that I always did the best job with her. I tried. I think I was so hard on her just to get her to fight back, and not to give up. But I do know she grew into a competitor. The Predictive Index© charts competitiveness. It shows you a graph. Abby Conklin's competitiveness rose three points in her junior year, from ten to thirteen.

By her junior year, Abby was an indispensable part of the team that won the first of our back-to-back national championships, upsetting Georgia and the college Player of the Year, Saudia Roundtree, in the NCAA 1996 championship game. Harlo was in the Charlotte Coliseum that night. He apologized to Abby right there in the stands, with tears streaming down his face.

It's a funny thing, but Abby never wore that first championship ring she won. All during her senior year, she hardly ever put it on. She was self-conscious about it. Through the ups and downs of her awful-wonderful '97 season, when I was so tough on her, she rarely wore it. You'd ask her where her ring was, and she'd say, "It's home on my dresser." It was like she didn't think she deserved it. Or maybe she didn't want to be complacent.

But Abby has two rings now. And she wears them all the time. She says she *wants* people to see them. She wants them to know she comes from the Tennessee program. She says it's a respect thing. It stamps her as a disciplined player, a proven winner, and a competitor.

A while back, I got a message on my answering machine from Abby. This is the last story I'm going to tell about her, because it's probably time we both move on. Which, I want you to know, is not at all an easy thing to do. I don't just blithely send our players off into the world with a graduation day snapshot and a handshake, and forget about them.

Abby is off playing for the Atlanta Glory now. She's a struggling rookie, but she's doing pretty well, even so. The other day when I got to my office, she had left a funny, rambling message for me. Abby has a high-pitched, semipermanently hoarse voice that is just naturally comical. I couldn't help grinning as I heard her voice, and I settled down in my chair to listen to her.

"Okaaaaay," Abby drawled. "I admit it. I miss Tennessee. Do you believe it? So what I'm calling to say is, can I come back now?"

She went on for a while, telling me about what she was doing and how she was playing. At the end she said, "So, anyway, I just wanted to tell you I was thinking about you."

After Abby's voice clicked off, I sat there thinking about her, too.

Then I hit the save button.

I kept it for a while. I wanted to play it for our assistant coaches, and I liked listening to it myself. Abby's voice on that machine sounded awfully young. But it was a competitor's voice. And it was the voice of someone I had come full circle with. It reminded me of everything I did right, and wrong, as her coach.

When you've shared four embattled years with someone, like I did with Abby—not to mention winning two national championships—when you've alternately loved her to death and tongue-lashed her, thrown a glass of water across the room on her account, and generally watched her grow up, you feel more than mere affection for her. Something of her abides in you.

Abby was brave. I have a real heart for the players who choose to come to Tennessee, because they make an ambitious choice. Some great young players are afraid to come here. The Tennessee reputation has intimidated them and been blown out of proportion in their minds. They are afraid they won't get enough playing time, or that they won't measure up. They are afraid of failure, and they are afraid of commitment. That's why I love the competitive spirit of a player like Abby Conklin. Abby wasn't sure of what she had in her. But Abby *reached*.

It's why I think a lot of Tamika Catchings, the Naismith Award winner for High School Player of the Year in 1997. Tamika signed on with us, even though we already had Chamique Holdsclaw. The question mark was, if you have Holdsclaw, do you have room for Catchings? Well, you make room for Catchings. But a lot of people told her during the recruiting process, "You're going to play behind Chamique."

Tamika had to *see herself* as being able to play here. She had to be enough of a competitor to say, "I'm going to prove I can play at Tennessee."

A competitor continually sets new goals. He feels the need to keep raising the bar. If the first goal is to make the team, and he achieves it, he immediately resets the goal to: I want to be a starter.

Our freshman class of '97 may be the most competitive group we've had at Tennessee yet. They were not a part of the last two titles. They came in wanting one of their *own*. All four of those players, Catchings, Semeka Randall, Kristen "Ace" Clement, and Teresa Geter, won state titles in high school. They know how to play in pressure situations and win championships. They've already learned a couple of things about themselves, but they want to learn more. They understand our standards, they know how tough it is, and they *still* want to come here. That means a lot to me.

One afternoon not long ago, I was particularly tough on Teresa Geter in practice. She got a little weepy. Afterward, we sat down and talked.

I said, "Teresa, if you want me to back off, tell me. Tell me right now, and I will."

Teresa looked back at me, and she said, "No, stay on me. Stay on me."

My kind of player.

● ● ●

I've had more experience with physical pain than most men. I've been paddled and whipped and hit so hard it lifted me off the ground. I've had my jaw dislocated, and I've blown out my knee, and I've given birth.

When I was nine, I accidentally drove a rusty nail through my foot. I was messing around with my brothers in the barnyard, and I jumped on an old plank. That nail rammed straight through my foot and went through the top of my sneaker. I looked down and saw it coming up out of my shoe.

My dad said, "She doesn't need to go to the doctor." But my mother insisted. I had a hole all the way through my foot. The doctor put some disinfectant on a needle, and then ran the needle through the hole, while I sat there with tears running down my face. I got a tetanus shot, too.

I hobbled around and did farm work on that foot. I didn't miss a day of school, either. In fact, I didn't miss a single day in twelve years. I set the all-time attendance record at Ashland City High. Rain or shine. I probably gave everyone in the class measles and chicken pox. Then I got to college. One morning I slept through my English class. I started crying because I had never missed a class before.

At home I fought for food at the dinner table with three strapping older brothers. We fought over the last piece of chicken. My brothers gave me no sympathy. Neither they nor my father had any idea of what to do with me, the fourth child and the first girl in the family of a cash-poor farmer. So they treated me like one of the boys or farmhands. My mother was busy working and trying to feed us all. She didn't have the time or the means to play dress-up with a little girl.

Only recently have sports audiences become accustomed to watching women explore their physical limits in competitive arenas, and deal with issues like playing with pain. A tremendous cultural shift has taken place in just the last twenty-five years, allowing us to run, jump, and throw without being accused of being unfeminine. We're just starting out, really. But I've known all along that women are capable of backbreaking manual labor and of withstanding the depths of physical pain.

Playing basketball in that hayloft, my brothers were out for blood. They taught me not to cry, and they taught me how to arm wrestle. I was the best fifth-grade arm wrestler in my class. You beat someone who is stronger than you by getting a jump on them. You give them a big jolt to start, and then you hold your ground. If you can hold steady, you'll wear them out. I beat almost every boy in school that way. There was only one kid who could take me down, an eighth-grader who weighed about two hundred pounds.

So don't tell me what I can or cannot do.

All of that arm wrestling taught me something: You can't always be the strongest or most talented or most gifted person in the room, but you *can* be the most competitive. There are bound to be days when you run into someone who is better than you. What can you do about it? You can compete, that's what. You can put forth so much effort that you cut your opponent down to size and force him to play below his own abilities.

Competitiveness allows you to influence your opponent.

We've had some great competitors, who were not great athletes, at Tennessee:

Sheila Frost was never an All American. She was just a steady presence in the middle. But during our run to our first national championship in 1987, she made the All Final Four tournament team.

Lea Henry was a tiny point guard, no bigger than 5-foot-4¾. She made the Olympic team in 1984 and brought home a gold medal.

Lisa Harrison was just a sophomore in '91, when we won our third national championship. She had twenty-five rebounds in two Final Four games.

There is always someone better than you. Whatever it is that you do for a living, chances are, you will run into a situation in which you are not as talented as the person next to you. That's when being a competitor can make a difference in your fortunes.

When I was trying to make the Olympic team, I knew there were people who were better than me. And younger. So I had to influence my opponents. During the trials I had to go one-on-one against Cindy Brogdon, who would go on to make the 1976 Olympic team and become a two-time All American at Tennessee.

There were twenty-four people trying out for the Olympic squad, and fourteen of them were forwards, like me. Only four would be selected. The coaches made us play a series of one-on-one contests to narrow the roster. I drew Cindy.

I'll tell you straight out, you wouldn't believe how superior a player Cindy Brogdon was to me. She never averaged fewer than twenty points in her collegiate career. But if I wanted to be on the Olympic team, I had to find a way to beat her, to force her to play below her norm. In a shooting contest, I wasn't going to outscore her. But I knew I could influence her on the defensive end. I could influence her ability to play offensive basketball.

Here's what I mean by the phrase "influence your opponent." In going up against a great offensive player like Cindy, I knew she couldn't score as well as going left. What I could do was force her to use her weaker hand and limit her to one shot. What I could do to stop her was to make her work so hard to get the ball that she'd be worn out just getting into position, before she ever took a shot.

I won, 5–0.

Influencing the opponent is why I stress defense at Tennessee. Everybody knows we get after it. We're not a passive defensive team. We're the aggressor. I have to drum our defensive philosophy into our players, and it's the least fun part of the day. People don't naturally want to play defense. It's tough, and it takes a long time to teach. I have to convince them of its importance year in and year out. Offense sells tickets, defense wins games, rebounds win championships.

Think of it this way. If you're driving down the street, and there's a roadblock, you have to make a detour. People will sometimes panic when they can't go the way they usually do.

That's the point of great defense. It makes people uncomfortable. Influencing your opponent is a matter of forcing them to do something they'd rather not, of making them go around instead of taking the easy path.

The reason I'm a stickler for defense, the reason I've always made it such a priority is that it is not a matter of talent, it's a matter of effort. It's within any team's power to be a great defensive team. You shouldn't ever have an off night on defense. There are times when the ball doesn't go in the hole offensively because you are cold or the luck isn't running your way. But defense is purely a matter of attitude. It's within your control.

When two teams are evenly matched, the hustle plays can win it. The defense, the rebounds, and the loose balls can decide the outcome. The team that makes the first effort, and the extra effort, will win.

One of the best competitors and defensive players Tennessee ever had was Melissa McCray. But I didn't know it at first. I went to see Melissa play in high school one night in Johnson City, Tennessee, and I had to send R.B. to buy a program, because I couldn't find her. Normally, the great ones find you. You walk in and sit down, and they're so good, they stand out. But I couldn't find her. I said to R.B., "Go get a program, I don't want to ask." The head coach at the University of Tennessee couldn't go to Johnson City and ask, "Which one's Melissa?" R.B. bought a program, and I found out which one she was, and I wasn't impressed at all.

But a few weeks later, I saw Melissa in the Tennessee State Tournament, and she scored thirty-eight points. Now I was sweating. I couldn't get to the phone fast enough to offer her a scholarship. I realized her talents weren't always obvious; she just took what was there, and no more. But she was the kind of competitor you seek out. I could tell, because she loved to play defense.

The biggest individual honor Melissa would win in her career was making second team All-SEC. But she became key in winning the NCAA championship in Tacoma in 1989, during her senior year. In the Final Four semifinal game, we had to play Maryland, the best offensive team in the country. The Terrapins came in shooting 54 percent from the floor. They were an absolute offensive machine.

We knew that the only way we could win that game was to slow them down defensively. We had to influence the opponent.

Maryland's biggest threat was a brilliant quick-footed guard named Deana Tate. I put Melissa on her. Melissa had guarded the best players in the country all season long. But Tate was lightning quick. In the first half, she ate Melissa alive. Melissa was not her typical intense self. She was back on her heels, instead of on her toes. She was shocked at how quick Tate was, and as a result, she was too cautious, trying to contain her instead of attacking. She needed to either give all, or nothing.

Very seldom in four years had I ever raised my voice at Melissa, because she always gave so much effort. She was a no-nonsense player, and a great leader, one of the best we ever had. But that night I stalked into the locker room at halftime, and I went after her.

I was taking a chance. But I had to get some kind of response out of her. So I talked to her at the top of my lungs.

"You better get with it," I snapped. "Something has to happen. You, of all players. Our best defender isn't ready to defend. That's just great. This team asked you to get out there and guard her, and you've stunk it up."

I spoke directly to Melissa, not the whole group. I singled her out. I knew which button to push. The thing Melissa cared about more than anything in the world was what her teammates thought of her. She didn't want to be the person who cost us the title. So I acted like if we lost, it would be her *personal* fault. As I talked, I could see every competitive bone in her body start to quiver. I continued to work on her throughout halftime. Everyone else just took notes.

Melissa handled it. When we left that locker room, she was determined to prove me wrong. She could have been almost dead, but Tate was not going to be the player who won the game for Maryland.

Tate had six points in the second half. She was not a factor. We went on to win that game, 77–65. It put us in the position to win the national championship over Auburn, which we did.

Another great competitor for us was Holly Warlick. I was never harder on a player than I was on Holly. But with her deeply competitive nature, she turned every emotion into positive energy. Holly really came to Tennessee on a track scholarship. She was a state champion in the 400 meters who walked on to the basketball team. As a freshman she ended up going to the national championships in both sports. Holly would exhaust herself from working out at both sports, and when she was most tired, I would tell her, "Reach down. You can get more. Don't tell me you've reached down as far as you can go."

Because Holly showed such a competitive spirit, I put a lot on her. I made her feel like she always had to do more than anybody else. And she never complained—she'd just go about her business. To this day I can heap as much on her as on any member of our staff.

When Holly was an undergraduate, I asked her to help me recruit a 6-foot-5 post player named Cindy Noble. When Cindy came to visit campus, Holly acted as her hostess. Cindy narrowed her decision to Tennessee and Ohio State, but at the last minute, she signed with the Buckeyes. Holly was furious.

Well, the next season Ohio State came to Knoxville to play us, with Cindy Noble.

Holly had ten steals in the game.

Cindy Noble transferred to Tennessee after her freshman year.

You have to love your adversaries. They make you better. They force you to improve, to stretch your capacities. Competitors respond to a challenge from their opponents, and to negative motivation as well as to positive. Competitors seek revenge for losses. They crave a compliment if they haven't gotten one. They are constantly asking, "Did I do the right thing? Was I was good enough?" Competitors want to prove everyone else wrong. They want to show skeptics "I am better than this. I am a winner."

If you want to be the best, you have to compete against the best, even if it means risking a loss. Why seek out weak competition? That's why we play such exhausting, competitive schedules at Tennessee. We routinely schedule twenty or more games a season against ranked opponents, because it makes us so much better in the end. En route to winning the NCAA national championship in Charlotte in 1996, we met a grand total of twenty-five ranked opponents in thirty-six games. The secret to our success in the post season is that we have already played most of the teams we will face. Frequently we have lost to them earlier in the season and are seeking competitive revenge.

There was no better example of loving our competitors than the '97 Tennessee team. Even now, I'm still trying to explain how that team won a national championship. There have been more talented Tennessee teams, no question. We had two freshmen and two sophomores among our first seven players. But what the '97 group responded to in the end was their brutal schedule—we played twenty-four of the top twenty-five teams in the nation. And this '97 group responded to constant predictions that they couldn't win it all. When we finally got to the NCAA tournament, they asked themselves, well, why not?

The truth is, we knew we had a chance the moment we learned we would face Connecticut in the regionals. Remember, Connecticut had killed us, 72–57, during the regular season. We had played so lousy that we racked up a season low for points and shooting percentage. But when I received the NCAA draw, I walked straight into our locker room.

I said, "Well, we're in the bracket with Connecticut. We'll meet 'em in the regional finals in Iowa. Provided we take care of business, one game at a time."

Our team was *excited* that we were in that bracket. Kellie Jolly said straight out, "We're going to beat UConn, and go to the Final Four."

Why? Because there wasn't a team we respected more than UConn. It got our competitive hackles up. We have a great rivalry with that team. I like and respect the Connecticut coach, Geno Auriemma. We recruit a lot of the same players. Our games are usually close and hard fought.

We had a 1–4 record against UConn going into that game. And we couldn't wait.

We knew they would have the pressure on them, because they were top-ranked and unbeaten. I said to our players, "You know, Connecticut is going to be thirty-three and oh when they face us."

Then I said, "I like our chances."

You could almost see the competitiveness rising in the Lady Vols. They were sick of hearing about what a disappointing team they were. They'd go to the mall, and people would say, "What's wrong with you guys?" To be honest, they had been underachievers for most of the season.

But against UConn, it was like all of their dormant competitiveness awoke. The lion started roaring at the bars of the cage.

A couple of days after the draw came out, a Connecticut newspaper labeled us "a pretender." Everyone who saw it sent it to us.

It was wonderful.

I announced to our team cheerfully, "We're pretenders."

I put it up on the locker room wall. After that, I didn't have to motivate them anymore. All I had to do was show them that clipping.

We won, 91–81.

Your competitors make you better. Having worthy adversaries stimulates your work ethic, and brings out qualities you may not have known you had. So don't resent them.

You should love your competitors. And you should thank them.

●　●　●

Competitors are essentially selfish.

I admit it. If I want something, I'm going to get it, and I lose sight of everyone and everything around me in pursuit of it. Competitors have a tendency to shy away from self-examination, because it can distract from that single-minded focus. So while I believe that competition is basically healthy and good, I also know that it is not easy on the people around me.

You may feel that competition conflicts with being a good, compassionate person. I have my own inner conflict on the subject.

But ask yourself, what are competitive instincts good for? Why were we given them? I believe that they are meant to help us battle adversity, to help us endure difficult situations, to help us get up when we've been knocked down, and to help us prevail over the blows that life deals us. Really, when I teach basketball, I am trying to teach our players about life.

There is a time and a place to be a competitor. I've had to learn to stow my competitive instincts at the office at the end of the day, because they are hard on my marriage. R.B. and I used to play racquetball all the time. I taught him how to play, and we would go into the basement of Alumni Gym and wail away with those rackets until we were both drenched in sweat. You could hear our sneakers squish when we walked. At first I beat him like a drum.

I was perfectly happy with that arrangement.

But then R.B. got better at it. He started beating me. And I didn't like it a bit. I discovered that I couldn't play racquetball with him and then go home and cook his dinner. If I lost, it made me tense. I couldn't separate the two. Finally, we had to quit playing.

Lately, we've started playing golf. We'll see how that goes.

There are times I have to ask myself if I'm too tough on the young women in our program. I've snarled at them pretty good, with the intention of making them competitors. I've walked out of practice and told our staff, "I was just too hard today." My staff is a good barometer. They will tell me, "Yes, you were too tough, or "No, they needed it."

So I struggle to keep my competitiveness in perspective and in the right place. But I don't ever want to lose it, or be self-conscious about it, because it has served me so well in surviving tough times. And I know that the young women who play for us may need it in their lives at some point down the road.

Competitiveness is not meant for peacetime. But it's an invaluable quality in coping with misfortune. Channeled correctly, you can use it to battle all sorts of hardship in your life, not just the athletic kind, or the corporate kind, or the managerial kind.

In Carla McGhee's case, her competitiveness literally helped her survive. When Carla had her car wreck, she and I learned about the real value of competitiveness, together.

In 1987, the fall of Carla's sophomore year, she was in a terrible collision. She and a friend were driving on the outskirts of town when a Jeep pulled out in front of them. They plowed into the jeep, and the force of the wreck sent Carla into the windshield. I was in Colorado Springs at an Amateur Basketball Association meeting when I got the news. I flew home and went right to the hospital.

Carla was so cut up and shattered and swollen I barely recognized her. She had broken bones all over her body. At first the doctors were just worried about keeping her alive. It was a life-and-death situation.

Once Carla was stable, they said she wouldn't be able to run again. They were worried about whether she would be able to walk. They told me, and they told her mother, that they didn't see how she would ever be able to play basketball.

"Carla," I said, "I don't care if you ever pick up a ball again. I just want you to be okay."

Carla couldn't believe I said that. Most people treated her as a ballplayer first, and a person second. She didn't know until that moment how much I cared about her.

I went to see her every day. I told her, "Just promise me you'll get your degree. Don't let this ruin your life." I also told her she had her scholarship for as long as she needed it.

But Carla already had what she needed: She had the drive to get through her long, difficult rehabilitation. It was a long road back. She had broken her hip and her jaw and damaged her voice box, among other things.

A year later, she was running.

Carla came back out to basketball practice. I was worried about her at first. "Don't push it," I said. But Carla had a sense of urgency. She needed to get back on the court, and to be a part of the Lady Vol team again.

As Carla began practicing, she ran up and down the court well enough, but she was fragile. She was clearly suffering from some lingering psychological effects of the wreck. She was scared to death of physical contact. Every time she drove the lane, she flinched.

I could see it, standing on the sidelines. Carla would move into the paint—and close her eyes. It broke my heart, because prior to the accident, she had been the player most willing to take a charge and get fired up.

Carla had had so many injuries to her face that she was gun shy. "I was afraid something in me would break again," she said later. But at the time, she wasn't really aware of it. We had to sit her down and make her watch herself on tape. Even after she saw it, she had a hard time conquering her fear. She had to work every day on regaining her physical and mental toughness.

I'm not sure what finally made the difference, other than Carla's sheer competitive spirit. I know I gave her a few tongue-lashings. I finally told her, "Either play, or don't play. If you're going to be out here, then play full out." One morning, Carla woke up tough again. She was a survivor.

Ten years later, Carla stood on a medal podium in Atlanta, with a gold medal around her neck. Usually, I save my deeper emotions for things other than basketball. But when I watched Carla play as a member of the 1996 Olympic team in Atlanta, I couldn't help but think about the long journey she had made, and I got tears in my eyes.

When you choose to be a competitor, you choose to be a survivor.

When you choose to compete, you make the conscious decision to find out what your real limits are, not just what you *think* they are. Competition trains you to accept risk and to endure setbacks. By embracing it, you can enhance your life. But it will also pull you through those painful, frightening everyday battles we all have to face at one time or another.

Ask yourself, are you a competitor? Are you selecting weak competition, or strong? Are you settling for less, or reaching for more? When you compete, refuse to limit yourself. Elect to overachieve instead of under-achieve. Believe me, you will surprise yourself.

Want to bet?

Q & A   *Bridgette Gordon*

Forward, two-time All American, 1988, 1989; Member, national champi-onship teams, 1987, 1989; Olympic gold medalist, 1988; Sacramento Monarchs, WNBA

Q: You almost didn't go to Tennessee, right?
BRIDGETTE GORDON: Yeah. I changed my mind at the last minute. I really wanted to go to Tennessee, but I verbally committed to Florida, because I was getting pressure to stay in-state. Then the phone rang, and it was Pat. She said, "Bridgette Gordon, what *are* you doing?" I could see her big blue eyes staring me down over the phone. I changed my mind right then and there.

Q: Was it the right decision?
BRIDGETTE GORDON: It was wild how much I matured there. I mean, I grew. I became wiser. I became a woman. Now I just laugh and say, "Pat was right. Pat was right."

Q: But she almost sent you home as a freshman, didn't she?
BRIDGETTE GORDON: We were playing a tournament in Hawaii, and she got my report card. My grade point average was 0.0 because I hadn't paid my library fines. But she thought I was failing. There was a knock on my door at midnight. Mickie and Holly said, "Pat wants to see you. Right now." So I went down to her room, and she said, "Bridgette Gordon, I ought to send you home on a raft with a slow leak."

XI

Change Is a Must

My husband won't part with his recliner. It's an old plaid chair worn so thin I can't bear to look at it. Not long ago, I tried to get rid of it. I did. I plotted its demise. While we were remodeling our house, we underwent a good deal of change. Fortunately R.B. and I are still on speaking terms, but the recliner remains a sore subject. What happened was, our interior decorator, Pat Lauer, wanted to redo the living room, replacing R.B.'s chair in the process. I thought this was a fine idea. I took the measurements on that old recliner and stowed it in the garage. But the decorator couldn't find anything like it—possibly because it was so outdated. Instead, we bought two brand-new recliners and covered them in a nice matching fabric. Well, he hated his. He said it was uncomfortable. It hit his neck wrong. We fussed over it, until I gave up. We had to dig the old one out of the garage, carry it back into the house, and put it downstairs in our den.

A couple of days later, he fell soundly asleep in the *new* recliner.

We all resist change. Change is the opposite of security and familiarity. R.B.'s chair was something familiar to cling to when everything else in the house was in upheaval. Even when you know you need to change, even when you *want* to change, it's hard to do. Why? Because it forces you out of your comfortable chair.

Change is good. It's underrated. It's got a bad name.

How can you grow, if you never change? Without changing something almost every year, Tennessee would never have won five national championships. We'd still be losing the big one. And without accepting some pretty dramatic changes in my own life, I wouldn't be the head coach of the Lady Vols. This chapter isn't about being born self-improved. I wasn't.

When I went off to college at the University of Tennessee-Martin, I left my family and high school friends behind for the first time in my life. Even though Martin was only a couple of hours away from Henrietta, it was a huge passage for a country girl. I was what you'd call a homebody. I had never traveled away from the farm, except for one week when I went off to 4-H camp—and even then I got homesick.

When I arrived at Martin, I found a reason to run home the very first weekend. I got a ride to Henrietta and walked in the door with my dirty laundry under my arm.

My dad said, "What are you doing here?"

I explained that I had just felt like coming home. But the real reason I'd come back was because I was scared, and he knew it.

He said, "Look. I don't want you on the road every weekend. And when you do come home again, don't bring your dirty clothes with you."

It was his way of saying "Stay there and grow up."

So I went back to Martin, and I stayed. It was pretty frightening. I didn't have a single connection on that campus other than the volleyball and basketball teams. I stayed in my room, and I went to class. I had never heard of fraternities and sororities. Fortunately a number of my teammates belonged to the Chi Omega sorority, which broadened my social horizons. That first spring, they convinced me to join. I'll tell you straight out, I was intimidated by that sorority. But I also knew I was ready for a change. I was tired of being known only as a tomboy.

I'd never really worn makeup, and my idea of a shopping spree was to buy a pair of striped pants at K-Mart. I really hadn't ever thought about how I sounded when I opened my mouth to speak.

I was in sore need of some social graces. Just imagine a 5-foot-11 teenager with a thick middle-Tennessee accent, so shy and modest she dressed in the closet. That was me. My old sorority sisters love to reminisce about how country I was. My college roommate and Chi Omega sister Esther Stubblefield Hubbard can tease me pretty good.

She claims I arrived at school with what I referred to as a "soup case." That's what I called my suitcase.

Esther says that one afternoon I burst through the door of our room and announced, "I done blowed four dollars, and I don't know how!"

I fought a running battle with embarrassment and insecurity every day. But I learned that overcoming fear is the most broadening thing in the world, if you make yourself do it. In the end the sorority was one of the best things that ever happened to me.

I grew more confident, I lost my shyness, and I became one of the livelier members of the sorority. I was the sort who liked to pull the fire alarm on a bet. The funniest part was, nobody believed I was capable of getting into trouble. One night, I pulled the main electrical switch in our dormitory. I completely blacked out Clement Hall.

It was a Sunday, and they had to get the electrician out of church.

Mrs. Bradberry, our house mother, said to me, "Pat, you've got to find out who did this."

"Oh, I don't think I could tell on anybody," I said demurely.

"You can tell me," she said.

"Miz B," I said. "Please don't make me tell you who did this."

In my defense, other people made me do these things. They would dare me. I would do anything on a dare. One night I drove on the sidewalk in my '67 red Plymouth. I got called into the dean's office for that one, but I learned to talk my way out of things. When you try to be accepted, you do some interesting things. That's youth. Eventually, you grow up and make good decisions instead of silly ones. Like having the sense to turn down a dare.

After a while, when I would go home to Henrietta, my old friends would comment on how I'd changed. I was obviously taking care of my appearance. I wore makeup. I was aware of my grammar, and I tried to speak correctly.

But I hated to admit it. When my old friends said to me, "Boy, you've changed," I got defensive. I'd reply, "No I haven't." As badly as I wanted to become someone new, I resisted saying it aloud. I viewed it as a sign of weakness if I had changed, no matter how obviously I was trying to alter my manners and appearance.

Today, if someone tells me I've changed, I take it as a compliment. The plain fact is, without change, the game of women's basketball would never have grown, nor I with it. We needed change. As an undergraduate at Martin, I didn't even have a proper basketball uniform. We wore sleeveless white polyester shirts with hand-sewn numerals. Since I couldn't sew, I used safety pins. On road trips we had limited money for hotels. We slept four to a room, and once we even slept in the gym on mats.

There is nothing wrong with personal or professional growth, as long as you are strong in who you are and don't lose sight of where you came from. Self-improvement doesn't mean abandoning your old identity. I've never deserted Henrietta, and I never will. But I'm glad I explored more distant boundaries.

When I graduated from Martin, I had to stretch even further. I had to transform myself from a college athlete and sorority girl into a professional woman, overnight. I was lucky to have two older women to convince me I could do it. Bettye Giles, the athletic director at Martin, and my Martin coach, Nadine Gearin, quietly recommended me for the assistant head coach's job and later for the head coach's job at Tennessee, even though I was only twenty-two. And they pushed me into taking it when I hesitated.

It meant leaving everything I knew all over again. Unlike Martin, Knoxville wasn't just a couple of hours from Henrietta. It was across the state, and it was a big city. It meant taking on the responsibilities of an adult in one giant step. When I accepted the job it was like Jekyll and Hyde. I changed from an undergraduate to a grim authoritarian.

I taught three classes, enrolled in three graduate courses, coached the team, and rehabbed my anterior cruciate ligament injury. I had to set priorities, understand time management, and juggle a schedule that went from stressful to overwhelming. It meant being in a leadership role constantly, and making decisions that affected not just me, but other people as well.

But what it really meant was that I was forced to grow up. I had to stop throwing switches and pulling alarms.

In some ways, that was too bad.

●   ●   ●

The funny thing is, as I have matured as a coach, I've gone back to my old alarm-pulling ways. I'm always looking for new ways to disrupt the other team.

My whole strategy is to force the opponent into a state of false emergency. As a sideline coach, I try to short-circuit the opposing bench and set off the alarms. I love it when our opponent has to do the basketball equivalent of calling the electrician out of church.

There is a phrase for it: It's called "changing the tempo," and there is an art to it. But breaking out of old habits or cycles is hard work, and frightening. We resist it out of laziness, or fear, or insecurity. We're afraid it won't work, or we're afraid of what people might say.

The willingness to experiment with change may be the most essential ingredient to success at anything.

For years my mentality was the opposite. I was predictable. I was extremely structured early in my career. The pressure of being such a young head coach made me very conservative, on both ends of the court. I believed, correctly, that every successful organization needed a system. So I had a system. But it was a system with no flexibility—and it was limiting as a result. I had to learn the value of strategic change and the element of surprise.

Back then I practically wanted to control the way our players thought. But basketball is a game of quick, fluid changes. Our players didn't have time to think, *Now what would Pat do in this situation?*

Today, I am a much better teacher. I impart what I know about the game and let them make intelligent decisions on their own. *That's* real teaching.

Not until I had the willingness to change was I a real success as a head coach. In my first few seasons, Tennessee was woefully easy to scout and prepare for. We had exactly one defense and one offense. We were a slow, plodding, methodical half-court team with two stationary posts. We deserved the nickname "corn-fed chicks." We massaged the basketball around the court, incapable of changing our rhythm.

Our predictability worked against us in two ways. Not only were we incapable of altering our strategy, but when people changed up against us, we'd panic. We were inflexible.

Mickie DeMoss accuses me of always doing things the hard way, and it's true. It's especially true in the case of our defense. I was always known as a man-to-man coach. But I was more than that. I was a *stubborn* man-to-man coach. I absolutely refused to play a zone. Until, one day, it got me in trouble.

The basic philosophy behind man defense is that you assign one defensive player to one offensive player and make the other team sweat to get a free shot. It sounds simple, but it's not. It's complicated, because there are a million options to defend. It takes time to teach it, and it's hard work to play it. You have to teach the various ways an offense will try to beat it. You have to teach how to play on and off the ball, and how to handle screens and cuts. You have to drill all game situations and all offensive styles and techniques that teams will use to break your pressure. It forces you to teach the whole game, every day. That's why I believed in it then, and why I still believe in it as our foundation now. But back then, I believed in it at the expense of flexibility.

Man-to-man defense was a principle with me. I liked the fact that it was a tough, disciplined scheme that was hard to learn. To me, a zone was weak. It was too laid back. A zone was easier to play than man defense, and it was easier to teach. Therefore, I regarded it as the lesser option. I was dead wrong.

I finally learned my lesson in a wrenching loss to Mississippi during the 1984 season. Tennessee was the superior team, no question. Our five players were better than their five. Moreover, we were playing on our home court. No way should we have lost that game. But that's exactly what we did, 67–65.

Ole Miss set screens all day long. Basically, they took advantage of our defense and turned it into a two-man game with a simple pick-and-roll. Throughout the game my assistant at the time, Nancy Darsch, kept saying, "Pat, we need to do something."

But I refused to go to a zone. I said, "We're going to win or lose in this defense." In reality, a change would have disrupted Ole Miss and taken them out of their offense. My refusal to change cost us a game.

I was more stubborn than I was smart.

So I learned the hard way. Later I watched the film, and I thought, "Why, oh why, didn't you go to a zone?"

That game made me realize how easy we were to scout. I knew that if I wanted Tennessee to improve, I had to loosen up. Today, I teach pressure man as our basic defensive foundation, but we install zones and change-ups and variations to go along with it. There are several things we can do to give ourselves different looks.

Change is risky. There's no question about it. But ever since that Ole Miss game, it hasn't seemed nearly as risky to me as standing still, or being overcautious. There's no worse feeling than second-guessing yourself after the fact, wondering if there was an adjustment you could or should have made.

In the 1991 NCAA championship game against Virginia, zone defense became an issue for me again. But this time, I made one of the riskier bench moves of my career. Virginia, captained by future Olympian Dawn Staley, led us for most of the game. We were in our usual man-to-man defense.

Throughout the game, Mickie and Holly kept bugging me to change to a zone. Every few minutes, one of them would lean toward me on the bench and try to get me to switch defenses.

"Pat, we need to go to our zone," Mickie would say.

"Not yet," I said.

Another few minutes would go by. Now it was Holly's turn.

"Don't you think we need to go to the zone?" Holly said.

"No," I said. "Not now."

It went on like that the whole game. They were on me constantly. "How about that zone?" they'd say. "Not yet," I'd say. They tapped me on the shoulder and raised their eyebrows at me. I just kept saying, "Not now."

With under two minutes to go, we were down by five points. But we kept our composure and got a couple of rebounds and turnovers, and then Dena Head made two critical free throws to tie the game, which I've already told you about.

Virginia had one last possession. I kept us in our man defense. "Stay between your man and the basket," I told our players. Virginia couldn't score.

We went into overtime, with a huge sigh of relief. As the players trotted over to the bench to get a drink of water, I huddled with Mickie and Holly.

"Okay," I said. "*Now* let's go to the zone."

They just looked at me with dumb amazement. The expressions on their faces said it all. Mickie told me later, she was thinking, *Well, you picked a hell of a time to do it.*

They didn't say a word to me. But their body language said plenty.

I thought, *Well, they finally got their zone. But I guess they don't want it anymore.*

It was a huge risk. It was the very last thing anyone thought I would call—which was exactly the reason I called it. I felt strongly that if we threw a different look at Virginia after they had played against our man defense for forty minutes, we could surprise them. Fortunately, that's exactly what we did. Virginia was affected by the change of pace just long enough for us to get a lead. We hung on and won, 70–67.

When you make a change, you force your opponent to hesitate. She has to adjust, and, in that small interval of time, you can seize an advantage. Success in any field is about who is best able to change fluidly. The better your competition, the more open you should be to change.

Here's another example: In the 1989 Final Four in Tacoma, Washington, against Maryland, I felt we needed to show a different face when the game began. Maryland was a pressing team, and we were a nonpressing team. But when the game started, we pressed. Why? I believe you press a pressing team. It gave them something to think about. It's like starting a fight by coldcocking your opponent.

Fact: Tennessee won its first three championships playing man—our bread-and-butter defense. We've won our last two with changing defenses, a variety of switching schemes. That's indicative of how the game is changing and how we have tried to respond. I'm proud to say we've become less predictable and therefore more difficult to scout.

Hopefully, I am now smarter than I am stubborn.

●   ●   ●

When you make a change, it's tantamount to admitting, "I can do this better." For that reason, some people feel that change is a sign of defeat. To me, it's the ultimate strength.

After our loss to Connecticut in the 1995 NCAA championship game, I decided we needed to study their triple-post offense. I'll tell you what I did about it. I made a change. I flew up to Chicago with our staff, and we spent a day getting tutored in the triple-post offense by Chicago Bulls coaches Phil Jackson and Tex Winter. Then we went home and added some of the triple-post concepts to our own offense.

The result was back-to-back national championships.

Once again, it was defeat that forced me into trying something new. We had suffered a string of losses to UConn, falling behind by 0–3 in the series, and it gnawed at me. I hate to even bring it up. I can't stand thinking about it. But I have to, in order to tell this story. They were simply better than us.

We lost twice to Connecticut in 1995, including a heartbreaker in the national championship game, 70–64, as the Huskies completed their undefeated run with Rebecca Lobo and company. We split meetings with them in 1996, including snapping our home winning streak at sixty-nine games. Then we beat them in a thrilling overtime game at the Final Four in Charlotte, en route to our fourth national championship.

Of all the teams we've faced in the last few years, UConn has been the hardest to defend—and that's the biggest compliment I can bestow on an opponent. It's hard for me, an unyielding defensive-minded coach, to say this, but the Huskies broke us down. They were hard to scout, and seemingly impossible to defend.

When we played UConn, for the first time in my career, I didn't have a handle on what the opposition was doing to us. I would watch film for hours and still not feel certain of what I was seeing. The reason was their sophisticated triple-post offense, which they had borrowed from the Bulls. The triple post, or triangle, as some call it, is a flowing, multifaceted attack that comes at you from all different directions.

I had a choice. I could resent UConn's success. Or I could learn a thing or two from it. I decided to learn.

In order to better defend the Huskies, I knew I had to scout their offensive system. So in September of 1996, I wandered into Al Brown's office, and we started chatting about the triple post. I told Al I felt we needed to learn more about it if we wanted to get a handle on Connecticut. Al mentioned that he knew Tex, one of Phil Jackson's assistant coaches.

"Why don't you call him?" I said. "Ask if we can come up there and learn the offense?"

Al called Tex, who graciously agreed to spend some time with us if we came to Chicago, so Mickie and Al and I got on a plane and headed north. Tex met us in their executive offices and escorted us into a film room.

All of a sudden, Phil Jackson rapped on the door and let himself in. "May I join you?" he asked. We hadn't expected to meet him, much less spend time with him, but Phil, as it turns out, had been watching us from afar. He had seen a couple of our games.

"I watched you on TV," he said. "So you want to talk about the triple post?"

I said we did. Phil walked into the room and began watching film with us. For the next few hours, we watched a series of offensive breakdown tapes and discussed the triple post. I was a sponge. I could not stop asking questions. It was the chance of a lifetime, of course. At the end of the afternoon, my head swirled. I realized I didn't want to just defend the triple post, I wanted to run it.

What I learned from Phil Jackson that day is that he has the capacity to allow people space; he has a patience and a tolerance for individuals, without abandoning his team principles. He lets people be who they want to be within his framework. For me, that's an area where I've had to change. Since that trip, I'm more tolerant than ever before.

As I looked at the triple post, it struck me that it was perfect for Chamique Holdsclaw, who is of Michael Jordan–caliber talent. So it made sense to rethink what we were doing. When you sign great talent, you have to find creative ways to use it. The smartest thing you can do is to adapt the job description if they don't fit your system.

We went home and installed the triple post. In learning it, we not only studied how to run it offensively, but we understood how to defend against it. The result is that we are a more versatile team than we've ever been.

But it's important to realize that our success with it didn't come overnight. It took time and effort for our players to make the change. But gradually we grew more comfortable with it. Since we've gone to it, we have finished runner-up and won back-to-back titles. To me, that confirms the value of the change.

Just like clothing styles, the game has fads. Just like bell bottoms are back in, so is a new offense. For a while it was the flex, then motion, and now, the triple post is the hot item. Curiously enough, there's nothing new about it: It was invented in 1948. So the more things change, the more they stay the same. And there's nothing wrong with changing *back*, either.

Here's the most important thing I gleaned from my afternoon with Phil Jackson, and it wasn't a strategy or a scheme. It was a simple truth: *It's what you learn after you know it all that counts the most.*

Stability, security, and *familiarity* are all words that should be faintly distasteful to you in any line of work. The most successful organizations are those that are always looking for the new idea, the new way of doing things—or at least improving upon what they know. There is the time-proven way of doing something, and then, eventually, there is always a better way.

We've tried a little bit of everything at Tennessee, in the name of progress. If there is a new method, we consider it. A couple of years ago, we put in place a "performance team," a crew of trained specialists, including medical and fitness experts, to get the optimum, physically, out of our players. We wanted them to have the most current medical advice and care. You wouldn't believe how rapidly ideas in that area change, especially for young women. Recommended eating habits, theories on weight training, and even the design of shoes, are continuously evolving.

Our trainer, Jenny Moshak, is a pretty strict nutritionist who does her best to keep our kids away from junk food. She can't stand to hear the words *fast food*. But college undergraduates are going to hit the burger joints, no matter what you do. Our team is always trying to stage meal insurrections. It's become a running joke. Not long ago, Jenny stood up in the back of our bus and tried to take sandwich orders.

The whole team started chanting "Cheeseburger! Cheeseburger! Cheeseburger!" They rocked until the bus swayed back and forth. Jenny had to cover her ears.

A few years ago, in the mid-1980s, Texas was a more fit team than we were. The Lady Longhorns used to kick us pretty good by outrunning us. We lost a couple of landslide games to them because they would make us look like we were standing still. Those teams, coached by Jody Conradt, taught me the meaning of up-tempo. I had some long nights on the bench watching us eat dust.

I couldn't stand it anymore, so I decided to do something about it. Here's what I did: I co-opted Texas's fitness program. I just plain took it. I got a hold of it from a friend, and I implemented it. It turns out that they were running a lot of middle-distance sprints on the track. They would run sprint after sprint, sometimes as many as seven 400s in a row. Once we started doing the same, our endurance went way up. Pretty soon we were staying with the Lady Longhorns.

Of course, that theory has changed, too. The current thinking is that distance running is not great for basketball. So we've changed yet again. That's okay, too.

I'll borrow anything from anybody. I don't care who or what the source is. Adopting a better idea than your own is nothing to be self-conscious about. Instead of being ashamed that someone does something well, or saying, "I resent him for beating me," what you should be saying is, "That looks like a good idea, why don't we try it ourselves?"

I borrowed an in-bounds play from Kellie Jolly's father, Ken Jolly, a former high school coach. When he was in Knoxville on a recruiting visit with his daughter, we talked basketball. I said, "What's your favorite in-bounds play?" He drew a baseline play he used with his team—a cutting, screening option. I said, "Oh, I like that." I put it in, and every time we run it, I give a silent nod of credit to Ken Jolly. That's fine. As long as we score.

The willingness to change allows you to turn a weakness into a strength. Think about it: Why would you live with a weakness, when it's within your power to remedy it? Only because you are fearful or insecure.

Converting a well-known weakness into a strength is great strategy. It lends you a constant element of surprise. In basketball, other teams scout us all season long for ways to exploit our vulnerabilities. We answer by trying to improve something specifically for use in the post season. In January and February, if I think our team is ready, I throw a new wrinkle at them. We will work on our defenses, individually and as a team, changing them, adding traps, anything that I feel might be good against our tournament competition. Or, let's say we have a player who's weak going to her left. We try to make sure she can go left by tournament time.

More and more, I realize that change is at the heart of being a good teacher. Really, all I try to do is make our players unafraid of it—from both a basketball and a personal standpoint. I tell them all the time, "Okay, great. You've mastered that. Now let's see if you can do this. Just try it."

You'd be amazed at how reluctant and fearful some of our players are. I can sympathize, because of my own limited experience when I went off to college. In 1991, when we won our third national championship in New Orleans, some of our players had never stayed in a four-star hotel before. Late one night there was a rap on my door. It was Marlene Jeter, a sophomore from Carlisle, South Carolina.

Marlene said, "Somebody robbed our room."

I hurried back to her room with her. But it was undisturbed.

I said, "Is anything missing?"

She said, "No."

I said, "Well, then, how do you know you were robbed?"

She said, "Somebody pulled the covers back on the bed."

Sometimes basketball is the least of what I teach.

I want our players to experience the unfamiliar and not be intimidated by it. That's why I vary our itinerary on road trips. If we are in New York, I insist we go to the theater as a group. On a trip to England a few years back, we toured Windsor Castle, even though we had a game later that afternoon. Whenever we visit Stanford, I make sure we take a bus trip to San Francisco. They aren't always happy about the excursions. But we do it anyway because I feel it's my job as an educator to expose them to as many varied experiences as I can.

Similarly our players need to be dragged out of their comfort zone on the basketball court. They fall into a rut. They all have strengths and weaknesses, and they tend to want to play to their strengths, naturally. If I don't shake them out of their routine, they'll never learn, and they'll never develop their game. To outsiders, I'm that mean lady on the sidelines, yelling at them again. But I'm determined to get the maximum potential out of them.

I don't care if I have to coax, pull, push, or haul it out of them. When I challenge them, what I'm really saying is, "You're better than this, and you don't even know it."

A great example was our All American from 1980–84, Mary Ostrowski. Mary was a player with great fundamentals, but she wasn't aggressive shooting the ball. She was passive. If she was standing right under the basket, she would still look to pass the ball. In December of 1983, we were in a tight game against Long Beach State. As the clock ticked down we designed a play to give Mary an open shot from the free throw line. When she caught the ball, rather than take the open jumper, she hit her teammate Lynne Collins in the back with a pass, which resulted in a turnover. We lost that game.

I decided I would *force* her to shoot. I threatened. I cajoled. I made her run sprints every time she passed off. In the end, I made it a requirement that she take at least ten shots a game.

She finished her senior year with a 17.8 points-per-game average, and she set an NCAA Final Four semifinal game record with a thirty-one-point performance. We finished runner-up two days later, losing to Southern Cal in the title game, but Mary made the NCAA All Final Four team.

Frequently, I will move a player to another position, just to force her out of her area of expertise and into the unfamiliar. It's the best way I know to develop her other skills. In our system, post players might handle the ball and perimeter players might post up. I'll have a back-court player spend part of practice in the front court. Or I'll move one of our front-court players to the perimeter. The reason I do this is, I want them to be able to adjust in emergencies. I hope they will develop their total game. The court is ninety-four feet long, and I want them to use all of it.

In any line of work, you have to be able to adjust to emergencies. Things rarely go as planned, no matter how meticulously you keep your appointment book or how organized your planner is. Accidents happen, people call in sick, appointments get missed. What then? The person who is prepared to cope with the setback will prevail.

That's why I even try to surprise our assistant coaches. I'll turn around and say, "Okay, Al, cover the jump ball." Al will have to step forward and teach our jump ball philosophy instead of me. I do it to keep our staff involved and the players engaged with the speaker. If the players hear the same voice over and over, they might grow numb to it. Especially if it's mine. Our assistants can give our ideas reinforcement and freshness, instead of saying the same old thing in the same old way.

In my business injury is the most common setback. We must constantly shift lineups based on the health of our players. For instance, in the first three games of the 1997 season, the Lady Vols suffered two heavy blows. Remember the greatest freshman class ever, the four top signees who arrived in August? By December two of them were injured. Kristen "Ace" Clement suffered a stress fracture in her foot, and Semeka Randall dislocated her shoulder.

They were a pitiful sight at practice, standing next to each other on the sidelines, all bandaged up. Semeka's arm was in a sling and her shoulder was heavily wrapped with ice packs. Ace hobbled around on one crutch. But we had to maintain a good attitude and decide we could get along without them. If we kept looking over our shoulders thinking, *if we only had Ace and Semeka,* we were sunk. We had to move on. Fortunately, Mickie is always good for an attitude adjustment. She does it with humor.

Mickie ambled over to see how they were doing.

"Hey, look," Mickie said. "It's the Johnnies."

Ace and Semeka looked at her, confused.

"When Johnnie comes marching home again, hurrah, hurrah . . ." Mickie sang.

From then on, they were the Johnnies.

What the injuries did was force us to become a more complete team. Suddenly Kyra Elzy had to grow into a leader. The guards on our bench, Misty Greene and Niya Butts, had to be ready and reliable. In the end the injuries made our team stronger and deeper.

Think about all the reasons we resist change. We're afraid. We're lazy. We're cautious. Change can make you feel out of control. But, in fact, if you learn to be comfortable with it, the opposite will be true: You will find yourself in charge of every situation.

Changing your rhythm gives you the ultimate in control. If you can dictate, even briefly, how a situation is played out, you have the advantage.

● ● ●

Don't just give lip service to change. A lot of people say, "Oh, I've changed," when really, they just got a haircut.

Genuine, fundamental change takes determination. It doesn't happen overnight. You have to constantly break old habits and instill new ones. You must wonder every day if you are staying abreast of the trends in your profession, or in command of altering circumstances in your life.

Examine yourself. Learn how to self-check. Seek others' opinions about what you could be doing differently. Look at what you *aren't* doing, so you can improve.

Three years ago I started videotaping our practices. I borrowed the idea from former Tennessee men's coach Kevin O'Neill. He'd say, "Last night I watched our practice tape. . . ." and I'd think, *now why is he doing that?* The first time I tried it, I immediately saw why Kevin did it. It gave me instant feedback. If I tell a player she played badly and she doesn't believe me, I can say, "I got it on tape." But most important, what I saw on that tape was myself.

How many times have you listened to motivational tapes on the way to work? People will listen to perfect strangers—like me—in an effort to change something about themselves. But they never listen to, or watch, the person in the mirror.

What better way to examine what you are doing wrong or right than to study yourself? When I looked at that tape, I saw yours truly in living color. It showed me when I was right, and when I was wrong, and when I was too tough. I saw some changes I needed to make right away. I was too vocal and too negative. You can only listen to yourself scream for so long, and then you think, *Wait a minute. Calm down.* If communication was what I really wanted, I needed to talk less. The tape made me extremely aware of what sort of teacher I am. It definitely toned me down.

The older I get, the more flexible I'd like to be. Change is a force of nature; the truth is that nothing, good or bad, lasts forever. There will be setbacks, injuries, and adverse circumstances, and the person who deals best with them will win out.

I've got more experience with change than most people. If I don't seek it constantly in my profession, I get left behind. Familiarity is not a good thing on the basketball court. It's a game of constant shifts and adjustments; the correlation between change and basketball is constant. But it applies to any field: If you aren't flexible, if you don't change your mindset to meet the circumstances and your personnel, *you will lose.*

Teaching college-age students has forced me to recognize how fast the world is moving these days. In some ways, they are *my* teacher. What's important to a forty-five-year-old woman and what's important to an eighteen-year-old are two different things entirely.

They say that the older you get, the harder it is to change. Me, I intend to move in the opposite direction. I hope I'm still changing in my rocking chair.

If you grant yourself the freedom to change, it will open worlds to you. Don't like your job? Change it. Don't like your attitude? Change it. Just because you start out having a bad day doesn't mean you can't change it. You can change the way you think; you can change your game plan. And you can change your life.

Don't just sit there in your comfortable chair. Do something.

Q & A   *Daedra Charles*

Center, All American, 1989, 1991; National Championship teams;
Olympic Bronze Medalist

Q: *How tough is Pat to play for?*
DAEDRA CHARLES: *I can remember a few times when she'd have us get up at six A.M. to run. We ran, and ran, and ran, and ran, and ran, and ran.*

Q: *Did she get on you?*
DAEDRA CHARLES: *She got on me. She got on me hard. When I went through it, I didn't like it and I didn't understand it. We actually preferred the older players on the team to get on us instead of Pat. They were seniors. They knew what they were talking about. If Pat says something to you, you just say, "My fault." You don't want to talk back. The talking back, she doesn't allow that. After you learn her ways, you say, "I know she's going to be on me. I'm going to do this right because I'm tired of her getting on me." And of course, that's exactly what she wants.*

Q: *Do you like Pat?*
DAEDRA CHARLES: *Some people don't like Pat. But let me tell you something, the reason I like her so much is, I found things in myself I didn't know I had. I didn't pass my [academic eligibility] test, and I had to sit out my first year. She said, "We're going to do whatever it takes to get you through. Tutors, whatever." She teaches you if you want something badly enough you can get it, but you've got to work. You go through it in her program. You go through it. But you use it the rest of your life. Some people don't get that about her. But all the women I know from Tennessee are successful and doing the things they want to do. All of us have our degrees. And most of us are playing in the pro leagues. So for those who don't like Pat, that's their own problem.*

XII

Handle Success Like You Handle Failure

A few years back, I received a pointed lesson in how to handle success. R.B. and I were having dinner with Mickie DeMoss and our old friend Hank Kress in Seagrove, Florida. It was the spring after I had coached the 1984 Olympic team to a gold medal, and I had gotten some attention and media exposure for the first time. So when the people at the next table started staring at me, I assumed they were gawking at the reigning Olympic coach.

I got up to go to the ladies' room.

"Hi, ya'll," I said, as I passed by the table.

"Excuse me," one of the ladies at the table said, "but you look *so* familiar."

"Oh, really?" I said innocently.

"I know I've seen you somewhere before," she said.

"I don't think we've met," I said.

"Don't you work at Ace Hardware?" she said.

"Not at the moment," I answered.

Behind me, R.B. and Mickie and Hank collapsed into gales of laughter.

Since then, I've had more than my share of success and recognition. But, frankly, I'm going to talk more about failure in this chapter. I'm going to dwell on some defeats and embarrassments. I know that sounds funny coming from someone who has spent an entire book discussing ways to succeed. But let me explain.

You can't have continued success without experiencing failure.

So you'd better get used to it.

There are different kinds of success. There is fame and fortune, which, as I have just demonstrated, is a pretty flimsy, short-lived kind of success. Then there is the more gratifying kind of success that comes from doing something you love, and doing it well. Still another kind of success results from committing to one person and raising a child with them. Yet another is finding a sustained faith in your church.

But notice something about all the various forms of success. They are *open-ended*. They aren't tasks that you finish. Success is a project that's always under construction.

Too often, we treat professional success as an isolated goal, an end. No wonder so many people have trouble duplicating success. They get to a certain point and they're satisfied. They quit working.

It's much harder to handle success than it is to handle failure.

You have to learn to handle them alike. Only by placing success and failure in their proper perspectives can you maintain the principles and priorities you arrived with.

It's tougher than it sounds. When you fail, you have a natural tendency to examine it more closely. You analyze it. You critique it. You look at every second of your performance, every possession, and every turnover. I'll tell you straight out, I've learned more from losing than from winning.

Whereas, if you win, you are not nearly as concerned with your mistakes.

Most of us overreact when we lose, and overcelebrate when we win. I used to have a hard time letting go of a defeat. Finally I had to force myself, and our team, to move on. We established a rule: We got twenty-four hours to enjoy a win or recover from a loss. A few of our teams even signed contracts agreeing to the rule. There are too many games and it's too long a season to brood about either one for long. It was probably more for my benefit than for the team's. I was living in the past, just beating every loss to death. I tortured myself and them.

But I've learned to welcome loss, and failure, and adversity. Why? Because they erase success. They make you start all over.

Success lulls you. It makes the most ambitious of us complacent and sloppy. In a way, you have to cultivate a kind of amnesia and forget all of your previous prosperity.

I'll demonstrate how hard it is to handle success: Tennessee has won five NCAA championships, but *we've only won once when we were favored to*. On every other occasion, we were upset. We've lost as many as four or five titles that we were predicted to win. But a healthy taste of failure has been good for us.

Failure is hard to swallow, but much easier to remedy. Failure is simple. It gives you a distinct blueprint of where you've gone wrong. Success is a much trickier matter. It's like balancing on top of a pole. It's one thing to climb up the pole, but quite another to stay up there. That's why it is so difficult to go undefeated. Your attention wanders, your original priorities become obscured, other people try to knock you off the top of the pole. Pretty soon you have lost your balance.

At Tennessee, we examine our successes as critically as our failures.

You know what my lingering thought is on our 1997 title? We turned the ball over too much. It still bothers me. That night, right before the trophy presentation, I got the stat sheet, and I glanced down and saw that we had twenty-nine turnovers, and I said, "Agghh!"

That's just me. I hate it when they don't take care of the ball.

It was a great run—and, yet, we're already a different team. In my profession, you have to treat success as fleeting, or you immediately sentence yourself to a subsequent failure. When you finish out a year, you enjoy it, and then you understand that it's time to move on.

Somehow, you have to make a commitment to get better every day, no matter how successful you were the day before. At Tennessee our system and our philosophy are designed to narrow our focus. We want our players to be so focused on improving their own game that they can't even remember last year. We want *today* to be so intense that they have no time to look back.

It's difficult to live in the past or the future, when you're just trying to get through the present.

The '97 team didn't handle success *or* failure very well, not until the very end. After the '96 championship, we spent too much time congratulating ourselves. In the off season, we did nothing to build on what we had done. We stood still. Every year we give the team an optional summer workout, just so they have some direction. We hand them a sheet with a suggested regimen. That year they didn't do it. Only two players, Kellie Jolly and Laurie Milligan, made a serious commitment over the summer to prepare to defend our title.

I knew what was coming. It was no surprise to me that we lost ten games. We weren't good enough or experienced enough to quit working, not with our schedule, and not with everyone gunning for us.

If someone is complacent, she doesn't fit well with me. Quite honestly, without naming names, we've had a couple of people like that, and they did not succeed at Tennessee. They were proud to be on the team, but they didn't have the desire to broaden their talents and open their minds. "Just proud to be on the team" almost ruined us.

They thought, *We always win. It'll take care of itself.* And then it didn't. Of our ten losses in '97, five of them could be attributed to the lack of commitment in the off season.

When our players finally did go to work in early January, only to lose so badly to Old Dominion, they went overboard in their emotional distress, as I've described. But that failure was the making of a champion in the end. We kept working, and, finally, the team found its equilibrium. When we played Old Dominion for the NCAA championship, that previous failure became our advantage.

Just to make sure our players finally understood what it would take to repeat as champions, I had a highlight tape made of our earlier loss to Old Dominion. I went to the HBO documentary filmmakers who had been following us all season, John Alpert and Marianne DeLeo, and I asked them if they could put something together.

"It'll cost you," they warned me.

"That's okay," I said. "No one will care, if we win another championship."

John and Marianne assembled a video of highlights and lowlights of our season. All of our successes and failures were there on tape. But the centerpiece was their footage of our devastated reactions in the locker room after we lost to Old Dominion in the regular season. I showed our players their own tearstained faces and wracking sobs.

Twice.

I took the tape into our team meeting room at the hotel in Cincinnati on the morning of the title game and put it in the tape machine. We watched it together silently. Then we boarded the team bus to go to the arena. The bus was equipped with a video system. As I got on the bus, I put the tape in the VCR and played it again. You could have heard a pin drop. We rode to the arena wordlessly.

It reminded them of how much failure hurt. It motivated them so much that we jumped out to a 20–8 lead and dominated Old Dominion in the first half. But as you would expect in any contest, Old Dominion made a run at us. They cut our lead to 49–47 midway through the second half.

But, motivated by the thought of failure again, we went on a 12–2 run and finally put the game away.

This time, in the off season, we worked.

●　　●　　●

Losing is not the worst thing that can happen to a team. If we lose, we have a better chance of winning it all.

People constantly ask me why Tennessee is so strong in the post season. It's the $64,000 question. The answer is that we have a method, and we have refined it. Here is our method: We make practice harder than games. And we play a schedule that forces our team to cope with both success and failure, and get over it.

I want our team to experience victory, and to develop some confidence. And yet, right about the time that they have the world by the tail, just when they have it all figured out, I don't mind if they get knocked down. It's the best lesson they can learn.

I have a love-hate relationship with losing. I hate how it makes me feel, which is basically sick. But I love what it brings out. It forces our players and coaches to improve and to make better decisions. Only through adversity do we arrive at a more complete perspective and understanding of the game.

We prepare for the NCAA tournament much like a teacher prepares students for final exams. We give them scouting reports for every game. Practice is like daily class, with assignments and a notebook. Every game is a test, and they have to do their homework to pass—they have to know the shooters and their patterns. But all the while, they're really preparing for the Final Four. In the end, I don't want to drill them. I want them to have the answers for themselves.

That's why I sometimes leave players with foul trouble in the game. I don't do it at the expense of the whole team. But I do it at those times when we can afford to teach someone a lesson. The lesson is this: She needs to make good decisions for herself.

So many times in life other people will make decisions to protect you. But if I'm always making decisions to protect our players from failure, if I soften their disappointments, they don't get better. My message, when I leave a player in the game is, "*You* figure it out." Eventually she gets it. Or she fouls out.

Losing makes you wiser. There is nothing to be ashamed of in short-term failure, or in making a mistake, so long as you deal positively with it. If our players don't get smarter, I find a way to enlighten them, even if it means slight embarrassment.

Once, I sent a message to Laurie Milligan via a referee. It was during an infuriating regular season loss to Connecticut in 1997. We trailed badly, and Laurie was trying too hard to catch us up. She kept jacking up desperate long-range shots that clanged off the rim. She wouldn't stop shooting. She meant well—but she was 0 for 9. It was time for her to get the message.

Finally I gestured to an official named Patty Broderick.

"Hey, Patty," I said.

Patty looked at me warily, with the whistle in her mouth. I am not known for my pleasant chitchat with the referees.

"Patty, c'mere," I said.

Patty drifted over toward the sideline.

I said, "You tell Laurie Milligan that if she shoots the ball one more time, she's on the bench."

Patty smiled.

"I'm serious," I said. "*Tell* her."

Patty told her.

There is only one acceptable way to deal with failure in my book: *Use it.* I've turned some of my own most embarrassing moments into successes.

As a player, I once shot at the wrong basket. It's true. I did.

UT-Martin was playing down at Memphis State. I was under the Memphis State basket when four of my buddies came through the tunnel of the gym. I had been looking for them all night—so much for my focus.

Just then, I got a defensive rebound. Unthinking, or maybe trying to show off, I went right back up and shot the ball. Fortunately, I was fouled and missed the layup. As the ball rolled off the rim, I realized I had shot at the wrong basket—and so did everyone else in the gym. I was mortified. The officials huddled to consider what to do.

I said, "I got fouled in the act of shooting. I get two free throws, and turned a negative into a positive."

They gave them to me. I made both free throws, and turned a negative into a positive.

The reason success is so hard to duplicate is because we tend to stop doing the disciplined things that made us successful in the first place. We lose our focus, like I did against Memphis State. Really, success is not overcomplicated. The truth is, it's a simple matter of focus.

A lot of people succeed once but never understand why. They don't examine what they did right or wrong. It's important to define your method and know what you did right, so you can reemphasize it.

It's amazing how much intensity comes from what you emphasize. If you pay fierce attention to a few important fundamentals, you can fight complacency. The most successful organizations tend to have a signature. They do two or three things extremely well. They don't try to be all things to all people. You can try to do fifty things not very well. Or you can emphasize a few things to perfection.

I'll give you an example: At Tennessee, we emphasize five critical things every year, no matter whether we have won or lost. We teach them meticulously. Mickie and Holly get so tired of our breakdown sessions that they call themselves the "Breakdown Bettys." They say they get the "breakdown blues." It's not the most interesting process in the world. But it helps us win championships.

The five things we emphasize are: pressure defense, dominating the boards, taking care of the basketball, taking good shots, and making layups and free throws. That's it. In everything we do, every offensive and defensive set we use, these are the points of emphasis. Now, defining your method and emphasizing it doesn't mean being inflexible. We might play pressure defense in a lot of different ways. We can full-court press, half-court trap, deny passing lanes. But it's all with the ultimate aim of putting pressure on the opponent.

You might ask, "Doesn't everybody want to out-rebound the opponent?" Yes. But it's how we emphasize it. We emphasize it in every single shooting drill. Our players follow and finish their shots—even in the most casual shoot around. If you don't finish a shot, you will earn my unfavorable attention every time.

You don't win basketball games on first shots. You win them on second and third and fourth shots.

And you can't achieve multiple success on first shots, either.

Follow-up is the secret to continued success in anything. That's why we set specific goals for every game. Win or lose, we evaluate whether or not we met those goals. That way, you learn to compete, not only against the opponent, but against yourself.

Chamique Holdsclaw is a good example. She is the best basketball player in the country. On most nights, she will outmatch her opponent But when you aren't challenged at the highest level, you can get into a rut and practice bad habits. You coast if no one is pushing you. So the trick for Chamique is to learn to play against herself, to try to better her own personal standards. If her career high is twenty-five points, she resets her standards.

Nobody has competed against their own standards better than Mickie and Holly. The fact that they have stayed at Tennessee and been just as dedicated in their thirteenth year, signing our best recruiting class ever, has been crucial to our ability to win multiple titles. They have never been complacent or satisfied. It's a classic example of refusing to allow success to undermine future success.

But there is one big problem with a second success, or a third one. Multiple achievement leads to spiraling expectations. With each additional feat, you create pressure to perform. It gets harder and harder to do what you're *supposed* to do. Eventually, high expectations are a killer.

In 1990, we experienced some of our highest expectations ever, and the pressure undid us. That year, the Final Four was scheduled to be held in Knoxville. We had a chance to play for a national championship in front of our home crowd. It was all anyone could talk about throughout the season. Every day someone at the grocery store or the gym or the dry cleaners would say, "We're going to be in the Final Four, aren't we?"

It wore on me, and it wore on our players. We felt like we had to get there for the good of the community, for the women's game, and for our own self-respect. But realistically, I knew it would be tough.

We didn't make it. We lost in the regional finals to Virginia. We were beat in overtime by a Cavaliers team led by Dawn Staley. It was my worst nightmare. We couldn't make anything go in. We missed layups. Nothing fell. As a coach, that's when you feel most helpless.

I was devastated. It had become personal. After the press conference, I got in a rental car with Mickie and Holly and our athletic director, Joan Cronan, and I just broke down. It's the hardest I've ever cried over a basketball game. I cried so hard that I trembled. It may have had something to do with the fact that I was three months pregnant. But it was also because I simply cracked under all that pressure.

What I learned from that day is that you can't perform when you think "I *have* to do this." You must handle pressure well enough to be in a loose, comfortable state.

We lost because we were focused on the long-range expectations instead of on what we had to do in that moment. It takes tremendous discipline not to let expectations sway you from your original purpose, and we didn't have it.

But we made up for it—we absorbed that failure and turned it into a success.

First, I required our staff and our team to stay in Knoxville that spring and be hostesses at the Final Four.

The next year, we came back and won the national championship— revenging ourselves on Virginia by winning the title game in overtime. That whole season was an exercise in coping with failure. Early in the year we played Louisiana Tech in a tight game that ended with two players at the free throw line. Their different reactions illustrate how to deal with pressure and expectations. We were ranked No. 1 and Tech was No. 2 in the country. Dena Head had a chance to win the game for us at the line. But she missed her free throws. A couple of seconds later, Tech's Venus Lacey was fouled and stepped to the line. She sank hers, effortlessly, to give Tech the victory.

In the post-game press conference, a reporter asked Venus what she was thinking as she went to that line.

She said, "When I go to the free throw line, I think of it like receiving an award."

In other words, she didn't focus on the pressure or the expectations. She focused on the positive.

Dena Head could have let that failure haunt her. Instead, she kept it in perspective and used it against Virginia. When she went to the free throw line in the championship game against Virginia, Dena was mentally prepared. This time, she sank the shots to send the game into overtime.

Ever since, we have spent a lot of time teaching our players how to cope with the burden of expectations. Some coaches try to shelter their teams from pressure. Not me. I want them to experience its full weight. It's the only way they will learn to master it.

People are appalled by our locker room on game day. It's a zoo. There are a million people milling around. Alumni, friends of the program, medical staff. The reason we allow it is because we want the players to become accustomed to coping with distractions and outside influences. "Handle it," I tell them. Eventually, they are able to screen out the distractions. When we arrive at the Final Four, they can calmly deal with the three P's: the press, their parents, and their peers. This is what we refer to as having and maintaining a "player's mentality." We talk about being a player first, instead of someone's daughter or friend. It means being able to go to the Final Four with all the distractions and to remember that you have work to do while everyone else is on vacation.

Some coaches don't want their athletes to read the papers. They're afraid that what they read could upset them. Not me. "If you're going to read the paper, handle it," I say. Whether they pick us to win, or pick us to lose, it doesn't matter—what matters is how *we* feel.

What we do in the post season is say, "Well, here it is. We've taught you all we know. Now go play." It's like teaching someone to drive. We want them to have all the specific answers, but more than that, to have an overall comprehension and confidence, so that they can contend with whatever circumstances might arise.

What we're after is a larger understanding, one that transcends the court. A habit of treating success and failure in the same way can sustain you through the inevitable fluctuations in your career.

Growing up, I never knew about the changes in my parents' fortunes. They worked just as hard when they were well off as they did when they were struggling. I valued that attitude later in life. When I flew to Los Angeles, on my way to coach the Olympic team in 1984, I wrote my mom and dad a long, long letter—just to say thank you. I talked about how their work ethic influenced my life, and how I regretted that they would not be there with me.

I've told you a lot about how tough my father was. But what I haven't expressed is how good he was to the people around him. When he finally sold the grocery store, there's no telling how many thousands of dollars people owed him. My guess is there was around $60,000 in debt left on the books. He floated everybody in the county. He would give anyone the shirt off his back.

That bothered me at times, when I was a kid, because we sacrificed as a family so that my father could help people in the community.

But on the plane to Los Angeles, it struck me that my parents were extremely principled and hard-working. They never rested. They understood that when you invest in and give to others, you are really investing in yourself. So I wrote them a long letter, thanking them.

I've tried to instill a similar ethic in our players. I want them to understand that success at Tennessee is not inherited or automatic. It's not like a coffeemaker. It doesn't come with a timer.

Each year, I hand our players a sheet of paper that tells them how much the university will spend on them. We total up recruiting, travel, hotels, meals, scholarship, books, tutors, medical—whatever it is. Broken down, in black and white, it adds up to $35,000 to $40,000 a year per player. Hopefully, it makes an impression on them.

It's not cash in their pockets. But it should make them stop and consider the sneakers on their feet. When they leave Tennessee, maybe they won't have a shoe contract. They just might have to buy their own sneakers. It's my way of letting them know that in the real world, no one will throw free shoes at them.

I only promise what I can deliver. I don't guarantee success. I tell our players, "If you work with me, I'll help you be the player you should be." I give them the tools and the opportunity and the knowledge to be successful. But at the end of their four years, they have to walk through that door to continued success by themselves. I'll get them to that point—but they have to take those final steps. And so do you.

To me, real success is when you become independently self-motivated. I tell our players, "You may marry rich, or hit the jackpot. But you'd better plan to handle things on your own."

I give our players structure and discipline. But I want them to be self-correcting; I hope that they learn to right themselves when they lose their direction.

Real success is when they don't need me anymore.

●   ●   ●

When Tyler was about four and a half, he and our nanny, LaTina Dunn, were out in the backyard playing by our pond. It's just a little circular man-made pool with some fat, sluggish goldfish in it, but he loved to hang over it, staring into its pitifully shallow depths. I kept saying, "One of these days, you're going to fall in." Well, finally, the day came when he did. He slipped and fell into the water. He panicked. He splashed around, his eyes squeezed shut. LaTina said, "Tyler, just stand up." He stood up, and the water only came to his knees.

LaTina laughed so hard, she bent double. Well, he started crying because she was laughing.

When I got home, LaTina told me the story.

I died laughing, too.

Tyler started crying again.

Later that day, we were driving to my mom and dad's place, and during a slow part of the drive I thought about Tyler in that pond, and I couldn't help it. I burst out laughing all over again.

He said, "Why are you laughing?"

I said, "I'm laughing about you in that pond."

He started to get tearful again. I said, "Son, let me tell you something. You have to learn to laugh at yourself. You're *going* to fall down again. And people will make fun of you for it. So you better get a sense of humor about yourself."

He just listened. A couple of hours later we got to my mom and dad's, and I was sitting around in the kitchen with my mom and my sister, Linda. All of a sudden Tyler came into the kitchen. He said, "Mama, tell Aunt Linda about the pond."

My son is a fast learner.

To me, humor is essential in handling success and failure alike. Fortu-
nately, there are lots of people around me who are only too ready to help
me make fun of myself.

On a boat, if too many people are on one side, you need load levelers.
Sometimes they are called trim tabs. They keep your bow down and level
out your boat, so you don't ride funny on the water. Well, R.B. and Tyler,
and Mickie, Holly, and Al, are like my trim tabs. I've always got one on
each side of me, and the boat never gets too unbalanced one way or the
other.

Continued success is about load leveling. It's about putting together all
the life skills we've talked about to our players throughout their careers:
respect, responsibility, loyalty, discipline. They are each building blocks,
forming a sound foundation. With that, you can build success after suc-
cess—because real success is about developing a value system.

Our value system is this: We work as a team, and we understand that
the world doesn't revolve around us as individuals. We surround ourselves
with good quality people, and we interact and work effectively with them.
We accept our roles, because we have gotten to know and believe in
ourselves. And at the end of the day, we hope to have personal content-
ment and happiness, not just trophies.

If you haven't made the correlation between being happy and success-
ful, then you aren't really successful. Material success varies from one
person to the other, but deeper success is a matter of what makes you
happy, of what brings a sense of satisfaction and contentment and peace. It
has nothing to do with financial gain. For me, that's nowhere near the top
of the list. A more gratifying, long-term success is the reward that comes
from feeling that I am a good mother, or a good coach, or a good friend.
More than collecting trophies, it's about seeing young people take those
independent steps and make good decisions without me.

It would be all too easy to get caught up in the glitter of what we've
done at Tennessee. Fortunately, I have a family and staff who keep me
trained on what our real goals are. They are always there to help me regain
my perspective—sometimes hilariously. Ever since that night in Seagrove
Beach, Florida, Mickie and R.B. haven't missed an opportunity to remind
me that I could just as easily be working at Ace Hardware. Whenever

Mickie thinks I'm taking our success for granted, or getting too big for my britches around the office, she knows exactly what to say to humble me.

"Hey," she says. "Aren't you the lady who carried the two-by-fours to my car?"

Q & A *Carla McGhee*

Forward, 1987, 1989, national championship teams; Olympic Gold Medalist, 1996; Columbus Quest, ABL

Q: Has anyone ever gotten the best of Pat?
CARLA MCGHEE: *Let me tell you something. There is one person who really has her number. Tyler. He's the only person who keeps her in check. She's a total sucker for him. She thinks she's in charge of that relationship, but she's not. That boy is running things.*

EPILOGUE

Reach for the Summit

Recently Tyler said something to me that every kid says at one time or another.

"I never get to do anything," he said.

Now, my son has been just about everywhere and done everything. He has been to Hawaii. He has been to Alaska. He has been to Disneyland. He made his first road trip when he was three months old.

"Ross Tyler Summitt," I said. "What little boy gets to do more than you? Name me a seven-year-old who has done more, in his short life, than you have."

Tyler looked at me cagily and said, "The UConn coach's kid."

You see what I have to look forward to

Success is all a matter of perspective. It depends on where you start from, and where you want to end up. Tyler has his own competitive standards. And I have mine. I have never had a losing season, at anything. In every basketball season I have participated in, I ended up with a winning record. Not too many people have enjoyed as much good fortune as I have, or been as driven. So my definition of success is not for everybody.

Success is a highly personal matter. Your own definition of it should be formed by your circumstances, and your desires and aspirations.

I'll give you another example, courtesy of Tyler. Every year, I rent a large house near Destin, Florida, for a two-week vacation. I invite my staff and some friends for the first week, and R.B. joins us for a family vacation the second week. Last year Tyler and I arrived ahead of everybody. I told him he could choose the room we would sleep in.

He went into the first bedroom, a beautiful room looking out on the ocean. He shrugged. Next he inspected the master bedroom suite, a lovely room with sliding glass doors. He shrugged again. Then he went into yet a third room.

It was a cramped little room, with nothing in it but a set of bunk beds. "Oh, *Mama*," he said, "*bunk* beds."

"Tyler, what about the master bedroom?" I said weakly.

"But, Mama, *bunk* beds," he said, imploring.

I slept in the top bunk. For a week.

For Tyler, success is bunk beds. For Tennessee, it's championships. So I'm not going to sit here and tell you what your definition of success should be.

But I can tell you this: The seeking of success for its own sake should not be a single-minded enterprise. In this book I've tried to talk about more than just how to succeed. I've tried to address the principles that I believe should accompany it, and I've tried to convey the price of it.

As competitive and achievement-oriented as I am, and as proud as I am of Tennessee's Final Four record, that accomplishment is not what I would hold out as my greatest.

Having a healthy son is.

Tyler is growing into a comical boy. He has a head of silky reddish-blond hair that I keep cropped short, so oftentimes in the mornings it stands on end. His complexion is fair, but his cheeks flush the color of ripe apples when he is excited. His eyes are watery-blue and grave, and he has a slight dimple in his left cheek, which he knows how to use to great effect. He is an affectionate boy who begins each day by crawling in my lap and putting his head under my chin. His sturdy little body isn't even as long as one of my legs. He's still so small that I can practically wrap my arms twice around him. He smells like warm, sweet bread, especially around his neck and ears.

All in all, he is a great success as a child.

Although if you ask me, he is getting a little showbiz. He spends way too much time around women who call him "Baby-doll." The other day he wrote a six-page novel, and dated it and signed it. It was called, "The Adventures of Me." Granted, he is only in the first grade, at that stage where his letters look like broken eggshells. But he is already ambitious. And why shouldn't he be? He has been to the White House three times.

On our last trip President Bill Clinton looked at Tyler, and then he looked at me. Then President Clinton smiled and said, "I feel like I'm watching your son grow up."

With that, Tyler looked back at Bill Clinton, the chief executive and leader of the free world, and winked at him.

As Tyler continues to grow, no doubt he will feel like he has to be an overachiever, like me. And that concerns me. He shows signs of being a lip-biter like his mother. He has a terrible habit of grinding his teeth in his sleep. So did I, as a child. It kills me to hear him. Six nights out of seven, he crawls into our bed, and I wake up to the sound of his jaw grinding. I have to gently slip my knuckle in his mouth to get him to stop. I lie there, in the middle of the night, with my finger between his teeth until he quits.

I want Tyler to be successful, but I also want him to be content and secure within himself. There is a part of me that doesn't care if he's a lifeguard, as long as he's a healthy lifeguard. I didn't know the meaning of fear until I had Tyler. After he was born, all of a sudden, for the first time in my life, I was afraid of flying. I got sweaty palms just thinking about leaving my son. So what worries me most these days is not whether Tennessee will make the post-season tournament or accomplish a three-peat. These things are important to me, but I worry more about my son.

My version of success is increasingly an internal definition, not an external one. I guess that's because life is getting shorter. I'm learning to simplify and to take vacations. Last year, when R.B. and Tyler and I were in Destin, I didn't make a single business call for a whole week. I have to confess, it didn't come naturally to me. But I've promised my family and our staff that I won't take on a big project next year. No more books or house renovations. Just coaching, and cooking, and raising our son.

I find myself less inclined to waste time and energy on things that aren't truly important to me and my family. For instance, I've been asked several times over the course of my career if I would consider coaching a men's team. I was even asked if I would be interested in applying for the men's job at Tennessee.

The only reason I would consider coaching a men's team is to show a woman could do it. But in the end I said no.

"Why is that a step up?" I asked.

Most of society thinks it's a bigger deal, because the men's game is more popular. But to me, I'm doing exactly what I should be doing. I'm an educator. I teach basketball, and through that, help young girls grow into women, and I broaden their ideas of what they are capable of. Why would I give up such a valuable job, one that I love?

There are too many people in this world who don't like their jobs, who dread going to work every day, or who feel that their work is unimportant. I count myself lucky. I have had a lifelong interest in other people's children. I could just as well have been that lady who carried the two-by-fours to your car at Ace Hardware. Instead, I found my passion. Now that I have a child of my own, my interest and passion has only redoubled.

So I'd like to finish this book by saying something to my son, and to all the players who ever came to me (and who ever will) hoping to achieve success.

My real victories and championships are not made of polished wood and metal. My victories are you.

I have not always made this obvious, I know. If there is one thing I would like to be more successful at, it's this: I would sincerely like to develop a greater understanding between me and our players. I would like them to understand what I am after, that I only get on them because I want them to be better.

I would like to say this to them: I'm kind of like that math teacher you had in eighth grade. You hated me. I tortured you. I made you do your homework on pain of death. I sent you to detention. I ridiculed you, I scolded you, I punished you, I kept you inside on sunny days. I told on you to your parents. I badgered you. I *never* left you alone. But then, it's hoped, you matured. And you realized how deeply I cared.

Above all, I would like our players to understand that I wish for them a broader kind of success than the one they experienced at Tennessee. What they do between the ages of eighteen and twenty-one should not be the pinnacle of their entire lives.

I carry a poem around with me, stuck in my weekly planner.

You can love me
but only I can make me happy.
You can teach me
but only I can do the learning.
You can lead me
but only I can walk the path.
You can promote me
but I have to succeed.
You can coach me
but I have to win the game.
You can even pity me
but I have to bear the sorrow.
For the Gift of Love
is not a food that feeds me.
It is the sunshine
that nourishes that which I must finally harvest for myself.
So if you love me
don't just sing me your song.
Teach me to sing,
for when I am alone,
I will need the melody.

—Dan Baker

The meaning of the poem is this: I can challenge you, and teach you, and discipline you. But ultimately it's up to each of you to make the right choices.

Success is a lifelong endeavor. You can't solve every problem in your life, and you can't make yourself perfect. I'll spend the rest of my life trying to conquer my quick temper. I know that. And I may get a direct compliment from my father. I know that, too.

Not too long ago, my parents came to visit. We had just finished the remodeling job on our house, and we were moving our furniture back in. A workman brought in a chair and said, "Where do you want this?"

I said, "Ask the decorator."

Across the room my father murmured something. I heard my mother snap, "Hush, Richard, it's none of your business."

I wheeled on my father.

"Daddy, what did you just say?" I said.

"Nothing," he said.

"Tell me," I said.

He bellowed, "What I said was, the day I let someone come in *my* home and tell me where to put *my* chair, is the day I know I'm crazy!"

So there you are. Clearly, he's still challenging me.

However, I am going to follow my own definition of success, and no one else's. Except perhaps, for Tyler's. As long as he approves, I'll keep coaching. So far, he thinks I'm a big success.

The other day, Tyler brought home a picture of me he had drawn in school. Under it, he had written something.

This is what it said:

"Go, Mommy, go."

The Definite Dozen

As we get caught up in day-to-day matters, we sometimes forget what's really important to us. I like to keep the Definite Dozen nearby as a refresher.

An overview of the Definite Dozen:

1. Respect Yourself and Others
- There is no such thing as self-respect without respect for others.
- Individual success is a myth. No one succeeds all by herself.
- People who do not respect those around them will not make good team members and probably lack self-esteem themselves.
- When you ask yourself "Do I deserve to succeed?" make sure the answer is yes.

2. *Take Full Responsibility*
- There are no shortcuts to success.
- You can't assume larger responsibility without taking responsibility for the small things, too.
- Being responsible sometimes means making tough, unpopular decisions.
- Admit to and make yourself accountable for mistakes. How can you improve if you're never wrong?

3. *Develop and Demonstrate Loyalty*
- Loyalty is not unilateral. You have to give it to receive it.
- The family business model is a successful one because it fosters loyalty and trust.
- Surround yourself with people who are better than you are. Seek out quality people, acknowledge their talents, and let them do their jobs. You win with people.
- Value those colleagues who tell you the truth, not just what you want to hear.

4. *Learn to Be a Great Communicator*
- Communication eliminates mistakes.
- Listening is crucial to good communication.
- We communicate all the time, even when we don't realize it. Be aware of body language.
- Make good eye contact.
- Silence is a form of communication, too. Sometimes less is more.

5. *Discipline Yourself So No One Else Has To*
- Self-discipline helps you believe in yourself.
- Group discipline produces a unified effort toward a common goal.
- When disciplining others, be fair, be firm, be consistent.
- Discipline helps you finish a job, and finishing is what separates excellent work from average work.

6.   Make Hard Work Your Passion
- Do the things that aren't fun first, and do them well.
- Think big, work small.
- Plan your work, and work your plan.
- See yourself as self-employed.

7.   Don't Just Work Hard, Work Smart
- Success is about having the right person, in the right place, at the right time.
- Know your strengths, weaknesses, and needs.
- When you understand yourself and those around you, you are better able to minimize weaknesses and maximize strengths. Personality profiles help.
- Be flexible.

8.   Put the Team Before Yourself
- Teamwork doesn't come naturally. It must be taught.
- Teamwork allows common people to obtain uncommon results.
- Not everyone is born to lead. Role players are critical to group success.
- In group success there is individual success.

9.   Make Winning an Attitude
- Combine practice with belief.
- Attitude is a choice. Maintain a positive outlook.
- No one ever got anywhere by being negative.
- Confidence is what happens when you've done the hard work that entitles you to succeed.

10.   Be a Competitor
- Competition isn't social. It separates achievers from the average.
- You can't always be the most talented person in the room. But you can be the most competitive.

● Influence your opponent: By being competitive you can affect how your adversary performs.

● There is nothing wrong with having competitive instincts. They are survival instincts.

11. *Change Is a Must*

● It's what you learn after you know it all that counts the most.

● Change equals self-improvement. Push yourself to places you haven't been before.

● Take risks. You can't steal second base with your foot on first.

12. *Handle Success Like You Handle Failure*

● You can't always control what happens, but you *can* control how you handle it.

● Sometimes you learn more from losing than winning. Losing forces you to reexamine.

● It's harder to stay on top than it is to make the climb. Continue to seek new goals.

All-Time Lady Vols (1974-Present)

PLAYER	SEASONS	PLAYER	SEASONS	PLAYER	SEASONS
Jody Adams	1989-93	Susan Foulds	1979-81	Lisa McGill	1976-79
Suzanne Barbre	1974-78	Valerie Freeman	1983-85	**Laurie Milligan**	**1994–**
Cindy Boggs	1974-75	Sheila Frost	1985-89	Zandra Montgomery	1977-79
Fonda Bondurant	1975-77	Amy Gamble	1983-84	Pearl Moore	1987-90
Sherry Bostic	1984-86	Marci Garner	1974-76	Karen Morton	1982-83
Nancy Bowman	1973-75	**Teresa Geter**	**1997–**	Sabrina Mott	1986-87
Gina Bozeman	1981	Bridgette Gordon	1985-89	Cindy Noble	1978-81
Diane Brady	1974-75	Liza Graves	1975-78	Kathy O'Neil	1976-80
Cindy Brogdon	1977-79	Kathie Greene	1975-76	Mary Ostrowski	1980-84
Niya Butts	**1996–**	**Misty Greene**	**1995–**	Jane Pemberton	1975-76
Nikki Caldwell	1990-94	Debbie Groover	1977-81	**Semeka Randall**	**1997–**
Sonya Cannon	1981-85	Tanya Haave	1980-84	Jill Rankin	1979-80
Tamara Carver	1990-91	Leanne Hance	1977-78	Linda Ray	1981-85
Kelli Casteel	1988-92	Jerilynn Harper	1978-79	Emily Roberts	1976-77
Tamika Catchings	**1997–**	Lisa Harrison	1989-93	Patricia Roberts	1976-77
Lesia Cecil	1985-86	Pat Hatmaker	1980-84	Debbie Scott	1988-90
Daedra Charles	1988-91	Debbie Hawhee	1988-92	Joy Scruggs	1972-75
Becky Clark	1979-80	Dena Head	1988-92	Jan Seay	1977-78
Regina Clark	1988-92	Lea Henry	1979-83	Shelley Sexton	1983-87
Kristen "Ace" Clement	**1997–**	**Chamique Holdsclaw**	**1995–**	Kim Smallwood	1995-96
Susan Clower	1978-82	Karla Horton	1984-87	Melissa Smith	1989-90
Lynne Collins	1980-84	Marlene Jeter	1990-92	Tanika Smith	1993-95
Shelia Collins	1981-85	Dana Johnson	1991-95	Kristie Snyder	1983-84
Abby Conklin	1993-97	Tiffani Johnson	1994-97	Kathy Spinks	1984-88
Pam Cook	1982-83	Michelle Johnson	1993,95	**LaShonda Stephens**	**1996–**
Bev Curtis	1979	**Kellie Jolly**	**1995–**	Sue Thomas	1974-77
Latina Davis	1992-96	Janice Koehler	1974-76	Pashen Thompson	1993-97
Susie Davis	1976-79	Tammy Larkey	1981-83	Mina Todd	1980-81
Freda DeLozier	1975	**Brynae Laxton**	**1995–**	Paula Towns	1980-84
Rochone Dilligard	1991-94	Cheryl Littlejohn	1983-87	Gay Townson	1986-87
Gail Dobson	1972-75	Michelle Marciniak	1993-96	Jennifer Tuggle	1984-88
Kris Durham	1987-89	Pam Marr	1982-86	Vonda Ward	1991-95
Tonya Edwards	1986-90	Dawn Marsh	1984-88	Holly Warlick	1976-80
Cindy Ely	1977-81	Melissa McCray	1985-89	Jackie Watson	1974-77
Kyra Elzy	**1996–**	Nikki McCray	1991-95	Lisa Webb	1983-88
Peggy Evans	1990-93	Carla McGhee	1986-90	Tiffany Woosley	1991-95
Sherri Fancher	1976-79				

Lady Vols NCAA Champions

1987
Tonya Edwards
Bridgette Gordon
Sheila Frost
Karla Horton
Cheryl Littlejohn
Dawn Marsh
Melissa McCray
Carla McGhee
Sabrina Mott
Shelley Sexton
Kathy Spinks
Gay Townson
Jennifer Tuggle
Lisa Webb

1989
Kelli Casteel
Daedra Charles
Regina Clark
Tonya Edwards
Sheila Frost
Bridgette Gordon
Debbie Hawhee
Dena Head
Melissa McCray
Carla McGhee
Debbie Scott

1991
Jody Adams
Nikki Caldwell
Kelli Casteel
Daedra Charles
Regina Clark

Peggy Evans
Lisa Harrison
Debbie Hawhee
Dena Head
Marlene Jeter

1996
Abby Conklin
Latina Davis
Misty Greene
Chamique Holdsclaw
Tiffani Johnson
Kellie Jolly
Brynae Laxton
Michelle Marciniak
Laurie Milligan
Kim Smallwood
Pashen Thompson

1997
Niya Butts
Abby Conklin
Kyra Elzy
Misty Greene
Chamique Holdsclaw
Tiffani Johnson
Kellie Jolly
Brynae Laxton
Laurie Milligan
LaShonda Stephens
Pashen Thompson